In the Trough

In the Trough

Three Years on Ocean Station

THOMAS F. JARAS

iUniverse LLC
Bloomington

IN THE TROUGH
THREE YEARS ON OCEAN STATION

iUniverse books may be ordered through booksellers or by contacting:

iUniverse
1663 Liberty Drive
Bloomington, IN 47403
www.iuniverse.com
1-800-Authors (1-800-288-4677)

Because of the dynamic nature of the Internet, any web
addresses or links contained in this book may have changed
since publication and may no longer be valid.

The views expressed in this work are solely those of the author
and do not necessarily reflect the views of the publisher, and the
publisher hereby disclaims any responsibility for them.

Any people depicted in stock imagery provided by Thinkstock are models,
and such images are being used for illustrative purposes only.

Certain stock imagery © Thinkstock.

ISBN: 978-1-4917-0653-4 (sc)
ISBN: 978-1-4917-0655-8 (hc)
ISBN: 978-1-4917-0654-1 (e)

Library of Congress Control Number: 2013915972

Printed in the United States of America.

iUniverse rev. date: 10/9/2013

Dad with brother Bill,
1935. (Photo from author's private collection.)

To my father

Peter John Jaras
1903–1978

His life was his children.

The Pacific Ocean. (Drawing by author.)

CONTENTS

Accept the things to which fate binds you, and love
the people with whom fate brings you
together, but do so with all your heart.

—Marcus Aurelius

A nautical definition for *trough* is a long, narrow depression or hollow between two ridges of water between waves. I was clinging to the Polaris compass on the open bridge of the USS *Vance* (DER 387) as the ship slowly turned through the trough in an attempt to come to a course with following seas. Time stood still, the rudder at hard left, and still we appeared frozen in the trough, our world heeling over 50°, the decks and the bridge being battered by ninety-foot-high walls of water. Behind each massive wave was another and then another, each waiting its turn to pound against our hull, all part of a September day on station on the edge of the Antarctic Circle.

A few months out of college followed by a sixteen-week course on how to be a naval officer, I was now standing bridge watches in the middle of nowhere, providing navigational aid for aircraft flying to the polar ice. After nine months battling these brutal seas, I had two more years in the equally remote and arbitrary northern Pacific Ocean. Here we were Cold War sentinels, part of the Defense Early Warning System, guarding the United States against nuclear attack. The only certainties were long periods underway, boredom, and difficult sea conditions.

The intensity of the experience was a personal trough of my own making. Here almost fifty years later, I recall my three years aboard the USS *Vance,* an extreme encounter that I proudly identify with. Yet I was repelled by the difficulty, loneliness, and unhappiness of the voyage. Was it an interesting trip? Yes, so long as you accept the journey for what it was, a subjective self-centered account. Is the tale true? Yes, if you can rely on my fading memory and remember you are seeing events through these old eyes. The *Vance* years have always stood out in my mind both as an adventure filled with challenges and accomplishments and as a bad dream. What I've experienced in life since tossing my sea boots overboard that last joyous day aboard influenced what I remember and how I interpret the events of those three years. Although writing does not come easy, I was drawn to the task to better understand the events of my shipboard days.

Have you ever been so seasick that nothing would stay down? That the dry heaves were so intense you believed the lining of your stomach was eroding? That in this debilitated condition you still had to do your job, pretending to be a naval officer? That after a week of misery, there was another week of the same ahead of you? And the real kicker: In the prime of life, why did I sign on for three full years of this grief? With my barf bucket beside me, I lay exhausted on my bunk, wondering how I managed to find myself committed to three years on the USS *Vance,* a World War II relic, a class of ship with the distinction of being perhaps the worst-riding ship in the US Navy and having the reprehensible peculiarity of being able to remain independently at sea longer than any ship in this man's navy (before there was a nuclear fleet). I wasn't shanghaied. I voluntarily signed up, but why?

Can our lives be determined by our dreams? I never asked myself this question until I was well into writing this memoir. The answer has to be yes. I was guilty of forever reaching for a dream, for something always just out of reach. In this dance through life, my dreams gradually changed and took on new dimensions; I would go scampering after these mutations, as a dog to a bone, until once again the dreams took on a new form. On and on it went, with me forever chasing. Maybe the chase is what counts.

We little kids lived in an imaginary world at the outbreak of World War II. Cap guns blazing, we ran around the neighborhood playing war, hoping to avoid being stuck on the side of the Germans or the Japs. I guess this was an early attempt to live in a different world. My first conscious effort to grab for a dream was at age nine, when I became obsessed with mountain men, those rugged, independent, society-detesting Rocky Mountain fur trappers of the early nineteenth century. The remoteness and self-reliance of these grizzly characters attracted me. I was fresh out of a three-year spell in an orphanage, which conditioned me to look to the future and dream of a better life. I devoured every book and movie of the early West and loved camping and hiking, the more remote the better. I gloried in my self-sufficiency in the wilds, feeling such joy in being able to survive without depending on others. My wildness, the countryside just beyond Cleveland, now all suburbs, was enough at first, until in my mid- and late teens, I found West Virginia and then New Mexico.

Unwittingly, my father promoted my dreaming. A Great Depression survivor, he preached being practical, but I focused on what had escaped him. Every day, I witnessed the life of this man I loved so much, this hardworking widower with three young children, whose inquiring mind had once entertained his own bundle of dreams, most unfulfilled. I came away determined to follow my dreams, a form of carpe diem. I wanted no old-age regrets over what I had wanted but put off and never tried.

The dreams lead me west to the Colorado School of Mines for two bruising years of the sheer joy of being on my own, while undergoing the excruciating pain of failing as an engineering student. Finishing my college education at Marietta College in southern Ohio, I immersed myself in world history to the point that mountain men were put on hold. The world beyond North America was more intriguing, something to experience now while I was still young. The thought of seeing the world as a tourist in my twilight years, the reward of a long career, was repugnant. Life was a crapshoot. Don't gamble and put off your dreams. My dreams did not include a particular profession. A career was too similar to my father's life of servitude, tied to piecework in a clothing factory for forty years.

Dream chasing led me to an intense three years at sea, a time of transition from boy to man, an experience I at first regretted and in time came to cherish. All these years, I have had a love-hate relationship with the USS *Vance*. Am I happy to have made the voyage? Yes. Knowing what I do today, would I have set foot on the *Vance*? Never. Those three years before the mast are what I share with you, the reader.

ACKNOWLEDGMENTS

As a historian, I have trouble letting go of the past. For years I thought about documenting the brief three years, 1961–64, I spent on the USS *Vance*, a little World War II navy destroyer escort radar picket ship, resurrected for a modest role in the Cold War. I had to reach age seventy before finding the time and incentive to take pen in hand. Waiting forty-seven years provided challenges, some of which were new and bothersome. Normally I approach a topic by gathering the documentation, then evaluating and organizing the material before writing the first sentence. In this instance, much of the information was in the recesses of my mind. These memories surfaced periodically, and I had no control over when this would occur. The primary catalysts were chats with old shipmates, reading the ship's deck log, and looking at old photos. The past came alive while I sat alone day after day at the computer, tapping out text. Progress was slow. Yet I was able to remember my way back to the *Vance*'s decks and feel her rolling beneath me.

At times, I think the ship will never let go of me. A few years ago, the last destroyer escort afloat in America, the USS *Slater* (DE-766), was towed up the Hudson River to Albany, New York, and moored permanently within two miles of my house. Was this an omen? I couldn't resist the desire to climb through the ship and revisit the past. Tim Rizzuto, executive director of the Destroyer Escort Historical Museum, which includes the *Slater*, welcomed me aboard and proved to be a valuable information source. The *Slater* and the *Vance* shared the same hull design and age; therefore, I had the opportunity to walk into the past, smell the paint and diesel, try out a bunk, and carefully climb down the engine-room ladders, where once I scurried down them without hesitation. Thank you, Tim, for your kind hospitality and assistance. Also, I wish to thank Karl Herchenroder, a *Slater* volunteer who once rode these ships, for sharing his technical knowledge of the Fairbanks-Morse diesel engines.

The structure for my story came from the *Vance*'s deck logs, located in the National Archives in Silver Spring, Maryland. The detail is uneven and scant, while the dates, weather conditions, and major events are on record. The deck logs proved invaluable to the development of the story line by providing a sense of order to my memory of events. To link a story to this structure, I relied on my memory and those of my fellow wardroom officers. Several of my shipmates helped joggle my memory over the last several years. Doc Gersenfish clarified a few medical events, and before he died, Harvey Payne recalled his days on the bridge. My thanks to Ray DeMott, who wanted to forget the *Vance* but willingly answered my inquiries.

Six shipmates read the text, expanded on the events, and verified what happened during these three years. Don Dunn recalled the difficult engineering and personnel challenges. His family, which includes three Annapolis graduates, enjoyed the first draft; and Don's son, Craig, suggested the title for the memoir. Larry Hanson was especially helpful in describing events in the operations department and the Miss *Vance* contest. He helped rein me in when I was too carried away describing the various personalities on this strange little ship. Robbie Robinson, who carefully read the draft, helped with the sequence of events, remembered how the captain treated his supply department, and clarified how funds were allocated.

Once or twice a year, Lee Cole and I spent the evenings laughing and reminiscing over drinks and dinner. We were engineers aboard together for over two years, as was Don Dunn. Lee contributed to the personnel stories, the shipyard overhaul, and floating on station in the North Pacific. Tom Milligan was especially helpful with the Deep Freeze deployment and the captain's actions. As navigator, he was an invaluable information source. Thanks, Tom, for the time and effort given to help me better understand events that I was part of, but not privy to what was happening backstage. Fred Levin helped me better understand some of Captain Beyer's concerns. For the photos, my thanks to Tom and Lee for digging out the old Kodachromes and to Anne Wright for the photo of Ross. I appreciate the legal assistance rendered by Lee Cole and my friend Sandy Poland Demars. Thank you both for reviewing the document from a legal standpoint.

The best and perhaps only resource that addresses the navy's role on the DEW Line is *Guarding the Cold War Ramparts: The U.S. Navy's Role in Continental Air Defense*, by Captain Joseph F. Bouchard (Naval War College Press: Newport, Rhode Island, Summer 1999). I found Captain Bouchard's work indispensable.

My thanks to the late Mary Jean Ainsley, who edited my draft and was the first to tell me I had a story worth publishing. Steve Phimister, a friend since the eighth grade and a retired navy four-striper, was helpful in matters of navy policy, the burden and responsibilities of command afloat, and the Cold War. His wife, the author Karen Jones, encouraged and guided me in the practical aspects of writing and publishing. Thanks to my college roommate and naval aviator Bob Yohe for ensuring that my social life was adequately recorded.

Unfortunately, many of the officers and crew who might have filled in the numerous blank spots in this memoir could not be found or have since passed away. One might think that living close together in a small steel cocoon, we officers would have similar stories to tell. Surprisingly, our individual departmental responsibilities in gunnery, operations, supply, or engineering tended to limit our awareness as to what the other guys were doing. At least, this was evident in our long-term memories. We tend to remember events as they relate to us. I was careful to verify the events I write about. Yet I found that three people agreeing on an event could come away with three different interpretations of what the event meant to them. So it is with my memoir.

We each came aboard with a different agenda. Some marveled at being at sea. Larry Hanson, Tom Milligan, and others enjoyed their years on the *Vance* and would probably write a very different account. Don Dunn, Lee Cole, and the other wardroom engineers will likely identify more with my story. Yet my story is unique because my joy was ashore. I was excited about where the ship went, the ports and countries visited. So beware, this is my memoir about a difficult and unhappy three years at sea that I am happy to have experienced. The views presented here are mine and mine alone.

I have done my best to stay true to events and yet avoid embarrassing members of the cast. I changed the names of a few shipmates and ladies who might have preferred to remain anonymous. It is not my intent to demean or humble anyone. Because of their ability to influence all life aboard ship, the commanding officers and their seconds-in-command are more closely scrutinized. Today there is a strong bond among a handful of men who sailed with me, if only because you had to be there to appreciate the journey. Fifty years ago on the *Vance*'s rolling decks, we were competitive, cocky young men, very different from the more gentle, forgiving nature of hopefully wiser old men looking back. This is how I remember it.

Finally, I wish to thank my partner, Marilyn Mattice, for her patience and understanding over the last few years when I brought the *Vance* into our little home for several hours a day. After plowing through pages of my first effort, Marilyn accurately pointed out that the story should be about me and that the ship was secondary. I began again, this time telling my story. Thank you, Marilyn.

Tom Jaras
Albany, New York
2013

CHAPTER 1

Arrival in Paradise

July 21–August 23, 1961

War is God's way of teaching Americans geography.

—Ambrose Bierce,
journalist and writer (1842–1913)

Cold War Living

In 1949, while I was dreaming of the cute brown-haired girl in the front row of Miss Lang's fifth-grade class at St. Jerome's Elementary School, the Soviets went and exploded their first atomic bomb. We, meaning we Slovenian and Irish residents on Cleveland's east side, had lost our leading position in the world now that someone besides us had a nuclear capability. But had we really lost our dominant world position? The commies' bomb achievement led to a second problem. The problem reminded me of the man who built a boat in his basement and then found the finished product too large to get out of the house. The Soviets had the bomb, but they lacked a delivery system capable of threatening the continental United States. Not understanding this fine point about delivery systems, we went about the urgent business of stockpiling canned foods and dreaming about home bomb shelters that only the wealthy could afford. We glossed over the tricky business of how to avoid breathing radioactive fallout. We avoided thinking too hard about what there were no answers for—similar to the approach our parish priest advised when we expressed religious doubts. We let ourselves be guided by government or the church, the organizations with all the facts.

By 1954, when I was painting rooms at the East Shore Motel after school at Collinwood High, the Soviets took advantage of my being preoccupied and introduced a new long-range

1

bomber capable of delivering nuclear warheads to our cities. The boat was out of the basement and threatening to sail. The news didn't stir up the neighborhood because we were already frightened just knowing the Soviets had the bomb. The government had never bothered to explain the need for a delivery system. Stockpiling food and digging bomb shelters continued, but with less enthusiasm. The Korean War came and went. The Cold War remained a threat to the neighborhood, but it was no longer a new threat. The Cold War was now a part of our lives, a necessary familiar part, like dikes to a Dutchman.

While I went on to complete high school and attended college in the mid- and late 1950s, the Department of Defense was busy countering the Soviet threat by establishing a continental air defense system. We civilians were too busy with our daily lives to be aware of these countermeasures, much less the details. We were all familiar with the much-lauded and highly inadequate air defense Nike missile systems that dotted the urban landscape. The Nike base in my Cleveland neighborhood proved to be an excellent relocation, a Siberian gulag of sorts, for some annoying eighty-eight squirrels my father trapped in our yard, transported in the trunk of our 1948 Plymouth, and released in the wooded area around the Nike site—squirrels condemned to life as exiles from our house on East 146th Street. The Nike missile defense, while inadequate for protecting the cities, at the time served to reduce our fear of being incinerated. I had no idea how the squirrels managed.

The Nike was a stopgap measure while the government built a better system, an offshore early warning system that would allow our interceptor aircraft time to destroy the Soviet bombers before they reached the continental United States. Of course, I was oblivious to this massive undertaking, having my own problems to contend with: the social tortures of high school, followed by the academic hell of a college engineering curriculum. My personal problems didn't stop the Defense Department in 1954 from establishing two radar barriers to guard the Atlantic and Pacific sides of America. By 1957, as I was trying to salvage my failing grades in calculus and chemistry at Colorado School of Mines, the North American Air Defense Command (NORAD) was established to operate a developing network of land-based radar stations in Canada and Alaska, with radar ship and aircraft platforms three hundred miles offshore and beyond, and interceptor aircraft bases. In the west by the late 1950s, the Pacific Distant Early Warning System, commonly referred to as the Pacific Barrier or Pacific DEW Line, extended from Alaska to the Midway Islands. A similar barrier was established in the Atlantic.

The US Navy appeared about as excited over this mission as I was over my calculus class, perhaps because of the tremendous resources required, the static task of manning a fixed position in midocean, and most important, the irritation of being under the overall control of the US Air Force. I imagine it was either get on board or let the US Air Force develop its own little navy to man the Pacific and Atlantic Barriers. In the Pacific, the US Navy's task was massive. It included assembling the navy's largest air squadron to fly the route and a squadron of destroyer escort radar picket ships to occupy ocean stations, all to be eventually headquartered in Hawaii.

Thousands of sailors, airmen, civilian technical support contractors, and dependent families arrived in Hawaii and the Midway Islands in support of the mission. In July 1958, as I relinquished all thoughts of an engineering career and transferred to Marietta College in southern Ohio, the USS *Vance* (DER 387) sailed from Hawaii to arrive on ocean station, the first ship on the Pacific Barrier. How was I to know that the *Vance* was to leave an indelible mark on my life?

Two years later, I was nearing my immediate goal, a college diploma. Beyond the campus, little had changed. Americans remained preoccupied with the Cold War. Since childhood, my generation had lived with this long -worrisome confrontational horse race. Dad would be in the backyard at night with binoculars to catch a glimpse of *Sputnik* passing overhead, an effective advertisement of Soviet superiority. The news media

3

provided an unending running commentary on the nose-to-nose arms race for technological superiority. The troublesome domino theory, foreseeing the continued ideological and political expansion of the communist world, was forever in the news. We saw it as a deadly spreading cancer. And there was the mother of all fears, nuclear war.

Accompanying these societal fears was an enduring fixed reality in the life of every young American male, universal military service. This was the norm. We saw our fathers and uncles serve in World War II, our uncles and cousins called up for the Korean Conflict, and now us in the continuing Cold War environment, all so rational at the time. The draft had always been part of our lives. We young males accepted that the draft was as inevitable as the daily sunrise. Upon graduation from college, I had the choice of two years as a draftee in the army or three to four years as an officer in one of the armed services. The choice was mine: to be drafted into the US Army meant two years as an enlisted man sleeping in foxholes on a huge army base in the south or an additional year as an officer in the same foxholes. The US Air Force offered better sleeping arrangements, a longer commitment, and no travel guarantees.

The choice was not difficult at age twenty-two. I wanted to see as much of the world as possible. I had no intention of committing to an early civilian career so that one day I could retire and travel as an old geezer. "Seize the day." "Damn the torpedoes; full speed ahead." Yes, I was and still am impatient. Where were the greatest travel opportunities for a penniless adventurous young man in a 1960s world, when international travel was expensive and the draft was ready to grab your body? Why, of course, the US Navy. Just read the posters: "Join the Navy and See the World." The slogan appeared to make sense because only the navy was mobile. In the air force or army, I could get lucky and snag an overseas assignment for a year or two in Asia or Europe, but the odds were against it. With no real guidance, I turned down naval air, the brown-shoe navy, thinking I didn't want to visit the airports of the world.

4

Besides, my eyes were not good enough for me to be a pilot. Based on my less-than-well-informed opinion, I selected the black-shoe navy, the seagoing navy, in the tradition of Nelson, Cook, and the long line of illustrious naval heroes and explorers available in Ohio only through books and the movies. I had never seen an ocean. The only saltwater in my life had been in our kitchen.

I can still hear the advice of Bill, my alarmed, older, pragmatic brother, who warned me, "You are wasting three years of your life while the competition is busy developing their careers. Join the National Guard or take the two years in the army." Bill, who would never have to put on a uniform, was safe from the draft. He was in law school, married, and starting a family. He meant well, although I had long realized we lived in different worlds. Bill was content in Cleveland and tenacious over a career. I had no career ambitions and couldn't wait to leave Ohio and the country.

Aloha, Oahu, and Vance

Hot tarmac, a light damp breeze, and the pungent fragrance of tropical flowers came in a rush as I stepped from the Boeing 707, after my first ride in a jet aircraft, into paradise at Honolulu International Airport, courtesy of the Department of Defense. The runways are shared with Hickam Air Force Base, where we deplaned. There was nothing special about the Hickam terminal area—just an open clean terminal softened by palm trees and shrubbery. The welcome committee consisted of two interesting, smooth tan-skinned girls in sarongs swaying their beautifully proportioned hips to the strum of a ukulele. One of the girls smiled at me, whispered aloha, and placed the traditional flower lei around my neck. I was euphoric, certain that I had lucked out and could look forward to three sweet years as a naval officer in the South Pacific before returning to civilian life. I knew this was paradise; after all, I had read everything Michener had written about the South Pacific.

5

Waiting for my luggage, I had time to reflect on the orders in my folder. They read: Upon graduation from Officers Candidate School (OCS), I was to report as the main propulsion assistant (MPA) to the USS *Vance* (DER 387) at Pearl Harbor after thirty days' leave. My fairy godmother, the Navy Bureau of Personnel, commonly called BUPERS, struck her magic wand, and here I landed, assigned to spend the next three years on a small unimportant destroyer escort in the Pineapple Fleet at Pearl Harbor. What more could I have asked for? I was several thousand miles from my industrial hometown of unhappy memories, Cleveland, Ohio, and stepping into paradise, the Hawaiian Islands, the heart of the fabled South Pacific. I was ready for the forever-blue skies, quiet lagoons, beautiful dark-skinned women, and clean sandy beaches. Here was liberation from family and Cleveland, a leap into a new and wonderful world, a paradise compared to what I had left.

The other part of the equation was this ship business. I accepted the risk of the unknown without giving the subject much thought. I had never been on a ship before. Yes, there was Lake Erie one city block from our house, and yes, Dad would hook up our Johnson five-horsepower outboard motor to a rented rowboat and we would cruise close to shore, fishing. Now I was about to graduate from a boat to a ship and from a lake to an ocean—no big deal. As for naval vessels, I relied on the navy to instruct me. Unfortunately or perhaps fortunately, OCS did not include shipboard training or ship visits. Instead, we learned the eighteenth-century naval vocabulary essential to being understood aboard ship: bulkhead not wall, deck not floor, ladder not stairs, overhead not ceiling, forward not front, aft not rear, and a hundred other quaint terms.

I joke now, but this preparation kept me from appearing a total fool my first months aboard ship. A large part of the curriculum was directed to teaching us enough to look and act like naval officers: correct vocabulary to sound nautical, proper wearing of the uniform so as to appear to be naval officers, and the rituals—when and how to salute, how to board and depart a ship, how to address your superiors and subordinates, and much more. These superficial skills were designed to quietly sneak new, know-nothing, sixteen-week OCS wonders aboard ship, while avoiding horselaughs from the crew and dressing-downs from the more senior officers. Once aboard, we were to learn how to be naval officers.

After four intensive months of training at OCS, I knew the pointy end was the front of a ship and the rounded end the rear, but I didn't know what a DER was and here I was with orders to one. I knew about destroyers, those streamlined, low-riding warships bristling with weapons and built for speed. On the naval base waterfront at Newport, Rhode Island, a DER had to be pointed out to me. It was a smallish, strange vessel with an unusually high midsection that destroyed any pretense of speed and maneuverability, more a plow horse than a thoroughbred. I briefly visited the ship, learning nothing and feeling like an intruder. With 150 sailors moving about the cramped decks of a working ship, a green OCS soon-to-be officer was just

Brief History of the USS *Vance*
The destroyer escort was a new vessel inspired by the need for a quick, economical way to protect shipping during World War II. A destroyer escort could be built in half the time and at one-third the cost of a conventional destroyer. Some 563 of these ships were built in sixteen shipyards between 1943 and 1945. About half of those with direct-drive diesel propulsion (*Edsall* class), including the USS *Vance*, were built by the Brown Shipbuilding Company in Houston, Texas, a subsidiary of Brown & Root. With a nine-million-dollar subsidy from the US Navy and no previous shipbuilding experience, the company built sixty-one ships during the war, an average of one a week.

The USS *Vance*, named for LTJG Joseph Vance, who was killed in action at Guadalcanal, had her keel laid down April 30, 1943, and was launched two and a half months later. After two war years in the Atlantic, the ship was dispatched to the Pacific in 1945, then decommissioned the following year and placed in the reserve fleet. After being mothballed for six years, the ship was loaned to the US Coast Guard from 1952 to 1954.

In November 1955, the *Vance* was converted to a destroyer escort radar picket ship, a DER. She had a new life because of her main propulsion system; direct-drive diesel engines gave her the ability to remain at sea for long periods without support. Recommissioned in 1956, the *Vance* operated on the Pacific Barrier, initially from Seattle and then from Hawaii, where I found her in 1961.

in the way, and I knew it. I never expected luxury, so the brief, superficial look at a DER didn't depress me. I tended to be optimistic in most situations, especially over future events that I was already committed to.

My assigned position aboard was a second mystery. What was a main propulsion assistant? At OCS I learned navigation, naval terminology, leadership, operations, seamanship, how to wear the uniform, how to shine my shoes and belt buckle, and how to blend into the woodwork, but no engineering and no mention of a main propulsion assistant. The navy posters dealt with fresh air and open deck scenes. OCS addressed the exterior or hull of ships but not what propelled them. Unfortunately Richard McKenna's wonderful novel *The Sand Pebbles* was still a year away from publication. Were it available, I would have had some idea of what was waiting for me belowdecks on the *Vance*. I dismissed the implications of being an engineer, again focusing on the positive, an adventure in the South Pacific and the belief that the navy knew what it was doing by designating me an engineer.

There was an additional reason to be positive and excited. I had received a letter from the *Vance* as I was graduating from OCS and about to be commissioned an ensign in the naval reserve. The commanding officer, or CO, a Commander Harmon C. Penny, wrote that I should report in July because the ship was deploying in August for a year to New Zealand in support of Operation Deep Freeze in the Antarctic Ocean. Now this was exciting: a polar expedition down under to New Zealand, Australia, Tahiti, and who knows where, a rare opportunity to experience areas of the world few Americans had visited. What more could I have asked for? My strategy of joining the navy to see the world was proving to be the correct one.

I left OCS with a commission from the president, a pile of uniforms, a set of dog tags, a seven-digit serial number, and a case of athlete's foot between the two smallest toes of my right foot. Today the commission is history, the uniforms wore out long ago, the dog tags were lost, and the navy dropped the serial number in favor of the social security number. Only the athlete's foot fungus remains.

My baggage arrived, a huge duffel bag and a suitcase, one hell of a load to carry and still appear military in this tropical heat. There was the chance that the *Vance* could deploy before my shipment of personal effects arrived. Consequently, I had to carry with me as much as possible: white and khaki uniforms for the tropics, blue uniforms and trench coat for New Zealand, work uniforms, three different color pairs of shoes, hats, gloves, civilian clothes, and personal gear. Still more had to be purchased if we were to be gone for a year. I dragged my baggage to a phone booth, found the *Vance*'s phone number via the base switchboard, and dialed.

Quartermaster Beeman, the petty officer of the watch, took the call and stated that the ship was moored in a nest of ships alongside a tender on Ford Island in Pearl Harbor. "Just take the Ford Island whaleboat shuttle from the Bravo Piers to the island." *Great, where's Pearl Harbor?* I was too green and perhaps too shy to insist on speaking with an officer. Later I learned that the captain reamed out Beeman for not passing my call on to him. The officers in the wardroom would have picked me up at Hickam Field and welcomed me to Hawaii. Not much help at the moment. The two long-gone aloha girls seemed to be the only civilians at the terminal. The whole scene was unnerving, a new and different climate, especially the military setting.

The immediate objective was to find the *Vance* as quickly as possible without drawing attention to myself, a new ensign in the new military environment. Gathering my bulky duffel bag and suitcase, I dumped the lei in a trash can to avoid calling attention to myself. I then located the bus to Pearl Harbor. The heavy load was a burden. When an enlisted man saluted me, I wasn't sure if I was to drop the suitcase and return the salute or just carry on with both hands occupied. Did OCS cover this situation? I couldn't remember, so I just pretended not to see the person. Perspiration began to show under the armpits of my khaki uniform. How was I to make a positive first impression in a wrinkled, sweaty uniform? I staggered on, trying not to appear the way I felt, lost and out of my element. Thankfully, I was in a short-sleeved khaki uniform, the accepted uniform on Oahu.

After I got off the bus at the main gate of the Pearl Harbor Naval Base, the marine guard checked my ID and provided directions to the Ford Island shuttle. I learned quickly that the shuttle was the curse of Ford Island. The island itself was a scenic spot, with the *Arizona* Memorial along old Battleship Row, a relatively quiet spot compared to the rest of the harbor with its busy shipyard, ship piers, and supply and support areas. The curse was in having to depend on a water shuttle to get on and off the island. For the single officers after a day's work, rarely was the trip off the island worth the few hours of liberty remaining. Returning on the shuttle posed the additional discomfort of dealing with zealous senior officers who happened to be aboard or drunken sailors returning from liberty. The one scrutinized your behavior; the other compelled you to scrutinize their behavior. Even worse was missing the last shuttle back at midnight. All one really wanted was to simply walk from your ship to the rest of the world.

Destroyers at Ford Island were moored in a nest of ships. A "nest" is several ships tied amidships to each other, usually a maximum of about six ships, with the lucky ship being the one moored to the pier. As luck would have it, the *Vance* was the second-to-the-last ship in the nest of five ships; the first, alongside the pier, was the USS *Hamul,* a huge destroyer tender providing repair services to the others in the nest. With duffel bag, suitcase, and orders occupying my hands, I squeezed up the tender's narrow gangway, dropped the baggage, and saluted the ensign (the American flag is also called an ensign) on the ship's fantail. Both arriving and departing a US Navy ship, one salutes the flag. At the quarterdeck, I requested permission to come aboard and cross over, returning the salute of the petty officer of the watch as he granted permission. I crossed the ship, carefully avoiding the beehive of repair activity on the open main deck, and finally saluted the flag once again before stepping onto the gangway of the next ship. I repeated the ritual crossing of each of the nested ships, first the USS *Nicholas*, a real destroyer, and then the USS *Falgout*, a sister ship and carbon copy of the *Vance*. Crossing each ship, I was careful to only glance briefly at the flurry of welding activity. I didn't want to arrive in a state of temporary blindness from staring at the torches.

On board the *Vance*, my arrival was entered into the quarterdeck log and my bags taken to the junior officers' bunk room. I was aware of being stared at by fifty pairs of eyes on the main deck and in the portside passageways as I was led to the officers' wardroom. Minutes later, another hundred pairs of ears received the news: a new ensign had just checked in, a short guy about 140 pounds, with a big nose. The crew had the advantage: only thirteen officers to focus on, while several months would pass before I met most of the crew. I could have been one of them, an enlisted man, had I flunked OCS or let the draft take me for two years. The reason I was standing there with shiny new ensign bars on my shirt collar was that the status of being a commissioned officer was as important to me as my need to see the world.

I had no choice. Being a commissioned officer was the logical next step after becoming a college graduate. I was the product of two achieving families, first- and second-generation Americans. The ghosts are real. My grandparents, uncles, aunts, and parents, especially my father, sacrificed much for the opportunity for me to go to college and hopefully have a better life. I have always been aware and appreciative of the debt owed to those who came before me. They asked nothing in return but to be proud of our accomplishments. The family was very aware of my new social status provided by a college education. My brother, sister, and I were the first generation with college diplomas. If I must be in the armed services, a commission seemed the only option. Yes, we hungered to be middle class.

I had just achieved educational parity, and now social equality was implied by my new membership in the tradition-burdened WASP officer caste of the United States Navy. World War II had opened the floodgates to an officer corps more representative of American society. The naval officer's costume and protocol were new and uncomfortable. I was role playing, trying to conform, to fit into a new society, new home, and new job for the next three years. Ambivalent over what to expect, I cautiously followed my escort as the ship's loudspeaker blared out, "All officers to the wardroom." *My welcoming audience was assembling.*

As welcome ceremonies go, this one was brief, routine, and lonely, similar to checking into a hotel, only the stay was three years. Captain Penny was all and more than I imagined—a tall, handsome thirty-nine-year-old cross between Dick Tracy and John Wayne. The man had a strong, square-chiseled jaw set on a solid body, a deep booming voice that I would learn to fear when he was aroused, and a smooth gentlemanly manner that exuded confidence. The next welcome-aboard handshake was from Tom Jewell, the executive officer, the second-in-command and always addressed as XO. The rest of the introductions were a blur: nine officers in work khakis milling around this confined space, all curious over what kind of a prize BUPERS assigned to live among them, but anxious to return to what they were doing before being summoned to the wardroom.

Left with Ensign Frank Collins to guide me, I was dispatched to the junior officers' bunk room to settle in. Collins, a short guy with sleepy eyes, had bellhop duty because he was the junior officer aboard. I was now the new "George," or junior man in the wardroom. Frank couldn't be happier; after nine long months as "George," responsible for shitty little tasks like operating the wardroom movie projector and eating last at lunch and dinner, he could now pass the baton to me. Date of rank was everything. Frank quickly pointed out which of the nine bunks, three desks, and three wardrobes were available, and then left. Alone to unpack in this metal box of a room affectionately called the junior officers' bunk room or boys' town, I unpacked and wondered what I was to do next. The ship's loudspeaker, called the 1MC, boomed in the bunk room, announcing the end of the workday and the commencement of liberty. I could hear sailors scrambling overhead on the main deck and in the crew's berthing compartment just outside the bunk-room door.

Sitting here alone seemed stupid, as did the embarrassment in attempting to find my way forward to the wardroom. Better embarrassed than stupid, I ventured out. The stairs, the ladder in nautical language, on the right side, I mean starboard side, were familiar. Ascending to a tight passageway on the main deck, I took a hard left and then another, stepping outside onto the hot deck plates of the fantail. Attempting a casual air of confidence, I asked the petty officer on the quarterdeck the way to the wardroom. "Sir, I'll have the messenger of the watch escort you there." *Never in a million years, sailor.* "No need of that; just tell me how to get there." Following directions, I ran the gauntlet, a hundred feet straight forward through two long narrow crew berthing spaces, with sailors standing aside to allow the officer to pass, an uncomfortable position for someone unaccustomed to deference. Then a sharp right at frame 57 over to the starboard side to the door on the left. The wardroom was empty.

Dinner was a quiet affair, only LTJG (Lieutenant Junior Grade) Hank Fox and me. The rest had fled the ship. The married officers went home to their families, and the bachelors off to their rented house in Waikiki. Two officers remained on duty, Hank and Frank Collins. Frank was busy sampling the crew's chow, a daily requirement for the junior duty officer, while two Filipino stewards served Hank and me in the wardroom.

Hank, or "Foxie," was the electronic material officer (EMO), the guy responsible for keeping the electronic equipment operable—a huge job, since our ship was a floating radar and communications platform. Five foot eight, with a slight build and thick-framed glasses, Foxie was a career navy electronics wiz who suffered the fate of being different. In time, he came to remind me of kids I knew growing up—intelligent, quiet little kids who built beautiful model airplanes and spent hours fine-tuning their little sputtering gas engines. Equipped with an orderly mind and a preference for tinkering with the equipment, Foxie was perfectly cast, a man drawn to fiddle with diodes as a moth is drawn to a flame.

At sea, Foxie proved to be a sociable soul, a regular at the evening wardroom bridge or backgammon game. Ashore, Foxie was shunned, suffering the fate of a good-hearted man who does not relate well to his fellow bachelor officers. While the other single officers, together in their rented house in the hills above Waikiki, ignored me these few weeks before our departure for the Antarctic, it was Foxie who showed me Oahu. He drove me around the island in his little convertible, stopping off at all the tourist spots for a drink or a touristy Polynesian show of drums, hips, and flaming batons. His kindness only became more evident over time. It was Foxie who offered the use of his hotel room or a ride in his rented car when in a foreign port. The music we all enjoyed and the record player that hung on ropes from the overhead in the wardroom were his. I treated Foxie with the dignity he deserved; yet on the beach, eventually I was as guilty as the others. I deserted him in my quest for more interesting company.

In the same vein, I can't fault the other officers for ignoring me on the beach my first weeks. We were shortly to depart on a nine-month cruise. Ashore, everyone was busy tidying up personal affairs. Aboard ship, I didn't know enough to make a contribution to the furious predeployment activity. I became an observer rather than a participant, standing around with my thumb up my ass while everyone else was busy.

On day two, I received the albatross around my neck without being aware of the magnitude of this burden, the assignment to my main responsibility. Ensign Chuck Laipply, the outgoing MPA, introduced me to my new division, twenty-seven sailors standing at ragged attention by the stack on the 01 level. I failed to notice how happy Laipply was to dump the main propulsion or M division on me. After a year as their division officer, Chuck was delighted to now move on to manage the repair or R division, the smaller and more manageable of the two divisions that comprised the engineering department. Chuck's introduction was short and to the point, no need for excessive words: "Men, this is Ensign Jaras, your new division officer." I kept my response to a short lie, "Happy to be aboard." In the two rows of sailors looking me over, most appeared curious and laid back, a few fawning, and a few indifferent. I could almost hear their thoughts: *Just another division officer coming through, a new green one every year.* During a normal tour of duty, these sailors would have three to four different division officers, all of them new to the navy.

In front of the two rows of sailors presenting the division was Engineman First-Class (EN1) Erwin Engles, the senior petty officer. His "Welcome aboard, Mr. Jaras," much to my relief, was short and flat. *Unearned flattery was the last thing I wanted.* At the time, I did not realize that before me was the person who, for three years, was to lighten the weight of the albatross around my neck. Of medium height, an average frame, and about twenty-eight to thirty years old, Engles had probably ten or twelve years in the navy working his way up the engineman rating, hoping to one day become a chief petty officer (CPO) and eventually retire on half pay with twenty years of service. Or if he were happy, perhaps stick it out for another five to ten years.

This interesting soft-spoken man was difficult to read. Most striking about Engles was his quiet reserve, which left me feeling neutral, neither welcomed nor rejected. It was not indifference, just another fact of life he must deal with, as common an occurrence as a rain shower in Hawaii. Every year a shiny new ensign showed up to lead the division. All divisions were assigned division officers, and I was the chosen one this year for M division. The only difference this time was that Engles was now, for the first time, the senior man in the division, the one who must deal directly with the green division officer. Obviously, this guy wasn't going to be my buddy; I just hoped we both had the same goals. At that moment, my only objective was to survive without looking too foolish.

Military appearance was not Engles's strong suit—presentable yes, spiffy no. He had a casual posture with a noticeable list to the port side, which might be blamed on the little black notebook always present in his left shirt pocket. The short cropped straw-blond hair, blue eyes, and light complexion suggested German-Scandinavian ancestry. In his South Dakota hometown, he probably graduated from high school, but I doubt that formal education held his interest. I was amazed by the large number of sailors recruited from landlocked parts of the country. Add me to the list. In his teens, Engles probably was attracted to cars, as were most kids in the 1950s. His skill with the written word left much to be desired, and his speech was typical sailor, plenty of double negatives and subject-verb mismatches. Unlike most sailors, he swore only when angry, and if he had tattoos, I don't recall seeing any.

Engles introduced me to my new kingdom, the engine rooms, an experience both fascinating and terrifying. With a show of jocularity and false confidence, I slipped through the hatch, down twelve feet of ladder, and looked around. Here was another world, quiet, almost church-like, with dim lighting, pipes and ducts running in all directions at once, and a strong fragrance. The incense of this church was diesel oil. A solemn environment of quiet order prevailed here, in contrast to the crowded havoc of humanity above on the main deck. I was on a catwalk, the upper level of a huge room, and still seven feet above a second, lower catwalk. Below, a path of deck plates hid the bilge, with its dark water resting over piles of iron ingots packed against the keel, the backbone of the ship. I had no notion that this collection of iron ballast was what kept the *Vance* alive in rough seas. The added weight permitted the hull to snap back after being rolled over by the force of the waves.

The room stretched the full thirty-six-foot width of the ship, by twenty-four feet long, and rose from the keel to the main deck, a full twenty-two feet. There were four of these huge spaces, about a third of the ship's total volume, crammed full with engines, generators, pipes, boilers, vent ducts, electrical switchboards, and auxiliary machinery. Yet the very size of the rooms appeared open and airy considering the closeness and economy in the layout of the rest of the ship's spaces.

My first engine-room visit was both deceptive and fascinating because I had never been in a large machinery space or power plant. We were at *cold iron*, meaning the *Vance* was moored, with all systems dormant. Electricity, water, and steam were provided from the pier. Four days later, this quiet church-like environment would vanish when shore services were severed and we were underway. The dreamlike tranquility of the engine rooms then changed to the screaming pitch of generators and the constant dull roar of diesel engines. I felt fear and depression. This huge complex of vital machinery was beyond my understanding. How could I be responsible for this strange world of machinery, an environment I didn't understand and probably never would?

Not knowing enough to manage anyone, I tried to look busy as the ship continued to prepare for the voyage. We steamed up the West Loch of Pearl Harbor to the naval ammunition depot. All hands mustered for a day of loading shells for our three-inch guns, torpedoes, depth charges, hand grenades, and small arms ammunition. I couldn't figure why we were arming for a scientific expedition to Antarctica. Still, this was more interesting than the engine rooms. Next came a huge consignment of foul-weather gear. Officers and the deck force were issued everything from sunglasses to Antarctic outerwear. Every inch of belowdecks space was crammed with spare parts, food, clothing, and fuel. We carried a nine-month supply of many of the items we normally take for granted, such as toilet paper rather than the cardboard-like product in New Zealand, leavened flour for baking, and lightbulbs that fit our lamps.

Monday, August 21, was the usual beautiful balmy Hawaiian day as the families of the crew flocked aboard for a day at sea off Waikiki. What do you do with a new ensign, his first time underway on a ship? Why you dress him up in a crisp, well-starched, white uniform and place him on the bridge as junior officer of the deck (JOOD), with a pair of binoculars around his neck. There I stood, a dashing figure, while the ship rocked gently at anchor off Waikiki Beach in a flat sea with but a wisp of a breeze. My job was to assure that the anchor was not being dragged, by periodically taking bearings on three landmarks: Aloha Tower bearing 345°, the pink Royal Hawaiian Hotel at 088°, and a swimming pool at 111°. A lovely day, and yet I was tired, sweating, and slightly nauseous. Five hours later, as we tied up at the pier in Pearl Harbor, I dismissed the idea that this was a prelude to seasickness. How absurd, we only streamed an hour from our mooring in Pearl Harbor and dropped anchor off Waikiki. Still, deep down inside, I probably knew and refused to acknowledge the possibility of being seasick. Three days later as we departed the Hawaiian Islands, I was still in denial.

CHAPTER 2

Underway

August 24–September 10, 1961

A sure cure for seasickness is to sit under a tree.

—Spike Milligan

Sea Sickness

Fuel and provisions on board, lines taken in, ship underway, the fading music of the navy band on the pier, and a final glimpse of farewell waves from Widows' Point as the *Vance* slipped through the Pearl Harbor channel. En route to New Zealand and the south polar region, we were scheduled to cross the equator in three days on a course for the island of Tahiti. We were two hours underway before I realized that perhaps I was a bit hasty in joining the navy.

Anxiety, nervousness, and fear are feelings we all experience at one time or another. They were all present and accounted for, swirling about in my head as I tightly grasped the ladder trying to steady my climb to the main deck and fresh air. My hands were moist. Sweat was running down my face. First, there was the fear of not understanding what was happening to me, then panic when I realized that I was losing control of myself. My feet had difficulty gripping the ladder as the rungs slowly tilted from side to side. Occasionally they gently rose up, slowing my ascent, then a downward thrust caused my grip to tighten on the handrails. My sole concern was to reach the fresh outside air as soon as possible. Nothing else mattered. If concentration were possible, I'd have recognized the symptoms: extreme nausea, dizziness, headache, and cold perspiration. *No time for analysis; get to the open deck and quickly.* I had to vomit and soon!

The moment of pure joy came with my head hanging over

19

the leeward side of the *Vance.* The delight was in realizing that I had barfed in an acceptable spot, the Pacific Ocean. Naval officers did not vomit on themselves. If they were prone to vomiting at sea, the navy in all its wisdom would not have insisted on white uniforms. Naval officers were dashing figures, Renaissance men, and gentlemen born to command, not barf. We smile as our ships plunge and buck beneath us; the rougher the ride the better.

As sick as I was, I could not imagine me, a naval officer, vomiting on the deck. Someone else, some poor sailor, would have had to clean up my mess because officers had an image to protect. Cleaning the vomit from the deck was not in the script. No one had to tell me this. I was not above cleaning up my own barf. It was just counter to everything the navy taught me about being an officer. This particular situation was not covered in the officer training classes I completed just a few short months ago. We learned the correct social posture, such as how and when to deliver our calling card on our first visit to our commanding officer's home. We received a lot of coaching on responsibilities, but nothing specific on how to handle an officer's previously eaten meal. The closest guidance I could recall was that the naval officer was a leader of men, a calm, stoic figure on a burning deck charging into hell's way. I suspect when under fire, one just wiped away the barf and kept on fighting. Impossible, absolutely ridiculous—I could not imagine this shining example of a seafaring man, in dress white uniform, on his hands and knees wiping up his lunch from the deck. Still, I would have been mortified to learn that some poor mess steward or deckhand was cleaning up after me. To guard against my worst fears, I found a bucket to carry, not particularly nautical and certainly not dashing, but workable considering my options.

The joy of having barfed in the correct manner was over quickly; a feeling of relief swept over me for a full five minutes. My world remained one of confusion. Vomiting was not relieving the nausea. The body, inner ear, and eyes were all sending different messages to the brain. My sensory perception was out of synch with the balance system in the inner ear, which was trying to compensate for the unfamiliar motion of the ship. Meanwhile, visual reports to the brain claimed the bulkheads and chairs were stable as always, when they were not. My brain was receiving conflicting messages from a visual system claiming the world was stable, while my inner ear was shouting that it was not. But there was hope. Without much conviction, my rational mind said, that seasickness was a temporary affair. This must be true because I was committed to three years in the US Navy and likely these years would be on said ship, the USS *Vance* (DER 387), with the motto "Watchdog of the Pacific." "Watchdog," translated, meant spending month after month bobbing in perhaps the worst sea conditions on earth. For my own sanity, I had to believe that seasickness was a one-time event, an introduction, a ritual, an initiation to the nautical world.

Unfortunately my seasickness lingered on for the next week until we reached land once again. I recall little beyond the days of suffering. Fresh air, looking at the horizon, nibbling on crackers, and medication were all advised by my fellow officers. Fresh air and the horizon I would get plenty of, because the ship's routine was sacrosanct: all line officers stood bridge watches. Seasickness was not an excuse. The general philosophy was that most everyone on a rough-riding destroyer experiences seasickness at one time or another, and they get over it. Life goes on. There was no need to make allowances for seasickness. Besides, I was observant enough and proud enough to never ask for special consideration. My bridge watches were stood with barf bucket close at hand. I popped Dramamine tablets, and they came back up twenty minutes later as greenish-yellow bile. Holding anything down was a challenge. No, it was impossible.

Attendance at wardroom meals was mandatory. Warding off the captain's cigar smoke and the heavy reek of cooked food, I nibbled on crackers, sipped tea, and then discretely barfed it up ten minutes later in horrible wrenching sessions better known as the dry heaves. When there was nothing more to bring up, the retching continued. Weak, dizzy, and disoriented, I dragged my body about the ship, with a death mask for a face. Whenever free from duties, I could be found in the junior officers' bunk room, in my bunk, commonly referred to as a fart sack. Lying flat on my stomach on the beloved bunk was the only refuge from pain and nausea. I lay there wondering if this nightmare would ever end. I drew no comfort reflecting on the fact that the greatest of all naval officers, Lord Nelson, who reportedly never knew fear, had suffered from seasickness and was incapable for many days of leaving his berth. I was no Nelson, who could stay in his fart sack until the cows came home. As a lowly ensign, the best I could expect was four hours in the bunk before my presence was required to stand watch, be in the engine rooms, or attend meals.

Meals proved difficult because of the aroma of foods. I found that seasickness seriously heightened my sense of smell. The odors hung in the air working their way up my nasal passages to bang against my brain. Each whiff appeared clear and distinct. Had Dante Alighieri been a sailor, one of the descending levels in hell in *The Divine Comedy* would have been eternal motion sickness, with a food-and-cigar fragrance room for the worst sinners.

For some unknown reason, the salty air and spray that encapsulated the ship, although raw, were not obtrusive. I could live with salt encrustation and did. Inside the ship's hull, the air-circulation system discharged the mixed odor of diesel oil and sweet jasmine. On a diesel-driven ship, there was no escaping the smell of diesel oil. I learned to live with it. Jasmine became a separate, special torment thanks to the friends and families who decorated the crew with sweet jasmine flower leis in the wonderful aloha farewell tradition. The legacy of the farewell event, as we cast off our lines, was rotting flower leis piled everywhere belowdecks, draped over bunks, in the trash, even in the engine rooms. As they rotted, sweet *aloha* quickly became a powerful, overwhelming, sweet, sticky stench in the ventilation system. My bunk reeked of jasmine. There was no escape. For a week, the sticky-sweet scent lingered, leaving its mark on me for life. Even now, over fifty years later, a strong whiff of tropical flowers will immediately place me seasick on the heaving deck of the *Vance*. Diesel oil, accompanied by the hum of vent fans, will also start me on the same journey, though more slowly.

Would the suffering ever end? Here I was on a large ship, 306 feet long, a 1,680-ton destroyer escort steaming in the calmest waters of the most tranquil ocean in the world, and yet I was deadly sick. The USS *Vance*, with gentle rolls and minimal pitch, was steaming smoothly at fifteen knots from Hawaii to Tahiti. The sea conditions would rarely be this fine again during the next three years.

King Neptune and Cdr. Penny at the equator, August 1961.
(Photo from USS Vance *Deep Freeze Cruise Book.)*

The Equator and Tahiti

At longitude 153° 40' 30" after three days at sea, what temporarily relieved my seasickness was the diversion of crossing
the equator on August 27, 1961. Captain Penny played his part
to the hilt, arriving on deck in white pants and blue uniform
jacket, a sword dangling from his side. In keeping with tradition, he turned the ship over to Neptune and his trusty *shellbacks*, those who previously had crossed the equator by ship.
The thirty shellbacks took over the ship, and we hundred-plus
souls suffered through a full day of initiation. The captain and
a few old-timers had crossed earlier in their careers; the rest
of the shellbacks were transfers to the *Vance* from previous
Operation Deep Freeze deployments.

I was distracted, but not cured of seasickness, by the initiation festivities, which ranged from shaving heads to total
immersion in baths of slime, to crawling over the hot decks.
Perhaps the most revolting task was kissing the "royal baby's"
greased belly, the belly belonging to EN1 Varn, an older, extremely fat sailor. Chronic seasickness must have helped because I managed to keep my hair. My mind was not on my
stomach for most of the day; the shellbacks had me in stocks,
with a barf bucket hanging from my neck and my uniform on
backward. Festivities over, Neptune returned the ship to the
captain, and we continued on to Tahiti. The mood was festive
and the ship a mess. We were a happy crew on an adventure.

Two days later as we steamed through the break in the
reef into Papeete Harbor, Don Dunn, the engineering officer,
noticed the ship was listing to starboard. Thinking that the
fuel tanks were not properly trimmed, he climbed out from
the engine room looking for the responsible sailor to trim the
tanks. Strangely, the port side of the main deck was empty, but
there was what sounded like moans and groans coming from
the starboard side. Most of the crew were pressed against the
starboard rail watching two Tahitian girls in the water. These
bare-chested girls laughed and smiled while splashing up out
of the water waist-high as they swam alongside the ship.

When Europeans first discovered Tahiti, a local custom was for native girls to strip to the waist before important persons or gods as an act of reverence, not sexual accessibility. If this remained the custom, it was lost on us. The crew couldn't have had a better welcome, despite our arrival as oversexed sailors rather than gods. I was told that we were the first American warship in Tahiti since World War II. I had no idea if this were true; the welcome suggested it might be. What a welcome! Sitting on the pier gazing at us was a beautiful Eurasian girl in a bikini. Eurasians are indeed beautiful people. My sailors claimed that all she wanted was two cigarettes for her services. While my eyes admired the bodies of these girls, my mind remained glued to the statistic that Tahiti had a very high VD rate.

The previous evening, the ship's movie was *South Pacific*. How timely. With the enchanting islands of Tahiti and Moorea within reach, division officers were instructed to prepare their men for the five-day visit through a lecture on the culture and customs of the islands, with the emphasis on what *not* to do. What stuck in my mind, but probably not in my men's minds, was the statistic that the VD rate was 85 percent on the island. I didn't know who came up with this number, but cautious me couldn't ignore the warning because naval officers do not acquire VD. Sailors like to observe that officers catch officer's or gentleman's disease, never VD.

I couldn't forget James, a black officer candidate in our company at OCS, who was a sharp guy with above-average grades and a better military appearance than mine. In 1961, the US Navy was sensitive to the lack of black officers in the ranks. They needed more, but were careful in choosing candidates to integrate the lily-white officer corps. James especially enjoyed our liberty weekends in Newport, where there was a fair-sized black community and few black officer candidates. One day after classes, I found James's mattress rolled up and his locker empty. All traces of the man had vanished. The rumor was that he washed out of the program and was shipped to the fleet. We learned that James contracted VD on liberty, and I assumed he went to the infirmary, not realizing that officers and certainly officer candidates do not acquire VD. In time, I learned that officers with VD often used civilian doctors, rather than seek military medical assistance, because the information might find its way into their service records. I arrived in Tahiti believing my own lecture, while my audience probably ignored it.

Despite our lectures and a warning from a Papeete official who briefed us on how widespread VD was on the island, the *Vance* managed to acquire a few cases of VD. The irony here was that the European navies were responsible for introducing VD to the Tahitians. The sailors from the British Navy frigate *Dolphin*, commanded by Captain Samuel Wallis, first introduced VD to Tahiti in 1767. The French navy made its contribution a few years later. The Spanish navy was right behind them. The *Vance* was just a recipient of an old tradition of the seafaring community.

I had the duty on board this first day while two-thirds of the crew swarmed ashore like a plague of hungry locusts. Duty was fine with me because the ship was moored to the pier. No more rolling. I ate and kept the food down for the first time since leaving Hawaii. My thin frame was almost ten pounds lighter from lack of food and dehydration. For the moment, food and terra firma were better than sex or sightseeing. Duty on board was eventful. We opened the ship to visitors as a goodwill gesture, our first and last open house in Tahiti. The natives stole us blind.

Had we read of the experiences of the first Europeans to visit Tahiti, we never would have opened the ship to the public. The frigate *Dolphin*, the first Europeans to visit the islands, encountered considerable theft of anything not tied down. Two years later and during subsequent visits to the islands, Captain Cook and his crew were continuously harassed by Tahitians stealing everything from nails to telescopes. Bougainville, who led the French expedition to circumnavigate the world in 1768, also experienced considerable theft from the Tahitians. Theft was an understandable and perhaps an excusable trait, as supported by Bougainville's writings popularizing the idea of the noble savage in Tahiti living in blissful innocence. The two Spanish expeditions to the islands in 1772 and 1775 didn't think so. They and the missionaries left behind on the island had constant problems with theft. Stealing was a game of sorts—dangerous if caught, admired when successful.

The *Vance* filled quickly with every conceivable street person on the island. Everything not tied down was pilfered. Battle lanterns hooked to the bulkheads and used for emergencies when the ship lost electrical power were easy prey. Every box of cereal and stray utensils in the crew's mess disappeared. The loss of the battle lanterns came to haunt me over the next two years because we never had the funds to replace them and they were an obvious discrepancy on squadron inspections. There seemed to be no malice in the theft, just a childlike curiosity and a big market day opportunity without a checkout counter. The concept of the noble savage was long out of fashion, but not theft. Sailors on duty were preoccupied trying to lure girls into the engine rooms, muffler spaces, and any other nook or cranny that offered a shade of privacy. I was everywhere, chasing women off the ship and trying to recover the loot.

That first day in Tahiti, I had a lesson in diplomacy by observing Captain Penny at work. I only knew this big, six-foot, square-jawed sailor from a brief welcome aboard, his role playing in the equator crossing, and his cigar smoke in my face at the wardroom dining table. The captain, a deep-voiced handsome man, knew how to entertain and be entertained in a foreign port. Once ashore, he had the whaleboat underway for neighboring Moorea Island with the actor James Mason and twenty sailors aboard. The movie *Mutiny of the Bounty* was being filmed on location. I was surprised Marlon Brando hadn't joined him. With limited whaleboat space and being the most junior officer aboard, there was no hope of my joining the group.

At a party the next evening hosted by the French navy, I learned the Tahitian war dance from a long black-haired beauty. I was no match for the French officers with tablecloths wrapped around their waists pounding out the dance rhythm. The French go native and enjoy themselves. We tended to follow the British treatment of native cultures by appearing more as nineteenth-century missionaries, who attempt to refashion native cultures to our own likeness. The French are more sensitive; they adapt to the new environment. We Americans followed in the British tradition with our own little puritanical twists. No booze on board our ships and little cultural sensitivity to or knowledge of the region despite our coming from Hawaii.

Captain Penny had asked if I knew any French; I admitted to taking high school French. Big mistake. Immediately upon entering port, I was named liaison officer to the French navy for our three-day visit. At the time, it seemed counterproductive to reveal that French was my worst subject in high school and that Miss Evans passed me with a "D" grade because she knew I tried and felt sorry for me. "Aye, aye, sir" seemed the appropriate response at the time. I had a great *bonjour* and a few catchy phrases, well-pronounced I might add, but little else. I could not understand spoken French. At least the Italians used hand gestures; the French offered nothing but that condescending look that said, "Poor culturally deprived fool." As the *Vance's* representative, I was invited to lunch on the French flagship, the frigate *Francis Ganier*, named for the great French naval officer and explorer in nineteenth-century China and Southeast Asia. His chief fame was associated with the Mekong Delta and French colonization of Vietnam.

I arrived decked out in starched whites, while the French sensibly wore short pants in the tropics, not a uniform option in our navy. We were a long-pants navy. My main concerns were to keep red wine off my uniform and to find an English-speaking French officer. I managed both. The ship was interesting, not much of a warship but nice for cruising the islands and lunch.

I enjoyed being the focus of attention that pleasant afternoon with Admiral Martinet, Commander French Forces Pacific, and his officers, dining on filet mignon, fries, and salad and making multiple toasts with a good red wine. Between toasts, I cleared up a small misconception. French sailors had their heads shaved when incarcerated (sent to the brig). Fresh from the equator-crossing ceremony, half our crew was shaved bald. There was concern that the *Vance*'s crew consisted largely of criminals.

The French officers had the envious duty of basking in the sun as they sailed between the various islands in the Society chain, showing the flag and attending social events. I learned that after five days or even five weeks in a port, one was still a tourist. We could not begin to appreciate the islands and the culture in such a short stay. Most of the crew must instinctively have realized this. They focused on women and booze, mostly booze, because the women were not that plentiful—or were they? So much for the South Sea tales of brown-skinned maidens and castaway sailors. My guess was that a few, and I mean very few if any, of our more bold and sex-starved sailors fulfilled their dreams in Tahiti.

Action in Papeete centered on Quinn's Bar, a popular watering hole on the waterfront. One brief evening at Quinn's was enough for me: a lot of sailors drinking, some happy drunks, some angry ones, a few fights, and much noise. Quinn's unisex restroom proved interesting, a slanted floor with a drain at the low end, where one must be careful to avoid spraying some local girl squatting on the floor next to you. I was beginning to understand the disadvantages of being an officer; there was no privacy on this little island. Your actions ashore became common knowledge on board the next day. Sailor escapades were of some interest, while officer events were front-page news and long remembered on our little ship.

Tahiti was interesting and in some ways a disappointment to me. Perhaps I foolishly searched for the simplicity and purity of Mr. Christian's Tahiti and Michener's romantic South

Pacific. Yet I was witnessing the end of an era of isolation. Years later, when working at the Smithsonian Institution, the maritime curator and I compared our Tahitian experiences. He had been second mate on a freighter that stopped in Papeete in 1934. The Tahiti we experienced changed gradually because of its isolation. In 1961, I was witnessing the start of perhaps the greatest change to the islands since the arrival of Europeans. A new runway had just been completed, permitting the first commercial-jet planeloads of tourists access to the islands. Previously, tourists reached Tahiti via a few visiting cruise ships. I was lucky to witness a bit of old Tahiti before the floodgates opened.

What there was of the real Tahiti was beyond Papeete, and the motor scooter was the preferred way to explore it. Narrow roads with a dangerous layer of dirt or loose gravel wound their way around the perimeter of the island. Under a new straw hat decorated with a seashell hatband, I set out our third and last day with a few fellow officers on rented Vespa motor scooters. What a great day exploring the coast and a bit of local history. At Matavai Bay is Point Venus, where the Royal Society, in 1769, sent astronomers to record the transit of Venus. The planet was due to pass in front of the sun, a rare event that can be used to measure the distance of the sun from the earth. The South Pacific was the ideal location for observing the transit. Captain James Cook, of His Majesty's ship *Endeavour,* was in command of the expedition. I believe this was the great navigator's first voyage to the South Seas. Always the dreamer, I was in the eighteenth century while circling the island.

Too soon, it was time to say aloha. The *Vance* was to get underway in the afternoon. Sailors were pouring in all afternoon from liberty ashore. The scene was unforgettable. Staggering-drunk sailors gathered on the fantail in grass skirts, underwear, or ragged uniforms. The "no alcohol on board" policy was strictly enforced, thereby encouraging sailors to be walking and crawling booze reservoirs, hoping it would be sufficient until we reached the next port. What a happy crew, singing and laughing, a few hanging over the side or just lying in their own vomit, one or two passed out. Shipmates hauled the dead-looking ones below to their fart sacks and dumped the soiled sailors into the shower stalls.

The last stragglers were motorized, leaving their rented motor scooters, mostly the surviving parts of motor scooters, in a heap on the pier before scrambling aboard. Unbelievably, a last rider gunned his scooter racing down the pier. Man and machine sailed twenty feet beyond the pier before dropping into the harbor. We fished him out, cast off all lines, and began edging away from the pier. My last glimpse of Papeete was of the Chinese owner of the motor scooter rentals standing over the heap of smashed scooters on the pier, shaking his fists and yelling at the *Vance.* Our propellers took hold, and we headed for the break in the reef at one-third speed.

We were underway ten days from Tahiti to New Zealand, following Captain James Cook, who 192 years earlier headed south aboard the *Endeavour.* After calling in on Tahiti to witness the transit of Venus, he sailed south to 40° latitude, but there was no land to be found. Captain Cook turned and headed toward New Zealand, which had previously been discovered by the Dutchman Abel Tasman. During the rest of the voyage, Cook and his crew charted New Zealand, sailed the east coast of Australia, and rediscovered the Torres Strait. We were following in his footsteps.

Cook made three voyages to the South Pacific, so I assume he didn't have a problem with motion sickness. Nor did I as we left Papeete, because an hour underway, as we were skirting Moorea Island, there was a fire in #1 ship service generator and we lost all power to the ship. I was too busy to be sick. The 200KW generator was my responsibility, although I knew nothing about the machinery. I looked concerned, but contributed little to the event. Once the problem was corrected and the ship steamed for a few hours, the seasickness arrived. I just traded problems.

Keeping food down was impossible. The dry heaves and

dehydration returned, only now landfall was ten days ahead, twice the distance of the Hawaii-to-Tahiti run. I continued to lose weight, a total of about fifteen pounds down from my normal weight. Life on board remained unchanged, the usual routine: watch standing, the required wardroom meals, and as much time in my bunk as possible. Wrung out, limp as a dishrag, I had no fight left in me. My bucket and I just went along with the routine in misery every step of the way. There was no joy in me. I would have willingly traded places with anyone anywhere so long as it was on terra firma.

Yet the panic gradually disappeared. There were no more surprises. Seasickness and I were now well-acquainted. In my only refuge, the bunk, I began to access how I managed to get into this predicament. I wondered if twenty-two-year-old Charles Darwin knew about seasickness before he signed up for the five-year cruise on the HMS *Beagle*. Could seasickness have been the reason he didn't bother to go ashore on some of the Galapagos Islands? We both voluntarily went aboard ships seeking adventure, as did Richard Henry Dana, who wrote about his two years on a whaler. Both of them profited immensely from their experience. Who was I kidding? There was nothing here for me but misery. I had three long years yet to serve on this rolling platform. Seasickness would never leave me. Deep down inside, the severity and duration of my condition told me that seasickness would follow me for life, like a dark cloud.

CHAPTER 3

New Zealand

September 10–16, 1961

If it would not look too much like showing off,
I would tell the reader where New Zealand is.
—Mark Twain, 1897

Approaching Dunedin

On the tenth day at sea, we made landfall after rounding the southern tip of New Zealand. The next morning the *Vance* was off Taiaroa Head, the headland at the entrance to Otago Harbor and the city of Dunedin. The area was named for Te Matenga Taiaroa, a nineteenth-century Maori chief. A Maori settlement existed on these headlands until the 1840s. In early 1770, Captain Cook stood off Taiaroa Head. He reported penguins and seals in the vicinity, which led sealers to visit the area at the beginning of the nineteenth century, followed by British settlers. Now we were plying the same shores. Since the beginning of Operation Deep Freeze in the late 1950s, the US Navy had been sending escort radar picket ships to Dunedin. Now it was our turn, the fourth ship to call Dunedin home for the duration of the supply season to Antarctica.

The crew was alive with interest; even the engineers, who rarely bothered to go topside, were on deck for a glimpse of the shoreline. I was no exception. The anticipation of visiting New Zealand left no room for concern over seasickness. We spotted the lighthouse built in 1884 and a signal station marking the entrance to the harbor. An old retired seadog living here on the edge of the ocean noted our arrival. Through binoculars, I watched him hurry to a flagpole and dip the high-flying New Zealand flag to us, and we acknowledged the courtesy by dipping the American flag on the mainmast. I could feel the twitter on board. Sailors hung over the rails talking while keeping their eyes on the distant shoreline. With nothing but hills to see at this distance, their imaginations had taken over. After all the speculation and months of preparation, we had finally arrived in the land of milk and honey.

At eight in the morning, the harbor pilot arrived on board, and we prepared to enter Victoria Channel. The 1MC blared out, "Set the special sea and anchor detail." There was a light frivolous tremor radiating from the crew as preparations for entering port were carried out by happy sailors on nimble feet. Those without specific duties lined the main deck, standing in formation in dress blue uniforms and white hats. Equally impressive were the deckhands, carefully manning the lines on the fo'c'sle and fantail so as not to soil their dress blues. Not a mean word could be heard. Nasty yes, but happy. The ever-present sailor banter, the "shits" and the "fucks," were lighthearted, without an edge. We were excited. This was what the sailor's life was about: the wonder and thrill

Operation Deep Freeze

The impetus behind Operation Deep Freeze was the International Geophysical Year 1957–58, a collaborative effort among forty nations to carry out earth science studies in various areas, including the North and South Poles. The United States, along with several other nations, agreed to go to the South Pole to study and contribute to the knowledge base of hydrographic and weather systems, glacial movements, and marine life in the region. The US Navy was charged with supporting the US scientists for their portion of the studies.

Operation Deep Freeze was the name for the US operations in the Antarctic. The name generally applied to the regular mission to resupply the US Antarctic bases. This was primarily a US military mission, and the US Navy had the dominant role. Navy Task Force 43, headquartered in Christchurch, New Zealand, carried out Operation Deep Freeze. From late September through March was the window of time available for resupply of the Antarctic bases.

Between 1957 and 1968, the US Navy employed destroyer escorts outfitted as radar picket ships to occupy a position, or ocean station, at 60° south latitude, 170° east longitude, in support of the flights to the primary American base in Antarctica. As the weather improved, the larger resupply mission was underway with icebreakers and supply ships, an intense summer effort to be completed by late February.

of new landfalls and new ports, heightened by weeks at sea between adventures.

The *Vance* entered the narrow, winding, fourteen-mile-long channel, first to Port Chalmers and eventually to Otago Harbor and the city of Dunedin. Port Chalmers, with a population of two thousand, was the main port for Otago Harbor. This saved large ships the added several miles up the winding and relatively shallow channel to Dunedin, a difficult mooring for large ships. We followed in the footsteps of a long line of famous explorers who sailed this channel before heading for the polar regions. The famous Antarctic explorer Robert Falcon Scott was here in 1901, and again in 1910, on his ill-fated final voyage to the ice. Shackleton was here in 1916. Admiral Richard Byrd's ships moored here on polar expeditions in 1929, 1934, and 1946–7. I felt that we were part of this long illustrious polar seafaring tradition.

Colonies of Northern Royal Albatross, seals, and penguins inhabit these headlands just off the harbor entrance. I could not see them, but I believed they were there. Captain Cook reported the sightings in 1780, and I was soon to discover that they were still in the vicinity. At the moment, there was no way I could look for wildlife or anything else from where I stood. My station for entering and leaving port was belowdecks in after steering, a space in the stern from which the ship could be steered in an emergency should the bridge lose rudder control.

Curiosity had the best of me. By climbing up through the hatch onto the fantail, I could see the countryside, knowing that I could drop down the ladder into after steering at a moment's notice. The view was great. Much of Port Chalmers is located on a small hilly peninsula. Close to the southeastern shore is a pair of islands, Saint Martin and Goat Island. It was springtime in the southern hemisphere, the hills a beautiful lush green, dotted with small houses and cottages. Greater concentrations of small homes lined the road and populated the town. At that moment, I began my serious lifelong love affair with terra firma. Never again would I take the land for granted.

Land was color, green, and lush, the ocean a monotonous dull gray. Land was people, variety, and choices. The seas were one-dimensional, routine, and restrictive.

Ashore, the excitement was even greater than ours. From the houses and along the road that follows the channel, people were waving to us. Everyone in the Province of Otago knew the *Vance* was arriving this morning. The schools had canceled classes for the occasion. Old ladies flashed the reflection of their bedroom dresser mirrors at us as a welcome. Small boats accompanied us up the channel, and everyone was waving. Cars along the road were honking their horns. Later, we learned that our arrival was big news and we, the lowly crew of one of the least important ships of the US Navy, were celebrities.

Why so? First, the New Zealand people were just naturally wonderful, hospitable people. Sharing the British cultural heritage, we were well equipped to benefit from their generous hospitality. New Zealand's isolation contributed in no small part to their excitement over our visit. This was 1961, just sixteen years after World War II. The memory of the US Navy, shielding New Zealand and Australia from the Japanese threat, was very much alive. It seemed fitting that we were here in that our ship, the *Vance*, was named after LTJG Joseph W. Vance Jr., who was killed in action aboard HMAS *Canberra* at Guadalcanal in 1942. Controversy over the Vietnam War and nuclear warheads

Dunedin, New Zealand

Dunedin, a city of a hundred thousand, began as a major whaling port in the early nineteenth century and in 1848 emerged as the principal town of Otago Province. Thirteen years later, with the discovery of gold in the province, Dunedin's population exploded, and it became the major city on the South Island. The city has had its ups and downs ever since, but one characteristic held true: Dunedin was Scottish. It was founded by Scots and remained Scottish. They even brought the damp, cool, coastal climate of the highlands with them. Scots and education go together, so naturally the nation's first university, the University of Otago, was founded here. What could be more Scottish than Robert Burns's statue, bigger than life, sitting in the center of town, his back to a church and facing a pub? If one needed more convincing, one could walk down any major street and observe the number of pretty, stout-legged girls with pink cheeks and fair complexions.

on New Zealand soil were future issues. We were the darlings of the World War II legacy, despite only three of our crew being World War II veterans.

A second factor was that in 1961, Kiwis were still isolated from the rest of mankind, and being some of the best-read people on earth, they were very aware of this. Visitors to New Zealand were rare because air travel was limited and expensive. Being at the southern tip of civilization, New Zealanders hungered for interaction with the outside world. They were the best-traveled people on earth, and this travel was largely by ship. Isolation was their lot, while self-awareness of this condition nurtured a knowledgeable, well-informed population.

After two hours of twisting up the channel, we moored portside to the pier in Otago Harbor and were overwhelmed by Dunedin's warm welcome. Moored at the best berth in the harbor, we were readily accessible to the population and they to us. Dignitaries, sightseers, the curious, and yes, women all came to welcome the *Vance*. The crew had a single pervasive thought: get ashore. There was so much to do and see and so little time. The shadow hanging over us was that any day now, with a break in the Antarctic weather, we would be steaming a thousand miles due south to our ocean station. Shore liberty became a precious commodity, and every man was acutely aware of it.

Sailors crowded the quarterdeck waiting for the 1MC to announce liberty. The uniform was dress blues, and the crew looked sharp. You could tell which sailors had a Far East cruise under their belt. Their turned-up blouse cuffs revealed beautifully embroidered dragons in bright gold and red thread, the work of Hong Kong tailors; it contrasted distinctively with the navy-blue wool uniform. Amazing how standard uniforms could be personalized. This was especially true of the circular white sailor hat, or Dixie cup. Some bent down the brim, achieving a rakish look, often accompanied by a tilting of the hat to one side of the head or better yet, wearing it low on the forehead. Others preferred a smooth, perfectly round brim, wearing the hat as designed to be worn.

Six Days in Dunedin

The task of the officer of the deck (OOD) was to ensure that deviations in dress were minimal, that the men were clean-shaven, and that their appearance was neat. The 1MC finally spoke: "Liberty commences. All ashore who are going ashore." Each man in turn saluted the OOD and requested permission to go ashore. A stream of blue uniforms rushed across the gangway. Civilian clothes were permitted, but only when worn once ashore. Most of the crew stayed in uniform; others changed at hotels or at private homes. Officers and chief petty officers (CPOs) were privileged to go ashore in either uniform or civilian clothes. After a few days ashore, civvies became the norm; uniforms attracted too much attention. The novelty of signing autographs for little kids on the street soon wore off. We wanted to blend with the population.

Some of our sailors knew their way around Dunedin and had friends waiting on the pier. After having once served on the previous year's DER, they had managed to transfer to the *Vance* for this year's cruise. I began to understand the attraction. In New Zealand we were celebrities or at least accepted in society and received more than a modest amount of attention. New Zealand was duty to kill for if you were a DER sailor in the Pineapple Fleet. Picket ship crews had thankless, long, boring cycles at sea, going nowhere, just floating on an abstract position in the middle of the northern Pacific Ocean. Ashore on Oahu, there were too many sailors, too high prices, and too few women. The lucky sailors had a berth on the squadron ship scheduled to deploy to New Zealand. Over twenty *Vance* sailors had been on previous Deep Freeze ships. They went south because New Zealand was a paradise for the single American sailor during this pre–Vietnam Era of the 1950s and early 1960s. Women were an important incentive, but more important, our sailors were treated with respect ashore, an elusive element in Hawaii.

Liberty ashore for officers included certain obligations. In dress blues, my first hours ashore, I was assigned to visit the Harbor Control Board with the captain and several other officers. After the toast, a social drink, and browsing the historic boardroom, we were off to make an appearance at several social clubs for more drinks, considerable talk about ships, World War II, and America, and some serious games of darts. Here, I developed a lifelong fondness for darts, learning from these older pros the fine points of the game while enjoying the camaraderie. As if to make up for my dull quietness aboard ship, with a few drinks in me, I became a social animal, launching quips with machine-gun rapidity and often unable to surrender the podium. Most days we were assigned various social events to attend, ranging from parties at private homes to more formal gatherings with officials and at private clubs. One could not buy a drink nor refuse one. Many a pleasant evening, I staggered back to the ship from obligatory social events.

These obligations served to rapidly integrate us into the community. Some of the more memorable social events were with the World War II veterans' clubs: fighter pilots and army and naval officers of the past. These men, fifteen to twenty-five years my senior, were now schoolteachers, businessmen, geologists, and farmers, a broad representation of Kiwi society. Their families had us to tea and dinner, and arranged parties in the country, a keg of beer behind the sheep-shearing shed, and days at the racetrack. Their hospitality was overwhelming. How do you repay such kindness? We couldn't. The best I could do was to volunteer to speak at the headmaster's school. Before fifty boys, ages ten to sixteen, I delivered a brief lecture on America, followed by a very long question-and-answer session. The kids were starved for information on America, having been weaned on World War II stories, Hollywood movies, and now the 1960s' racial unrest in the great white democracy of the North.

Marriage to a "Yank" was a worthy objective in some circles. A few of the *Vance's* sailors returned to Dunedin to marry girls they met from the previous year's Deep Freeze ship. The rest of us just wanted to enjoy the ladies of Dunedin. During our official invitations, I met a few gracious families with lovely daughters, but the opportunity or chemistry was not there. My first unofficial social event ashore was a private party that the *Vance's* communications officer, Larry Hanson, heard about.

Larry, a six-foot-four Dane with a thin coating of blond hair, was a Californian who attended OCS a year before me. He was the friendliest and most approachable of the bunk-room officers. I believe this was partly due to Larry having an inquiring mind. The man was intelligent and very analytical. I liked him immediately because he showed an interest in me and provided helpful suggestions to this new ensign. Larry was a Stanford man, who planned to return for an MBA when his three-year navy obligation was over. How he plotted his future interested and impressed me. "Dad and I plan" prefaced the description of his career plans. My assumption was that he was following in his father's footsteps or his father was very experienced in the business world. Above all, I was impressed that Larry seemed to know exactly what he wanted and how to get there. In contrast, I was footloose and indecisive, an adventurer with an uncertain future. His kindness and consideration I truly appreciated. Yet we never formed a close friendship. There existed a formal wall of sorts. Larry could be reserved, even cold at times. He was a good man, yet so different from me, more calculating and with a structured life, whereas I was more spontaneous and without future plans.

Larry learned of a party from some of his men in the communications division. The party was held in a small barren apartment, two flights up, in an older building in the center of town. We had great expectations based on the stories floating about the ship glorifying Dunedin as a sailor's paradise. Also, there was a sense of urgency in the air; the clock was always ticking, and our days in port were limited. I had to make use of every moment ashore. I never let a liberty day go by without making an effort to drum up some activity, preferably one that included women.

The party consisted of twenty or thirty dancing and drinking people crammed into a couple of empty, shabby rooms. There was no furniture except for the record player and beer keg; it was probably a vacant apartment only used for the party. Occasionally the apartment blacked out until someone fished up another shilling for the electric meter. Initially I was hesitant because several of the men who greeted us with a drink were *Vance* sailors. At least they weren't from my division. Still, I was leery of the situation and uncomfortable. Giving orders the next day to sailors you party with the night before was asking for trouble. Larry seemed comfortable with the situation, so we had a few drinks and met a few local girls.

I loved to dance, as did my partner. She was short, with soft brown hair, about my age, sweet face, and lovely slim figure that pressed hard against me. My god, was she warm. I believe she might have been as sexually excited as I, but that was highly unlikely. No one could have been that horny. Women always interested me from the fourth grade on, but unfortunately always from afar. I didn't date girls until college and had but one steady girlfriend, and that lasted only for a single semester. I had no experience with, only considerable interest in, women. After twenty-three long years on earth, I thought I had at last found paradise. So the stories were true about New Zealand: there was a beautiful woman behind every tree waiting to throw herself at you.

After a few drinks and dances, breathing hard, we left the crowded apartment for the alley next door. There was real passion here; kissing, fumbling hands worked the bra off, dress was hiked up, and panties were down to the knees. Our wild passion was interrupted by voices entering the alley from the party. *Wake up, Tom!* With great difficulty and sadness, I realized that we didn't belong in this alley. What I sought was a private act, not a public event to be circulated throughout the ship. I imagined myself at quarters the next morning facing twenty-seven sailors, snickering and exchanging smiles and making comments just out of my hearing.

My brain once again began to function. She too cooled off, claiming it was late but insisting we meet the next night outside the movie theater where she worked. I skipped along on my way back to the ship, thinking how much I liked this wonderful country. On the way back to the ship, I met Larry Hanson and the bottom fell out. While I was in the alley with my dream girl, Larry had been warned about her being married, with two kids and an unhappy, jealous husband. This wasn't my idea of a romantic relationship! Besides, highly visible naval officers did not become involved in local scandals. I kept my date the next night to confirm the information and said aloha. A sensible act, yes, but I was not happy; the price was high for celebrity status and having a bit of personal pride.

I continued undeterred in the quest for female companionship. Naval officers appeared to be in high demand. There were but a handful of us. A blind date was arranged for a private party a few days later, this time with a cabaret performer. She was a knockout, a beautiful young woman, five foot four, with a perfect figure and lovely long blond hair. Forty people sat on the floor of this upscale home talking and drinking, as the host entertained us by hanging by his heels from a high ceiling pipe in the living room. Again, a few *Vance* sailors were present, as well as six fellow officers. The conversation wasn't especially interesting; she was stunning and knew it. On the taxi ride back to her house, we did some controlled kissing, and I marveled at being permitted to unlatch her bra and fondle those lovely breasts to my heart's content. Unlike the typical American coed of the 1950s, her breasts were available for exploration on the first date. Most single girls in Dunedin either lived at home or rented rooms in private homes. The cabaret dancer was housed in one of the latter, and there was small chance of my being invited into these chaperoned quarters.

The *Vance* went to sea the next day. When we returned, we had one more date, an official appearance at the racetrack, me in uniform and she in a to-die-for sexy open-front dress. What a beautiful woman, who enjoyed the public attention associated with our celebrity status. Unfortunately we had little in common. The little girl in her had fled years ago. Instinctively I knew we were going nowhere together, yet to voluntarily let go of something so gorgeous was impossible. The *Vance* again was underway for patrol duty, and her life continued without me. She probably realized there was more to life than waiting for some short, cute but not handsome, navy ensign. Besides, our celebrity status gradually faded the longer the *Vance* was in Dunedin. So ended a beautiful dream. I bounced back well from the disappointment, having had considerable practice in losing dream girls. Perhaps I would have better luck next time in port.

CHAPTER 4

First Antarctic Patrol

September 16–October 13, 1961

The wonder is always new that any sane man can be a sailor.
—Ralph Waldo Emerson

Campbell Island

There was a chill in the air, two o'clock on this mid-September Saturday afternoon, with the clouds promising rain by evening. We ignored it. Who cared what the weather would be? Our time ashore had ended. Dunedin would soon be behind us, not forgotten, just shelved for the next month. The special sea and anchor detail was being set. When entering or leaving port special care is taken to ensure the ship enters and leaves port safely. Engineering must be ready to respond to propulsion and rudder demands from the bridge. The deck force must handle the lines from the pier and be ready to drop the anchor should the need arise. Radar, sonar, and the signal bridge must be prepared to assist in the navigation and piloting of the ship. Preparations for getting underway had everyone busy. I was inspecting the engine rooms and my other division spaces to ensure that we were ready for sea. Everything must be secure, either tied down or locked in place. Once we entered open water at the mouth of the channel, the ship would begin and continue to roll until we entered a protective channel again. Loose equipment was dangerous.

As I dropped down the ladder into the forward engine room, the screaming pitch of the ship service generator became deafening. After a cursory inspection, I climbed back out to inspect the next engine room. A personal detailed inspection of all my spaces was impossible. I had to rely on Engles and the other senior petty officers to ensure that the job was complete. With the special sea and anchor detail set and all division officers having reported to the bridge that their spaces were secured for sea, I retreated to my post in after steering.

With all stations manned and ready, the 1MC blared out that the ship was ready to get underway. Harbor pilot on board and lines taken in, Captain Penny maneuvered the *Vance* from her berth and out of the harbor into the long channel heading to the open sea. A sense of exhilaration blanketed the crew. Dunedin was forgotten for the moment. We were about to begin an adventure, following in the footsteps of a long line of Antarctic explorers and adventurers. The *Vance* was heading south into wild-ass seas, the first and earliest ship of the season to brave the Antarctic waters. Even the navy icebreakers had to wait until the summer weather made the journey to the ice practical. An experienced few on board understood that September was very early to be heading for 60° south latitude, a mere 6° from the Antarctic Circle. The rest of us had no idea of what lay ahead. The excitement and romance of following Shackleton, Scott, Byrd, and others stifled any pessimism. We had no clue that this was the last time we would be excited over an Antarctic patrol.

As the *Vance* steamed slowly down the narrow winding channel, sailors lined the rails standing proudly at parade rest, legs spread, hands behind the back, the bell-bottoms of their navy-blue uniforms flaring in the breeze, their white hats at a rakish tilt, an impressive show for the Kiwi audience at the southern tip of New Zealand. We basked in a glorious fourteen miles, running the gauntlet of waving children and housewives mingled with the honking car horns as they kept abreast of us along the channel. You would think our little ugly World War II vintage ship was the battleship *Missouri*. I watched this pageant from the open hatch on the fantail. Despite knowing that seasickness awaited me at the mouth of the channel, I too was caught up in the excitement of this undertaking, as the *Vance* steamed proudly out to do battle with the wildest seas in the world.

Our boss, Rear Admiral Dufek in Christchurch, wanted the *Vance* on station early, to allow the first flights of the season to begin with the first break in the weather. Already in the Roaring Forties at the southern tip of New Zealand, we headed directly south to steam through the Furious Fifties and then sit on ocean station at the edge of the Screaming Sixties for as long as our fuel permitted. The navy weather people in Christchurch crystal-balled the timing. We just complied with orders, not knowing what lay ahead. We didn't give the task much thought because orders were orders—or perhaps we were invincible.

I was invincible for a few hours until the ship cleared the channel; then, past Taiaroa Head, the choppy seas began. After two hours of being tossed around, I heaved up lunch and retreated to the fart sack until my next bridge watch. Most junior officers were also in their bunks. I think of these first hours in rough seas as the quiet time. Conversation was avoided, humor nonexistent, people grumpy. No one enjoyed the rapid transformation from protected waters to turbulent seas. I wasn't alone being seasick. I hoped that only a few days would be needed before the food stayed down to get me past my misery. Unfortunately, we were scheduled to anchor at Campbell Island within twenty-four hours, and the seasickness period would likely begin once again upon leaving the island.

Our assigned ocean station for providing navigational assistance to navy airlifts to McMurdo Sound on the Antarctic continent was at 60° south latitude, 170° east longitude, about a thousand miles south of New Zealand, roughly halfway to McMurdo Sound. On the journey to and from ocean station, the *Vance* was scheduled to stop at Campbell Island to ferry mail and limited supplies to the fourteen scientists manning the weather station on the island.

Twenty-seven hours and 430 miles from Taiaroa Head, the special sea and anchor detail was set for entering Perseverance Harbor, the closest anchorage to the meteorological station at Campbell Island. In the early afternoon, the weather cleared enough to see rugged hills backed by weatherworn cliffs and seabirds by the thousands. On the fantail sailors, creative as ever, were having fun with their fishing rods, casting into the air with chunks of bread tied to the lines. The hookless missiles were snatched from the air by albatrosses, petrels, cormorants, and especially the evil skuas. The fantail was alive with circling, screeching, angry birds. Several tugs-of-war were in progress, the huge birds giving up at the last moment when reeled in to within reach. More and more birds were attracted to the melee for an easy meal. A cloud of birds poured off the distant cliffs heading toward the *Vance*. Apparently free meals were a rarity on the island. The sailors were the first to tire of the game. The birds, angry and then bored, gradually disappeared after a clamor of irate screams over having to return to the cliffs empty-handed.

We dropped anchor in twelve fathoms of water.

> **Campbell Island**
>
> Campbell Island is the southernmost of the New Zealand sub-Antarctic islands, 52° 32" south, 169° 10" east. It was named for the Campbell Company of Sydney by Captain Frederick Hasselborough, a sealer, who discovered the island in 1810 and happened to drown there the same year.
>
> The coastline consists of impressive tall cliffs and several fjord-like valleys, Perseverance Harbor being the largest. Sealing in the area went on for about thirty years in the early 1800s. A few exploratory expeditions spent time on the island, including the British James Clark Ross expedition of 1840–42. A French expedition was on the island in 1873–74, to observe the transit of Venus.
>
> Throughout the nineteenth century, whalers used the island until around 1914. Farming was introduced, lasting until 1931. Abandoned sheep and the Norway rat played havoc with the natural vegetation and the bird population over the last century. Eventually the sheep were removed by the 1990s and the rats eliminated in a major poisoning operation in 2002.
>
> During World War II, the island was manned as a coastal watch station. After the war, a meteorological station was established. In 1958 a permanent station was built and staffed. In 1995, a fully automatic station was installed. Today, there are no permanent residents on Campbell Island.
>
> The island is home to considerable wildlife, including southern sea elephants, sea lions, three species of penguin, a variety of seabirds, and the world's largest population of Royal Albatross. The area is one of five sub-Antarctic island groups designated as a World Heritage Site by UNESCO.

Dead ahead on a hill above the harbor were a few low-lying buildings, with a boat ramp stretching down the hill to the harbor and a small dock. From this foreboding treeless, rocky, wet, cold, and desolate environment appeared a small boat. Eventually the sputter of the outboard motor could be heard as the boat closed on the *Vance*. Two tall bearded men in heavy windbreakers were helped up to the main deck from the rope ladder hanging over the starboard side. We were their first human contact in seven months. After introductions, they made a beeline to the ship's store, loading up on cigarettes and candy. Eventually, most of the fourteen island men visited the store while we off-loaded mail and supplies.

The ship's whaleboat was lowered, and the captain, two officers, and several sailors headed for shore. I was dying to go ashore but knew better than to ask. There was a line of more senior officers waiting their turn, and I happened to be the junior officer aboard. It was instructive to note who the privileged few were in the whaleboat. Robbie, our supply officer, was at the captain's elbow, ready to handle any supply requests, admittedly a necessary function, yet I was resentful. Milligan, the ship's navigator and a favorite of the captain, was there. The senior chief, Stanley, who ran the ship's office, and the captain's personal yeoman, YN2 Hamel, also had seats in the whaleboat. The leading aerographer's mate, AG2 Martz, a popular *Vance* personality, managed to join them. Later in the day, others were ferried ashore for short visits, while the captain and his court stayed ashore socializing for the duration of the visit. Had I been invited ashore at Campbell Island, I too would have seized the opportunity.

In the cold and damp afternoon, I stood the first bridge watch, taking bearings on the neighboring hills to assure we were not drifting from the anchorage. The wind never let up, swinging the ship around on sixty fathoms of chain, like a big dog pulling on its leash. On the bridge I monitored the whaleboat's progress ferrying sailors ashore in shifts for short visits. I realized there was no chance for me given the limited hours of daylight left and the number of officers waiting their turn. I joined the navy to see some of the world, traveled halfway around the world barfing my guts out, and here I sat within a five-minute boat ride to one of the rare opportunities of a lifetime to explore a remote Antarctic island. Would I ever have this opportunity again? So close and yet out of reach.

On board, we waited nine hours for the captain and his entourage to return and get underway for ocean station. Night descended, dark, cold, windy, and miserable. Eventually I heard the whaleboat's diesel start up and a bobbing light work its way toward the ship. Finally the boat was alongside. Climbing aboard was a noisy boatload of happy sailors, led by the skipper. Captain Penny, a born diplomat, was never one to turn down a friendly drink, especially in support of American-Kiwi friendship. Apparently, the visitor-starved fourteen-man meteorological station staff baked a cake in celebration of our arrival and rolled out the rum keg to help wash it down. Despite several months of isolation, the Kiwis' remaining booze supply was more than enough for the captain and his entourage to become well-oiled.

I attempted to reconstruct the events of that night, fifty years ago, when we set the sea and anchor detail, hauled the whaleboat aboard, and weighed anchor to be the first navy ship to get underway from Campbell Island at night. The skipper was attempting to navigate the ship in the dead of night, out of this desolate (no navigational aids) harbor, which we were totally unfamiliar with. Moreover, the captain, the navigator, and several others had just returned from several hours of drinking ashore.

As the ship got underway, I was in after steering, isolated from what was happening on the bridge. To reconstruct and better understand that scary night, I went for help to Tom Milligan, who was the navigator on the bridge, and to Larry Hanson, the communications officer. Likely, Captain Penny had planned to spend the night anchored in Preservation Harbor and then proceed to our ocean station the next day. It is difficult to believe that the captain and his navigator would spend the day drinking, knowing they had to take the ship out of an unmarked and unfamiliar channel that night.

USS Vance *at anchor at Campbell Island, September 17, 1961. (Photo from author's private collection.)*

Apparently, we received a message informing us that the timetable for the first flight of the season was moved up due to the earlier-than-expected improved weather conditions at McMurdo Sound. Tom Milligan did the numbers and advised the captain that we had to leave that night or we would be 150 miles from our assigned ocean station. We had to be on station when the first flights would be homing in on us as their navigational aid. The skipper had the ship prepared to get underway.

It was dark, and the wind had dropped off some. The quartermasters could see well enough to take bearings on a few prominent island features, and the radar painted a clear picture of the channel. The normal process for leaving the channel was for the navigator to recommend the courses and speed and for Combat Information Center (CIC) to concur or suggest a different action. Transiting this channel at night was dangerous. The skipper wanted to ensure no one else would share the blame if anything went wrong, so he conned the ship. He took full responsibility.

Now Captain Penny was no shrinking violet. He was loud, and that night, some say he was no louder than usual. Others claim he roared, "I intend to be the first captain in the navy to get underway from Campbell Island at night." The bridge crew suggested that the situation was scary but under control. Others emphasized the importance of Senior Chief Saunders guiding the ship from his radarscope in CIC. Once the *Vance* started to roll, everyone relaxed, realizing we were now in the open sea and safe. I of course reached for the barf bucket once again. Once clear of the island, Captain Penny addressed the crew on the 1MC, thanking them for their help and stating that if anything had happened, he wouldn't have had a leg to stand on.

In time, the night exit from Perseverance Harbor became just another humorous sea story and a positive macho factor adding to the popularity of an already-popular captain. Yet our concerns that night were very real, so real that Larry Hanson, who was responsible for classified publications, went around the ship collecting and locking the classified material in his safe in case the ship went aground or sank. There were some frightened people on board the night of September 17, 1961.

Alone on the Bridge

"Mr. Jaras has the *deck* and the *conn*," was shouted out, a singsong response from the petty officer of the watch to ensure that everyone on the bridge knew who was in charge. The event was entered into the ship's log. Having the *deck* meant that I was the OOD underway responsible for the ship. Having the *conn* empowered me to pilot the ship. It was the midwatch, Tuesday September 19, my first solo on the bridge as the OOD underway. After the first few weeks at sea as a JOOD, I was deemed responsible enough to solo, an accomplishment more attributable to Captain Penny's self-confidence and trust in his officers than to my qualifications.

Behold, there I stood, a new ensign, a rank the navy views as "lower than whale shit," on the bridge alone and responsible for the ship. Proud and tense I stood my bridge watch, hoping nothing out of the ordinary would require my attention. The OOD must be aware of which engines, generators, sonar, and radars were online, what equipment was down for repair, the ship's course and speed, weather conditions, and anything else that might affect the ship or crew. In lousy weather, the OOD could expect a call from the captain, via the sound-powered phones or over the voice tube from his cabin, chewing the bridge officer out for picking a lousy course or simply suggesting a course change if he were in a good mood.

The captain had the worst ride on the ship. His stateroom was perched high on the 02 level behind the pilothouse, sonar room, and the bridge. Forty-plus feet above the ocean, his cabin swung from side to side in a huge arc, whereas the rest of the crew slept closer to the waterline. This miserable location was the price the captain paid in order to keep an eye on the bridge watch and his own career. The navy ordains captains to be gods; with this power comes sole responsibility for the ship. Little wonder the captain always lives within reach of the bridge, the ship's control center.

The last thing I wanted was Captain Penny calling to criticize my handling of the ship. With the wind a steady forty knots and the waves at thirty-five feet, this first solo watch was a busy night. Enroute to ocean station, the orders were clear: maintain course and speed regardless of the nasty ride. We had a timetable to keep. The navigator dictated the course; the seas were horrible. My job was to maintain the course, although I could make minor speed adjustments to minimize the wear and tear to the ship. I was certain the captain would at any moment yell at me through the voice tube for the lousy ride. I doubt he slept that night; yet the skipper never called the bridge. I guess he knew that there wasn't much I could do to achieve a smoother ride.

View from the bridge on ocean station, October 1961. (Photo from author's collection.)

The next morning the waves were over forty feet high, and the wind continued to blow hard. From where I stood on the open bridge, the waterline was forty-four feet below. So what was the big deal if the waves were forty feet high and the bridge forty-four feet? A forty-foot wave measures eighty feet high from the bottom of the trough to the top of the wave. Heading into the oncoming seas, the bow dipped down into the trough and then rose to meet the crest of the wave as it crashed over the bow. The idea was to try to keep the bow at about one *point* (11°) from taking the wave head-on. The ship then climbed slightly higher up the side of the wave before the crest broke over the bow. The angle minimized the jarring impact as the front half of the hull slammed down into the trough again. In short, taking the wave slightly off the bow provided a smoother ride.

Taking a Beating on Ocean Station

Wednesday, September 20, we arrived at ocean station after two difficult days of steaming, bucking a nasty sea. The weather continued to be miserable; the waves rose to forty-five feet and the winds increased to forty knots. We were taking considerable punishment bouncing around in the middle of nowhere. Ocean station was a patch of water sixty miles in diameter, at 60° south latitude, 170° east longitude, roughly one thousand nautical miles from New Zealand, halfway to the major American base at McMurdo Sound. Our job was to remain on station as long as possible. The Antarctic weather window was short and unpredictable. Supply aircraft could fly only when the *Vance* was on station to provide weather information and navigational aid.

Bridge watches on ocean station required little more from me than ensuring as smooth a ride as possible within the sixty-mile diameter patch of ocean. More challenging was finding ocean station and staying within its boundaries. Thankfully, this responsibility belonged to the navigator, Tom Milligan, not me. Milligan, who was both gunnery department head and navigator, spent considerable time on the bridge trying to determine our position, a serious challenge due to the lack of navigational aids. At the time, LORAN (long-range radio navigation), the system then most used for ocean navigation, depended on our intercepting low-frequency radio transmitters from multiple shore stations to fix the ship's position. Unfortunately, reception of the signals in the southern hemisphere, especially the rarely traveled Antarctic Ocean, was not possible.

The time-honored reliance on celestial navigation, obtaining angular measurements (sights) between the horizon and a common celestial object, usually the sun and at night the moon and planets, also proved problematic. The Antarctic summer allowed a brief three or four hours of darkness, during which time the sky usually was too overcast to clearly see celestial bodies. Milligan, using what celestials he could, relied heavily on *dead reckoning*, the art of calculating our position by the ship's course and speed, taking into consideration sea conditions, currents, and other fudge factors. This was an art and Tom proved to be quite the artist, although I know he sweated out the intervals between decent celestial fixes.

A likable, intelligent, pug-nosed, baby-faced officer, Tom Milligan, understandably, was Captain Penny's favorite. Tom, a reserve officer with almost two years on board, was destined to spend two more years on a real destroyer. I respected his ship-handling and navigational skills and envied the confidence the skipper had in him. I think Milligan was probably successful at whatever he undertook. Perhaps this helps explain my seeing him as a bit haughty those first months aboard.

As I said, the OOD's job, once Milligan found ocean station, was to hold as smooth a course as possible within this sixty-mile diameter. The first several days on station we had to contend with hazardous seas, now forty-five feet high, and the wind howling at forty knots. We also were to conserve fuel, the objective being to stay on station as long as possible. The fuel supply dictated the length of the stay. This was why the DER, specifically the *Edsall* class, was the chosen ship type and why the *Vance* and the other few dozen DERs remained in operation sixteen years after World War II, instead of being ground into razor blades along with the hundreds of other World War II–vintage destroyer escort ships. The *Vance*, a direct-drive diesel ship, was able to chug along at five knots on one engine, expending minimal fuel.

By operating only one of her four diesel engines at minimal speed, our standard fuel-conservation practice, we could stretch the on-station time to a maximum. One engine meant only one of the two propellers was turning and at a very slow speed, sacrificing maneuverability for a class of ship that was already noted for its poor handling under the best of conditions. My task on bridge watches was to try and keep the ship at minimum speed, only increasing speed as necessary the ensure that the ship answered to the helm.

We steered into the oncoming monster waves riding high, then dropped off the crest to nose into the trough, only to rise again, quiver, and then drop once again. So long as the ship met the waves slightly off the bow, we were on the best-possible course, a terribly rough ride but acceptable under these conditions. The quiver and the hard slam of the hull were unnerving as the *Vance* shook her bow free of the brutal wave and plunged down into the trough. Then she did it again and again, as if the old gal wanted to destroy herself. I could not ignore the doubts running through my mind. How much of a beating could the hull of this old ship take? The shipyard had slapped her together in three hurried months

Radar Picket Ships*

The navy had learned the value of radar picket ships during the last year of World War II, when destroyers equipped with air search radars had provided invaluable early warning of Japanese air attacks. Fast, heavily armed destroyers had been needed to escort the attack carrier task groups, which were always the first to sail in harm's way, but smaller, more economical ships could be used as radar pickets for slower amphibious and replenishment groups. Design studies for the radar picket destroyer escort (DER) were begun in the last year of the war ...

The US Navy decided to convert mothballed *Edsall*-class DE, whose diesel engines gave them twice the endurance of the steam-powered *Buckleys*. The *Edsall* class had originally been commissioned in 1943–44 and placed in mothballs after the war.

The *Edsall* DERs carried a crew of 150 men, and their diesel engines gave them tremendous endurance, an operating range of 11,500 nautical miles at eleven knots. The design was not without problems. The DERs were crowded, were difficult to steer at speeds below eight knots, and had very little reserve buoyancy (for stability in a flooded condition). However, these limitations did not detract from the outstanding operational performance of the DER, which provided significant capability in an economical package.

* Paraphrased from *Guarding the Cold War Ramparts: The U.S. Navy's Role in Continental Air Defense*, Captain Joseph F. Bouchard, U.S.N. (Naval War College Press: Newport, Rhode Island, Summer 1999)

during World War II, and that was a long, long time ago. At that time, the idea was to get hundreds of these escort vessels to sea as soon as possible to protect the Atlantic convoys from German U-boats. The *Vance*, an economical short-term assembly-line solution for convoy protection, was never meant to be in Antarctic waters in September eighteen years later.

Here was the *Vance*, a ship overdue to join the hundreds of other World War II–vintage destroyer escorts in the scrap-metal market, testing her rivets, welds, and basic design flaws on perhaps her roughest ride to date. We were riding a 306-foot, 1,680-ton ship dropping off an eighty-foot wave crest, with the propellers, commonly referred to as screws, suddenly spinning wildly in the open air. They lost all resistance as the bow nosed into the trough, causing the stern to kick up free of the ocean before slamming down, the screws once again grabbing at the ocean and propelling the *Vance* forward ever so slowly up the wall of the next incoming wave. The explosive force of the forward half of the hull slamming down jarred the crew; 160 pairs of hands instinctively hung on, feet braced, awaiting the next inevitable wave.

The crash of the hull against the waves was unnerving. More upsetting was the *Vance's* quiver, a lull in the action that moment when the ship was suspended on the crest of a huge wave. I could handle the loud collision of steel against water; there was no time to think, just to hang on and react. The quiver was different; the pause led to thinking and therefore questioning. The quiver permitted, no, it demanded my attention. The quiver came in the quiet seconds that seemed like eternity, the bow hovering in the air before crashing down once again into the sea. A few moments of utter silence, nothing moving, like a roller-coaster car at the peak of the highest track, those few seconds balanced on the edge of the sheer drop before the descent. Suspended here was the *Vance*, a huge steel box shielding a little self-contained community of human beings. In these quiet moments, I could hear the ship groan. One felt or heard the barely audible sound of quarter-inch steel hull plates stretching, support frames straining, the keel and main deck flexing. The quiver was a fore-and-aft twisting action of the hull as the ship fought to be free of the pounding waves

The quiver reminded me of a dying whale breaching for the last time, one final mighty thrust to the surface, the huge body briefly suspended, twisting in the air, as if trying to free itself from the sea, then exhausted heavily slamming down onto the sea one last time. The next year in the North Pacific, I witnessed a dying whale making this last mournful thrust, breaking the surface, reaching up for the last time, only to fall back with finality into a calm sea, with sharks clinging to its body. The ship's quiver differed in that it was repetitive, occurring over and over again every few minutes as the ship breached the huge waves.

The quiver was scary because time stood still. All movement stopped; the wind blew unnoticed with the angry seas behind and below us. I was sensitive to the slightest hull vibration. The usual sounds of the hull banging against the waves were suppressed. The message was in the form of a question. How much of a beating can the old gal take before the keel snaps and we all go under? The universe was still, silenced for that brief moment, as if awaiting a decision from the sea-gods on what to do with us.

This degree of concern was not readily evident on board. If there was fear or uncertainty among the crew, we suppressed it. Never would a sailor share his fear or serious doubt with a fellow crewmember. At times, I noted a hint of fear or doubt on individual faces when we took a particularly hard roll and the ship was slow to recover. As the ship edged back to right herself, faces relaxed again. I suspect that most of us were fatalistic and just accepted the ride. No one aboard was qualified to evaluate the ship's capacity to endure this punishment. We passively accepted that the designers and builders knew their trades and that the navy would never permit a flawed ship to sail the Antarctic. No one spoke of the seaworthiness of the *Vance*. Dwelling on the subject was unproductive. There was nothing you could do about it. I read somewhere that fear is prevalent when there are options. The navy assigned us this mission. We had no options. In time, the continuous pounding became the norm, and we adjusted our bodies and minds accordingly. We accepted our lot.

True fear in heavy seas was to be caught in the trough. To remain on ocean station, the ship periodically had to reverse course and steer with a following sea. With one engine at five knots steaming into the seas, the actual speed over ground was about two knots, requiring thirty hours to go across the sixty-mile diameter of our ocean station. We would then turn and run downwind, with following seas and a helping current. Our speed over ground was then about twelve knots and relatively comfortable for the five hours it took to reach the other side of the station boundaries, before again turning back into the miserable oncoming seas.

Executing a 180° turn in heavy seas, using a single engine making five to eight knots, could be difficult. A warning went out over the 1MC: "Stand by for heavy rolls as the ship comes about." Everyone braced, and the cooks ensured that their pots and kettles were secure and less than half full. Throughout the turn, the ship was being battered broadside by the waves. The most dangerous moment of the maneuver was halfway through the turn, with the ship broadside in the trough. In this position in the worst weather, an eighty-foot-high wall of water was striking the ship amidships. This was dangerous! The ship heeled over as much as 50° before slowly righting herself as she turned out of the trough.

With a single engine operating, the turn was agonizingly slow. Not until you felt the ship's bow slowly pulling away from the trough was there a sense of relief. An option was to bring a second engine online to execute the turn more quickly. A second engine meant expending more precious fuel, thereby reducing our time on station, so we rarely took this option. Once committed to the turn, it was too late to add the second engine. To start the engine and bring it online required at least fifteen minutes lead time. Tom Milligan recalls once making the mistake of trying to turn in heavy seas with a single engine online. The ship met the side of the wave and spun 110° to the left with the rudder at full right, losing control of the ship. The ship was then caught in the trough, dangerously heeled over until a second engine was online permitting her to escape the trough.

Our most serious situation in heavy seas was the loss of electrical power. All shipboard functions then ceased, including the engines and steering. The ship would lose headway and slip broadside into the trough. At least once in the Antarctic, we lost all power in heavy seas and slipped into the trough. The crew walked on the bulkheads as the ship heeled to 66° and hung there suspended. This was true terror. A single feverish thought would grip you; only a fool was in complete denial. Would the ship right itself? Were the seas adding more and more weight to the heeled-over hull so that we eventually would capsize? The silence and darkness inside the hull added to the drama. We lived day and night with the constant hum of machinery: engines, generators, circulating pumps and motors, air-conditioning units, piped-in music, and more. With all systems dead, inside the ship was tomb-like, dark silence that lasted seemingly forever.

How far could we heel over before reaching the point of no return? The DER hull was unique on paper. Theoretically the *Vance* could safely roll 90°. Unlike passenger ships, large warships, and cargo ships, the World War II destroyer escort was designed for excess stability. When recommissioned as a DER, the *Vance* was modified by adding equipment and living space above the main deck and considerable antenna systems, all top-heavy additions. To compensate for the four hundred tons of additional topside weight, the engine-room bilges were filled with fifty tons of iron ingots for ballast. The added weight above the main deck increased her desire to roll over, while the ballast in the bilges brought her upright more quickly. As a result, the *Vance* snapped back upright very quickly, the period of roll being eight-and-a-half seconds. The roll period is the time required to roll from full over on one side to full over on the other side and back again to the original position. The period of roll would always be the same whether the *Vance* rolled 5° or 30°. The DER period of roll was probably the quickest and thereby the most uncomfortable ride in the fleet. By comparison, a typical passenger ship has a twenty-eight-second period of roll.

While a ship's *roll* is the ever-present rocking from side to side, to *heel* is to lean or tip temporarily to one side, as opposed to *list,* which is a permanent tilt to one side, generally caused by the position of a ship's cargo or fuel. The *Vance*'s ability to snap back quickly provided an uncomfortable, but seemingly safe ride. What was scary was the ship heeling for an extended period. When the roll exceeded 30°, the roll amplitude increased, and you began to worry about when the ship would begin to right itself. This was what happened when the ship was caught in the trough. The high seas battered the windward side, preventing the ship from righting itself. Milligan recalled witnessing a roll of 72° the previous year in the North Pacific. Larry Hanson recalled a similar event, a 73° roll also in the North Pacific. My guess is that other DERs experienced similar rolls. Informally, by way of old World War II sailors, I heard that 75° was the largest roll taken by a destroyer escort, and this was during World War II, before the DER modifications.

If the *Vance* heeled much beyond the 60° to 70° roll, then the added weight of seawater on the decks and the drag created by submerged antennas and equipment shifting would further reduce how far the ship could roll and still return. A theoretical 90° roll limit was determined by testing the ship in port alongside the pier. Sea conditions, ice on the superstructure, cargo placement, and ballast all influenced stability. Those who knew about the theoretical roll limitations just accepted the number to mean that the DER was more stable than most ships. What else could you do?

When we were stuck without power in the trough this first

Antarctic patrol, suspended at 66°, there was enough time—an eternity—to play games with your mind. Everyone was dodging moving objects and holding on, waiting and hoping for the first indication that the ship would begin the slow process of righting itself. The wait was long and the crew surprisingly quiet. The only movement was in the engine rooms, where the engineers frantically worked to bring a generator online. A long fifteen minutes passed before power was restored and the ship began forward progress and responded to the rudder. Ever so slowly, she righted herself while pulling gradually out of the trough to turn into the following sea.

Shipboard life returned to normal, the usual uncomfortably severe rolling and pitching. No one talked about being scared. Personal fear was suppressed or dismissed. Some probably adopted a fatalist perspective, figuring we had little choice as to where we were and what we were doing, a military organization carrying out its assignment. Others, including myself, preferred to have faith in the navy, rationalizing that the ship was seaworthy, designed and maintained to operate at these difficult latitudes. Other DERs had survived the Antarctic duty in previous years. Strange that I had this faith in the navy. It was counter to my reaction in tall buildings, where I hesitated to press my body against a window or porch railing, subconsciously questioning the design, workmanship, and quality control. Would the window pop out or the rail give way because of a design flaw or a sloppy installer? My best guess was that we, the crew, were lulled into feeling secure and safe by the constant day-in-day-out battering of the ship's hull against the seas. Our world was one of constant motion, so repetitive that the rolling and pitching became the norm. We had a bad moment losing power and landing in the trough during a major storm. It was now over, just one of those experiences that gave us bragging rights at the local tavern or wherever an audience could be found. Fortunately, no one ever learned what the real maximum roll was for the DE or DER hull.

When the seas were high, my four-hour bridge watch passed

quickly since I was too busy to keep track of the time. I watched the forty-foot waves break over the bow and race freely over the next hundred feet of the deck. The forward gun mount, with its protective bulkhead, took the worst of the pounding. Then the wave would reach up over the hedgehog mount on the 01 deck and then leap to the next level to slam against the bridge bulkhead in front of me. At times a wave would surge clear over the open bridge and threaten to break the glass windows in front of me. Water seeped down through the canvas overhead as the last of the wave's force landed on the 03 level above the pilothouse. The bridge was awash with water sloshing across the deck from port to starboard and back again as the ship continued forward and I hung onto the Polaris compass behind the bridge windshield, awaiting the next wave. The windshield wiper would be going berserk, to no avail. I could see nothing but churning water. As the waves exploded against the bridge, I backed away from the windows, fearing they might shatter. They held. This was not a silly precaution. Twice the windows shattered during my tour aboard.

I stared out the bridge window in frustration as the windshield wipers continued to work furiously, about as useful as if mounted in a washing-machine window. As the bow dipped, we began the descent into the trough, and visibility returned until the next wave arrived. With each wave slamming over the bridge, I asked myself if this would be the one to crash through the windows. All I could do was keep the ship heading slightly angled into the oncoming seas, or with the captain's permission, reverse course and let the waves attack over the fantail.

Steering the fishtailing *Vance* in a following sea was a difficult undertaking. Either way, taking the waves slightly off the bow or stern was the smoothest and safest ride possible given the sea conditions. Rarely were rough seas easy to read. Usually there were cross patterns of waves. While steering to meet one set of waves correctly off the bow, a second overlapping set was banging into the hull broadside, creating a miserable ride. The trick was to make certain you were dealing with the dominant wave pattern, and if conditions kept changing, you were aware of it and altered the course accordingly. There were times when the seas were unreadable and experimentation was called for until settling on the best of several miserable courses.

When battling rough seas, the open decks were dangerous. Only the lookouts remained outside; the two on the bridge were generally safe at forty-four feet above the waterline. The after lookout on the 01 level could retreat to a protective doorway. The main deck, especially the fo'c'sle and fantail, were constantly swept by wave action. No one ventured out on the open deck without permission from the bridge. There were times the lookouts retreated from the open bridge to the pilothouse because of the danger of being washed overboard.

The first iceberg, sighted September 25, 1961.
(Photo courtesy of Tom Milligan.)

Antarctic Ice

On Saturday, September 23, the wind dropped off and the seas settled, permitting us to shut down the engines and drift to save fuel. Amazing how the seas were now calm after a week of truly miserable weather. Two days later, the morning of the twenty-fifth, my starboard lookout found our first iceberg on the horizon. Surprisingly, the radar watch in the CIC didn't find it first with the surface search radar. I guess that helps explain why navy ships insist on having lookouts. Once found, it was determined that there were two icebergs out there. Twenty miles off the starboard bow, they at first appeared as part of the horizon, but gradually enlarged. These monsters, big flat-topped square miles of ice, had broken loose from the Antarctic continent. Sailors scrambled onto the open deck to witness the event. Watching Captain Penny on the bridge in his enthusiastic swashbuckling state of mind, I was certain he would love to put a foot on an iceberg. The danger to our thin-skinned ship or to the whaleboat for such an attempt was too great to seriously attempt a landing. Instead, Captain Penny had us close in for a better look and some gunnery practice. The forward gun mount pumped eleven three-inch rounds into the first iceberg. The effect on the iceberg was like peeing into the ocean. These monsters just floated by, continuously depositing huge chunks of ice in their wakes, leaving us to carefully dodge these dangerous baby bergs.

Four days later, additional icebergs were spotted as we steamed toward the Antarctic Circle at 66° 33' south latitude. Wanting to go to the Antarctic Circle, the skipper sent an UnODir (Unless Otherwise Directed) message to Deep Freeze Command stating where he was going. He sent the message late on a Friday, knowing no one would read it over the weekend. We would be back on station Monday before headquarters had the opportunity to tell us otherwise. They weren't pleased but couldn't say much because the skipper followed the rules. Captain Penny was enjoying himself, and the crew certainly wanted bragging rights for having crossed the Antarctic Circle. This was as close to the Antarctic continent as we would ever get. The weather was agreeable except for a brief ice storm, which had the deck force chopping off an inch layer of ice that coated the ship. Ice buildup was a serious concern. The added weight decreased the ship's stability.

As the *Vance* steamed farther south, the temperature dropped; the ocean surface took on the consistency of pea soup, a thick sluggish mass nearing 28°F, the freezing point for saltwater. Some staterooms had ice form on the bulkhead insulation. Our water intakes for the boilers and evaporator froze over, requiring periodic blasts of steam to keep them open. Later in a calm sea, we encountered pancake ice, also called lily pad ice, depending on the size. The surface, to the horizon in all directions, was covered with floating circular cakes of ice, five to fifteen feet in diameter and a few feet thick. In my bunk against the starboard bulkhead below the waterline, I could hear the ice bumping and scraping against the hull. Here, alone and away from distractions, I could focus on our vulnerability, realizing for the first time that only a thin sheet of World War II steel plating separated us from an unforgiving freezing ocean.

Pancake ice looking aft from the 01 deck, October 1961. (Photo from author's collection.)

The captain showed an interest in this new novelty. He suggested to Ray DeMott, the operations officer, that he go over the side and stand on one of the larger floating ice cakes. I understood the morale aspect of the captain's idea, having an officer venture onto the ice. It helped break the boredom for the crew and presented a photo opportunity. Ray was a lanky, quiet, soft-spoken New Yorker, who attended OCS like most of us. He was saying farewell to the navy on our return to Hawaii, having extended his three-year tour on the *Vance* for the Deep Freeze cruise. I liked Ray. He was thoughtful, fair, and approachable.

Ray accepted the invitation to stand on a potentially unstable block of ice floating in 30°F seawater. A plunge into the cold sea could be fatal, especially with the ice cakes grinding against one another. With a life jacket and tethered to a line, Ray carefully slipped over the side onto the dangling rope ladder. He balanced himself for a few wobbly moments on an unsteady ice cake before leaping back to clutch the ladder and climb back aboard. The chosen block of ice was too unstable for this game. Still, Captain Penny and the crew were delighted. Ray, back on the fantail, took the event quite naturally. My guess was that after a year and a half with the skipper, Ray wasn't surprised by the request.

I wondered about Captain Penny taking such chances. Why the occasional risky antics? He was a competent, well-liked commanding officer. His clowning around did appear medicinal for a hardworking crew on a long and boring mission at sea. The skipper once told Tom Milligan that he always took his ship into dock at twelve knots, rather than the conventional five-knot approach, and then backed down full, a good-looking approach if all went well. If he hit the pier, well, he figured he wouldn't make admiral anyway. Penny was always a full-speed-ahead kind of guy, and the crew loved him for it.

We left the pancake ice before nightfall and the surface freeze. The *Vance*, not designed for this environment, wisely headed north to the slightly warmer waters of ocean station. On station, the sea became choppy and the barometer continued to drop. Ugly weather was here once again. Saturday, October 7, the seas rose to thirty feet, with thirty-five-knot winds. I was off watch when the forward gun mount cover caved in from wave action, rendering the gun inoperable. The welds on the aft mast braces broke and had to be held in position with cables until we reached port. Then sonarman second-class Ballard injured his back from a fall during a hard roll. Faced with a possible broken back, the best our corpman could do was administer pain drugs, while the shipfitters rigged a hinged bunk on gimbals, thereby reducing the influence of the ship's roll. Nothing could be done to lessen the fore and aft pitching as the ship's bow banged into the waves. Ballard had to endure several more days at sea. Deep Freeze Command insisted we remain on station.

Others had more minor injuries, a broken wrist and a few cracked heads, including mine. Conning the ship on the eve watch, I was hanging onto the starboard bulkhead as the waves battered the bridge area. With water underfoot, I lost my grip and slipped as the ship collided with a wave. My feet went out from under me and I was flat on the deck, sliding rapidly across the bridge as the ship rolled to port, cracking my head on the port bulkhead. I was out cold, my body sliding from one side of the bridge to the other and back again every eight and a half seconds. No one noticed that the OOD was missing because the pilothouse portholes were closed to avoid taking in water as waves crashed over the bridge. After five minutes, the watch crew discovered me when I wasn't responding to the lookouts' periodic reporting of the status of the running lights. The corpsman patched my minor head wound and served me a shot of brandy from the medical stores.

Low on fuel, we started for home, arriving off Campbell Island on October 12. Anxious to get Ballard to a hospital, we managed to conduct our business and were underway for New Zealand within an hour and a half. Our first and worst Antarctic patrol was almost over.

CHAPTER 5

Comrades

October 13–December 14, 1961

Friendship is born at that moment when one person says to another,
"What! You too? I thought I was the only one."
—C. S. Lewis

Boats and Jim

At five in the afternoon, the light rain was almost a mist in the cool air. The tired and battered *Vance* was secured to the Dunedin pier before a small crowd of girlfriends, suppliers, and the curious. Quickly the gangplank was lifted off the fantail and lashed to the pier, followed by a stampede of sailors clamoring to get ashore. The clock had begun to tick for our whole nine days in port. In the shadows of the pier buildings, I noticed a sailor, his white hat protruding over the turned-up collar of a navy peacoat. He had quietly watched the *Vance* tie up to the pier with a clinical eye. As this large hunched-over figure slowly approached the quarterdeck, I noted he carried a manila envelope, his orders. The peacoat bore a second-class bo'sun's patch. BM2 Oldervick reported aboard for duty, a big confident six-foot sailor with a surprisingly quiet, patient, almost gentle manner, a style foreign to navy bo'sun's mates. This was how I first met Oldervick, one of the most impressive men I had the pleasure of serving with on the *Vance*.

Oldervick was no novice; he reported aboard as the senior petty officer of first division, the ship's deck force, commonly referred to as the "deck apes" for their gentle mannerisms. Rarely was a second-class petty officer the senior man in a division. The *Vance* had departed Hawaii with the CPO billet vacant, not a serious problem because traditionally deck force sailors were noted for their strong leadership capabilities.

71

Other divisions left without a strong first-class or chief would be more likely to have serious technical and leadership problems.

The bo'sun's rate can be traced back to the days of sail and wooden ships. Today's bo'sun's mates continue to perform the basic seamanship tasks. Our sailors of the deck force remain as colorful and bold as their predecessors, usually men touched with a romantic spirit. Their career path was less appealing; there were few advancement opportunities. CPOs with only ten years of service were common in the newer highly technical rates, while competent bo'sun's mates, such as Oldervick, with fifteen years of service, were lucky to advance to chief in a twenty-year career because of the limited openings and strong competition.

In a rate renowned for its strong leaders, Oldervick quickly proved to be among the best. He was big in a chunky way, a bit of a paunch, thin sparse hair and a fleshy face framing deep-set, alert, happy eyes and a round pink nose. Beneath this sea-weathered exterior was a storehouse of world-class dry humor and an easy, quiet smile. Patient, low-key, and thoughtful, Boats was worshiped by his men. I always enjoyed our interaction. He knew I had a sense of humor, so we tended to banter over minor problems, a source of recreation for us both. Typically Boats would casually mention some engineering shortcoming, hoping to upset me. For example, my enginemen would come topside in their work clothes, leaving grease marks on his clean decks, a minor matter routinely handled between leading petty officers. Boats knew I didn't need another problem and that I would defend my men, so he would intentionally mention the incident, sit back, and await a reaction. I would return the favor in the time-honored rivalry between deck apes and engineers.

Bo'sun's mates were often loud, flamboyant men playing out a time-honored perceived role. Cowboys and Texans have been accused of doing the same. Bo'sun's are capable of using every cuss word in the English language. I never heard Oldervick publicly curse or lose his cool. If he were provoked, his face turned red and his voice became a bit crisper as he internally struggled to maintain self-control and refrain from a verbal or physical outburst. When presented with a stupid order, he would offer a reasoned second opinion only if he thought the officer or chief were receptive. If not, Boats just quietly carried out the task, never resorting to "I told you so" when the task proved a bust. I knew nothing of Boats's private life except that he had a Japanese wife, whom I learned of months later in Hawaii, seeing her waiting at the Pearl Harbor pier each time we returned from a long patrol. While most sailors openly embraced their wives and children on the pier, Oldervick and his wife discreetly met in an isolated spot off the pier, saving their embraces for a more private moment at home.

The day after Boats's arrival, I was greeted by the welcome news that a new ensign, junior to me, had just reported aboard. Fantastic news. I was no longer at the very bottom of the pecking order, and more importantly I had company. New officers reporting aboard at about the same time tended to establish friendships, an "us against the world" defensive position, necessitated by the new environment and the formal pecking order, which dictated status by your date of rank. Those of us at the bottom clung together by necessity.

The new arrival, Ensign Jim Kunz, was two months junior to me, fresh out of OCS. That's where the newness ended. Jim had served a few years as an enlisted man in the Navy Ceremonial Guard in Washington, DC. On his thin, erect, five-foot-ten frame, the uniform always fit perfectly, wrinkle-free, with creases where the navy deemed they belonged. Jim, charged with managing the deck apes, was a squared-away officer eager to exercise his new authority, an eagerness tempered by an awareness of how to manage men. Blessed with prior exposure to the navy, an easy division to manage, and Boats Oldervick to guide him, Jim had a much easier passage from civilian to shipboard life than I. Moreover, he rarely was seasick.

Jim and I became close friends, surviving the *Vance* together for over two and a half years. Although close friends, we were very different people, who probably wouldn't have struck up a close friendship in another setting. There was a Prussian military boot-clicking side to Jim that was totally foreign to me. Perhaps his strong Catholic background, fine-tuned by the Jesuits at Marquette University, helped explain Jim's comfort in a military environment. He seemed always to know right from wrong, allowing few gray areas into his life. Jim was a military man, strictly adhering to the rules of military life. Ashore in Pearl Harbor, if a sailor unintentionally walked by without saluting, Jim would stop the man, chew him out, and at times even report the man to his commanding officer for discipline. In the same scenario, I would ignore the unintended slight. Jim needed to uphold the rules, while I was frankly embarrassed to discipline someone over such a minor infraction. If the infraction could undermine my ability to do my job, I would act. I had serious misgivings over the concept that the insignia on my collar commanded respect regardless of my conduct. I could earn respect from my sailors as did Jim, but he enforced the letter of the law, believing in and being comfortable within the system. I was not comfortable and only grudgingly showed deference to a more senior officer whom I did not respect. In short, Jim was a better officer

Author (on left) and Jim Kunz at sea, March 1962. (Photo from author's collection.)

than I. He was made for the navy, and I was not. In 1961, I had yet to understand this part of myself. What cemented our friendship was his fine sense of humor and enough self-awareness to apply the brakes when having carried the Prussian act too far.

Being single, Jim was also eager to search Dunedin for young Scottish maidens. We spent a few days attending required events, the racetrack, a private home party, and the usual darts and beer with the World War II veterans. Maidens were in short supply the six times I was able to get ashore this time in port. We stood a four-section watch in port, the captain being liberal with our workday by permitting as much liberty as possible. Still, I envied the few officers who didn't stand watches, especially the *pork chop*, the popular term for all shipboard supply officers. Our *pork chop*, Robbie Robinson, a married man several years my senior, had served in the enlisted ranks, gone back to college, and then was commissioned via OCS. His was a tricky job that touched on everyone's daily life. Food, fuel, spare parts, ship stores, our pay, and every little personal item on board funneled through his department. He worked diligently at keeping the captain happy. In Dunedin, the true beauty of the *pork chop* position was the ability to be ashore any and all the time dealing with suppliers of food, fuel, and services. A line of vendors formed wanting to please Robbie. The man had entries to hospitality options I could only dream of. I liked Robbie, a pleasant man and always friendly to me. Perhaps what I liked best was his height. He and I shared the distinction of being the shortest officers aboard. He claimed to be five foot seven, as did I. We both were probably about a quarter inch less.

My Second Patrol

The nine Dunedin days rocketed by. On October 22, the crew was at morning quarters for roll call, followed by preparations for getting underway. At one in the afternoon, lines were cast off as the *Vance* backed away from the pier, then pivoted slowly, one screw turning forward the other aft, pointing the bow toward the channel leading to the sea. As before, sailors in neat blue uniforms manned the rail, this time with quiet, sober expressions. The thrill of an Antarctic adventure had left the *Vance*. The pleasures of Dunedin were behind us, and another grueling patrol lay ahead.

Twenty-six uncomfortable hours later, my stomach empty and head throbbing, we anchored at Campbell Island. Within five hours, we were underway once again. I was concerned that the island stops were now shorter. Captain Penny probably had seen enough of the island and its rum supply. The good news was I would avoid a second round of seasickness leaving Campbell Island if our visit were brief. The downside was, would I ever have an opportunity to visit this interesting island? As I watched the supplies being ferried to the island, our chief master-at-arms climbed down into the whaleboat with his duffel bag, ready to spend a month exploring the island. The captain could spare his senior chief for this once-in-a-lifetime vacation, but not the new ensign, who at this point of my education was near useless to the ship. I knew I didn't rate the privilege and as an officer would never be given leave while the ship was on patrol. Still, I was green with envy.

While the chief was exploring the penguin rooks of Campbell Island, at sea we were amusing ourselves with the albatross that followed the ship as we steamed toward ocean station. What a strange bird: a huge wingspan, sharp eyes, and an amazing ability to appear tranquilized. On the bridge, I was conning the ship in thirty-foot seas, with a strong wind off the bow. At fifteen knots, we hung on as the ship nosedived into the trough and reared up onto the crest of the next wave. On the crest of the huge waves, there calmly floated two or three albatross just passing the time of day and probably wondering what the big deal was with us riding this mechanical bull with such grim determination. Undisturbed, the big birds just bobbed along as if in a country-club swimming pool floating on an air mattress with martini in hand, not a care in the world.

Albatross are great sailors but they have a fatal flaw, an irresistible curiosity beyond belief, but who wouldn't when having to exist in a gray world of barren ocean and dull skies? The bridge watch lookouts, forty-four feet up on the open wing of the bridge, were the first to discover this alluring nosiness. Albatross would glide through the air parallel with the ship's course to within ten feet of the lookouts, appearing suspended in air while critically looking us over. By the sailor waving a few inches of white cloth close to his body, the overly curious bird would glide to within arm's reach. All hell broke loose as the sailor grabbed the huge bird, a squawking, sharp-beaked, eight-foot flapping wingspan of a very angry Royal Albatross. Generally, the pissed-off bird broke free, and after a few minutes of high-pitched verbal complaint, resumed his station, now leery of sailor tricks. Out of boredom one day, the crew had some fun releasing an albatross in the officers' wardroom. Removing the huge panicked bird and his fleas added some humor to a normally dull day. I've read about hunters in the 1800s attracting antelope on the western plains by waving a white cloth or ribbon, but never albatross.

At eight in the morning on October 24, while approaching ocean station in very difficult seas, we sighted HMNZS *Rotoiti*, the New Zealand *Loch*-class antisubmarine frigate that had relieved us on station. She was departing as we returned to take her place. This first time viewing another ship in rough weather left a lasting impression. I began to appreciate the beating our ship was taking by watching the *Rotoiti* as she fought the seas. This New Zealand frigate was similar to the *Vance* in that she had twin screws and was about the same tonnage, but she was not direct-drive diesel-powered. She looked a lot sleeker than the *Vance*, but then most ships did. One hundred yards off our port beam, the *Rotoiti* was crashing through the heavy seas. Her bow plunged over the crest of each wave, leaving the fantail and the screws high out of the water. Free from the water resistance, the screws spun furiously until the fantail dropped back into the sea and the bow lifted out of the water, exposing the sonar dome under the keel. What a ride! We felt for the Kiwi crew and then realized that we were looking into a mirror. The *Vance* was taking the same beating and would be for the next three weeks.

Wonderful *Rotoiti*, she was to relieve us as the station weather ship three times during our Deep Freeze tour, allowing the *Vance* some much-needed and well-deserved time in port. The Kiwis had the better schedule: three patrols on station to our six. Our time on station was longer because the *Vance*'s direct-drive diesels were fuel savers and we carried more fuel than the *Rotoiti*. They were at sea for fifteen-day patrols, while ours varied from twenty-one to twenty-eight days. We were very aware of the differences because our precious time in port, from six to nine days, was governed by how long the *Rotoiti* could stay at sea. We grumbled, wishing that we were in the New Zealand Navy and not on this workhorse of a US Navy ship.

Grumble as I might about the shortage of time in port, I appreciated the *Rotoiti* sharing this miserable duty with us. Regrettably, we were unable to know our counterparts on the New Zealand ship. Only once were both ships in Dunedin at the same time, and of course, I was too busy on the beach to visit the Kiwi ship. One of our sailors was lucky enough to be traded for duty with the *Rotoiti* in exchange for one of their sailors. The Kiwis sent over one of their very best, Petty Officer Cheater, a clean-cut, smart sailor with a great personality. We did the same in sending them a squared-away aerographer's mate. Trading aerographers was a wise move because these were some of the sharper sailors on board and probably socially more compatible and less likely to be an embarrassment to either navy. The trade worked well; their jobs were identical. Both ships were important sources of weather information. The aerographer crew launched and tracked weather balloons every four hours, often working on dangerous wave-swept decks. Exchanging sailors was a friendly gesture between two navies.

Later that day, we arrived on station. The air temperature

was in the thirties, the water 49°F, and the seas remained high. My lonely bridge watches resumed. Six hours a day, seven days a week, we junior officers stood a four-section watch while underway. Once on station, the more senior officers stood four-section watches in CIC, a warm but claustrophobic space in the bowels of the ship, forward where the ride was nasty.

The hours on watch dragged by slowly from boredom, four hours of standing alone on the cold enclosed bridge. "Enclosed" meant a canvas roof cover overhead and a couple of plywood doors to the wings of the open bridge. Behind the bridge, the watch section huddled in the warm pilothouse, a social setting compared to the OOD's isolation on the open bridge. Time dragged most when the seas were readily manageable, there being little to do but keep my eye on the course being steered and daydream about the next time in port. Night watches were especially long, with bridge activity at a minimum. Thankfully at night, every fifteen minutes the lookouts each reported that the ship's running lights were functioning, a testimony to their being awake with the sing-song calling out, "Starboard running light bright light, sir," reassuring me I had company.

Because of their cold, exposed stations and to minimize the boredom, lookouts were rotated into the pilothouse every half hour. I had better protection from the wind on the covered bridge. Wood grates covered the deck to improve my footholds when water washed over the bridge, and there was a small twelve-inch-square space heater welded to the bulkhead. When the seas behaved, I gathered a little warmth by resting my butt or hands (not room enough for both) against the heater. In rough seas, the heater was abandoned for better handholds. The only other bridge luxury was the captain's chair, a sacred cushioned throne welded to the deck and reserved for the captain and no one but the captain. The longer the midwatch dragged on, the more tempting the chair, knowing the captain was asleep. The real danger was becoming comfortable and falling asleep in the chair. I was fainthearted enough to avoid the temptation. Instead, I wedged myself in between the gyro compass repeater and the forward bulkhead of the bridge, counting the hours till my relief appeared.

Another disadvantage of clinging to the heater was that I was several feet away from the gyro compass repeater. I couldn't monitor the ship's course with my butt on the heater or if dozing in the captain's chair. In mild weather, if I didn't keep an eye on the course being steered, some bold helmsman, out of boredom, would be tempted to play a favorite game, turning the ship a full 360° without the OOD knowing it. Having this trick executed during your watch was truly embarrassing. I am fairly certain it never was successfully pulled on me.

Once I caught the helmsman, TMSN Jiracek, 40° off course. I knew he was attempting a 360° turn on me. Jiracek, the best helmsman aboard, had the balls to try it and was known to have been successful several times. He risked being written up and disciplined for this little game, but the guy was a free spirit and I liked him for it. A chewing out and a laugh was my response, knowing he couldn't be sure I wouldn't take the matter further. If he were successful, word would have rapidly filtered through the crew that I was sloppy enough to have a 360° pulled on me. A few officers did have the 360° turn pulled on them, some more than once.

There were a number of social dos and don'ts associated with officers standing bridge watches. It was the little things that eventually carried big messages. For example, don't use a coffee cup with a saucer on bridge watches where everyone else used mugs. Don't ask for special consideration, like sending the watch standers to the galley for coffee and cream or some other little personal errand. Deckhands weren't domestic servants. Place your order when the petty officer of the watch announced a coffee run. Special requests for cream or two lumps of sugar were not appreciated. Sailors were not required to do personal services nor could they refuse an officer's request anymore than I could refuse a favor asked by the captain. We officers already had special status. Asking for more invited problems. Empty your bladder before going on watch and be careful on your coffee intake. You quickly learned which officers were calling around to find someone to take the watch so they could leave the bridge to take a pee. After a while, we made ourselves scarce to such requests.

Watch standing on the bridge was an opportunity to know the deck force. More of my time was spent with the deckhands on the bridge watch than with my division of engineers. I met with my division at quarters each workday morning and with a few of the more senior petty officers during normal work hours. Because officers did not stand engine-room watches, I rarely had an opportunity to spend time with my men. In contrast, on the daily bridge watches, there were opportunities to interact with the watch section as we chugged along at five knots hour after hour. Most of this chatter was group banter; individual conversations between officer and enlisted were rare. Comments and short quips were the norm, serious discussions unusual. In this highly structured organization, information passed over predetermined channels. The seaman talking at length with an officer was suspect. The first interpretation by more senior petty officers would be that the man was bitching about something that should go through channels. His peers would view the act as sucking up to officers to curry favor. In confined environments, such as our small communications shack, where an officer and the enlisted men worked closely together on a daily basis without an audience, more personal discussions were possible.

Group banter was the norm with three or four sailors in the pilothouse joking with me or challenging my knowledge regarding some nautical fact. I once won a five-dollar bet that I could tie a bowline knot faster than the leading bo'sun's mate, BM2 Seales, who had twelve years of sea duty under his belt. I set him up, knowing he had learned the conventional way to tie the knot. As a teenager, I had learned from a lumberjack a quick novel way to tie this lifesaving knot. I won the bet but refused his fiver, my payment being a little more respect and leaving a few sailors wondering that perhaps there was more than they'd thought to this green young officer.

Some of these bull sessions were motivated by the sailors' curiosity regarding officers. Officers ruled the ship. They lived in separate, more spacious quarters, and their food was cooked and served in isolation from the crew. Filipino stewards made up their bunks, cleaned their rooms, and hauled their dirty clothes to and from the laundry. Officers had a private lounge area for movies, card games, or whatever. It stood to reason that young men were curious about this private privileged world. Our conversations revolved around hometowns, schools, New Zealand, seamanship, and what they were going to do with their lives after the navy. Occasionally I was able to help someone with a bit of career or college advice. My subliminal message was that I was just like them, the product of a working-class family. The only difference was that because I had a college education, I was a commissioned officer. With the draft, we all served one way or another, but we were basically the same, just guys from different hometowns putting in our time. I had a job to do. A large part of it was to ensure that they did theirs.

On this second patrol, we did our thing, bobbing about on ocean station guiding aircraft to the ice. In the bunk room, we wedged books between the mattress and the outside bed rail to keep from falling out of our bunks when the seas grew angry. I would be seasick for the first two or three days of a patrol and uncomfortable for a few more days. If the rough weather persisted as it did these last several days, I would be uncomfortable but rarely sick. The bunk was always the best place to wait out miserable weather. The seas continued to be difficult, but never to the extent we experienced on the first patrol; still, the Antarctic Ocean was nasty. Leaving station on November 9, we made a hurried two-and-a-half-hour visit to Campbell Island, picked up the chief and the mail, and then headed for sweet Dunedin.

Green Jeans

After twenty-one days at sea, on November 12, we again doubled up our lines to the Dunedin pier. This was one of several pivotal days during my years on the *Vance*, although the magnitude of the event escaped me and everyone else at the time. Lieutenant Mel Huffman was on the pier waiting to report aboard as the new XO. Tom Jewell, with orders in hand, quickly departed after two years on board. As second-in-command, the XO runs the ship for the captain, who technically has no specific duties beyond overall responsibility for the ship. A foreman of sorts, the XO is the captain's confidant, who ensures that the commanding officer's wishes are carried out. To be effective, he must be a hard-nosed boss who does not get too close to the ship's officers. Tom Jewell was an excellent XO, respected by the crew and especially appreciated by the wardroom officers. At the time, we didn't realize how much we valued him.

Unfortunately, Mel Huffman was no Tom Jewell. Where Jewell was tough when required and sufficiently aloof to be effective, Huffman was not a strong personality and too overly friendly to be effective. They had very different backgrounds and personalities. Tom Jewell, at age thirty-two, was a comer in the navy surface fleet, a college graduate who received his navy commission via OCS and eventually attended the navy's line-officer school. Mel Huffman had been in the navy much longer, enlisting in 1947 and seven years later receiving his commission via OCS. He was an extremely friendly and approachable man, slender, of medium height, and certainly experienced. It was soon apparent that we had ourselves a very different second-in-command. The man appeared to be more interested in being our buddy than our boss. In time, the wardroom officers, inspired by the jovial, naïve TV character from the popular children's TV show *Captain Kangaroo*, began in private to refer to the XO as "Mister Green Jeans."

Mel was a strange duck from the start, but tolerable under Captain Penny's rule. I was certain that within a few days the captain knew what he had been handed by BUPERS, that venerable organization responsible for all personnel assignments. I doubt that Captain Penny cared, because he had orders to depart the *Vance* in another month. We officers realized at the time that we had a strange but friendly new boss.

Another Ensign Reports Aboard

The captain had other concerns, one of which was the new CIC officer, Ensign Fred Levin, who also was waiting for us on the pier. Captain Penny was furious because Ensign Levin had arrived in New Zealand a month earlier, when the *Vance* was at sea. While waiting for the ship, he was temporarily attached to the Deep Freeze Task Force Headquarters in Christchurch, New Zealand. He then secured a flight to McMurdo Sound, missing the *Vance*'s second patrol. Here was a new ensign missing the ship's movement while enjoying a holiday on the ice as we busted our asses at sea. Fred Levin became the only *Vance* crewmember to set foot on the Antarctic Continent, something we all wanted to experience. To rub salt into the wound, Fred eventually received a unit citation, a medal, because the command he was temporally assigned to for two weeks received this special achievement award for their Deep Freeze accomplishments. Of course, I was envious of Fred having made it to the ice. I guess we all were.

Fred was fortunate that our next patrol would be Captain Penny's last. Just one patrol with a pissed-off Captain Penny, and Fred would start afresh with a new CO. I cringe to think how Fred would have survived under the reign of Penny and Jewell. Missing the ship's movement was a major strike against him. Penny could have made Fred's life on board the *Vance* a living hell.

Aside from the rough beginning, Fred proved to be an interesting, intelligent, and lovable addition to the wardroom. He was senior to both Jim Kunz and me, having attended CIC School following graduation from OCS in the class before me. Fred, who was eventually referred to as "Friendly Freddie," was a chubby Jewish man with a pink complexion and thinning hairline. He wanted to be everyone's friend, and therefore was susceptible to more than his share of abuse in the wardroom. He proved a refreshing addition because he put a positive spin on life in general; he was a happy man with a sense of humor. Fresh from two months of specialized CIC training, Fred, with the help of a strong chief, managed a small group of intelligent, motivated radarmen.

With the arrival of Fred, there were now three new junior officers. The basis for a friendship was there between quiet intense me, Jim the Prussian, and happy Fred. We were destined to spend almost three years working together and sharing the junior officers' bunk room. Yet we knew little of each other's past. I never understood how Jim came to be in the navy honor guard and knew little about his earlier life. Fred was friendly, but also cagey, avoiding details on his past military experience after college. Gradually, it became evident that Fred was an astute observer with a master plan for a naval career, a persistent and perceptive person who took the time to study and work the system. I both admired and was exasperated by the man. Like the albatross unable to stem its curiosity, Fred could not resist an opportunity to impress and please his audience. The urge to please and impress had Fred at times offering more that he could deliver, a dangerous trait when working for a demanding captain.

Fred brought kindness and thoughtfulness to a hard wardroom environment. In spite of Fred's seniority, he willingly assumed the role of "George," the junior officer on board. George traditionally bought all the soap used in the junior officers' bunk room, operated the movie projector, was served last at meals, and performed other little services. It was a mild form of hazing that junior officers endured, reinforcing the concept of seniority and group cohesiveness. No one wants to be in this "lower than whale shit" position, yet Fred accepted it in good spirits and I respected him for it. The three of us shared the

George duties until our return to Hawaii, where we picked up a fresh load of ensigns.

I Meet Miriam

Our time in Dunedin was to be a short seven days, peppered with a few social gatherings and obligations. At the best hotel in town, an early twentieth-century Victorian with the bathrooms down the hall, I met Miriam, the hotel receptionist. This tall, big-boned, twenty-year-old, dark-haired Scottish girl and I hit it off from the start. Here was a fun-loving working girl with a nice figure, supporting a popular 1960s beehive hairdo on her five-foot-five body plus high heels. When she was dressed for work, the collective ensemble towered over me, reaching into the ionosphere. Sensitive to the latest fads or fashions that filtered down to this isolated corner of the globe, wardrobe was important to Miriam. I couldn't care less about the hairdo, clothes, or the makeup, although the height business did bother me a bit.

Here was a cute, bouncy girl with a solid Scottish body, a body that I hoped to enjoy when we had some quiet time alone. Miriam, who was from Christchurch, rented a room in a private Dunedin home. With the room came a vigilant old landlady, who lacked compassion for love-starved sailors. We had access to the kitchen and living room. Miriam's room on the second floor was off-limits. The landlady never left the house. If we arrived early, the old gal would offer tea and sit around until I left. Late one night, arriving well after the landlady's bedtime, we got comfortable together. Stretched out on the sofa, my foot upset the brass coffee table, causing a loud bang followed by the landlady's high-pitched voice from upstairs. "Who's there?" Frustrated, I quietly exited, cursing the lack of privacy in Dunedin and hoping for better luck the next trip ashore.

In my horny state, I secretly envied those sailors who seemed to attract every loose girl in Dunedin and placed few boundaries on their personal actions. If anything, public knowledge of their sexual activities ashore only enhanced their reputations among their peers. The crew seemed to be enjoying themselves ashore, while I felt like a Victorian throwback. A few lucky sailors were more discriminating. They found nice girls to date, showed an interest in the country and culture, sought opportunities to travel, and became involved in local activities. Some of these relationships resulted in marriage. The older, more mature, married sailor might play tourist and drink with the locals, and a few would have relationships with local girls. Most indiscretions found their way back to the families in Hawaii, compliments of other sailors writing home to their wives.

Sarge and the Carbine

Regardless of our life ashore, the leash was short. We always returned to the ship each evening, with a few holding out until morning muster. Upon returning to the *Vance* after leaving Miriam's in frustration, I noticed Scullion, the popular second-class gunner's mate, perched on top of the after-gun mount drunk, looking down onto the quarterdeck. Scullion, known to all as Sarge, was a compact five-foot-four Irishman. With fourteen years of service, eight of which were in the army, he was not a kid. Square-jawed and charismatic, Sarge could pass for an Irish sergeant in John Ford's Monument Valley movies about the US Cavalry.

Sitting drunk on top of the after-gun mount, Sarge was peering down onto the quarterdeck waiting for his division officer to return from liberty. He was shouting, "I'm going to shoot the little bastard." The chief on the quarterdeck watch typically would have the drunken sailor hauled off to the showers and sobered up, except that Sarge happened to be perched up there with a loaded M1 carbine in his lap. As a competent sailor responsible for our little arsenal on board, Sarge had just helped himself to his weapon of choice. After a brief futile attempt to talk him down off the gun mount, I retreated, leaving the task to Boats Oldervick. An officer was not the best choice to defuse the situation. Boats, in his quiet unruffled manner, gradually engaged the intense, weeping gunner's mate in a conversational way. Eventually Sarge handed down the loaded carbine and was helped to his bunk to sleep it off.

The unspoken opinion on the fantail that evening was, let's just forget this ever happened. Had the sailor been a fuckup and not one of the *Vance*'s most colorful and popular characters, there would have been no regrets if he were to face a court-martial. The incident was never formally reported, and I never learned what set this drama in motion. This was Sarge's third Deep Freeze cruise. He couldn't have been on the *Vance* more than six months. The little Irishman was back to work the next morning, and nothing more was said of the incident. Had the captain been notified, he would have had to address the event, perhaps with a court-martial.

Doctor Aboard

Before we were underway again for the next patrol, the navy sent us a medical doctor, Lieutenant Gil Gersenfish, in response to the broken back accident suffered on our first patrol. The injured sailor had been treated in Christchurch and then flown to Hawaii for medical treatment. Gil was to be with us for the remainder of the cruise. This easygoing Jewish doctor with a friendly smile was fresh from medical school, an internship, and then a brief stay with the navy in San Diego. Gil had a few weeks of naval officer's training under his belt, having mastered how to salute and how to recognize the hierarchy of ranks requiring a salute. Doc, as he was soon to be called by officer and enlisted alike, reported aboard and was ushered to the wardroom to meet Captain Penny. He extended his hand with a big smile and said, "Hi, Captain, I'm Gil Gersenfish, but you can call me Gil." The rest of us in the wardroom, on hearing his clueless greeting, froze and looked wide-eyed at the overhead, waiting for the captain's reaction. Captain Penny stretched his long frame, jutted out that square Dick Tracy jaw, and shook Gil's extended hand, welcoming him aboard with a knowing smile. Then, as if the heavens had opened and in a tone of finality, he responded, "I'm Captain Penny. You can just call me Captain." So began Doc's first navy shipboard adventure.

Fortunately in the navy, neither doctors nor chaplains are taken seriously outside their professions. They have nothing to do with operating the ship. Gil was a doctor relegated to sick bay. He quickly gained the respect of the crew, but in a more casual manner than the other officers. In the wardroom his rank, a full lieutenant, junior only to the CO and XO, was unimportant except for where he sat at meals, near the head of the table. Doctors were officers who helped individuals; the rest of us just managed men.

We were to enjoy Doc's company during his several months aboard. Normally the *Vance*'s medical staff was a single senior corpsman. Gil was here solely for the Antarctic cruise. I particularly liked the Doc, who, besides being a nice guy and competent doctor, shared the joys of acute seasickness. Misery loves company. Since he was from Cincinnati, the *Vance* was Doc's first taste of the blue-water rock and roll. The romance of an ocean voyage was difficult to experience on a bucking ship in the Screaming Sixties.

As Gil stowed his bags in forward officers' country, the *Vance* cast off her lines for my third and last patrol with Captain Penny. The date was November 19, a breezy Sunday afternoon. The ship bucked gently as we entered the open water rounding Tiroa Heads. Now we had Doc for company as several of us emptied our stomachs and then some. I felt sorry for Doc, experiencing seasickness for the first time. He looked lost. I knew his mind was riveted on the basic questions. Will it ever end? Is there no escaping this misery? How can I endure the next few years aboard ships suffering like this? I sensed a special amity with Doc; his experience with the sea was similar to mine in severity.

Life aboard was improving as I grew accustomed to being seasick. Every time we were underway, I was sick for two to three days. Once I digested a meal at sea, I was okay—not perfect, just okay. There was no avoiding this curse. Barfing was inevitable and especially violent if we encountered rough seas the first few days out. After a few days, rough weather didn't bother me. Not that I was smiling; I just didn't heave up my lunch anymore. We all felt lousy when in rough water. Upchucking was another matter. Rarely would I meet a sailor who wasn't somewhat affected by rough weather. Most masked their discomfort. The skipper had the benefit of privacy should he feel ill. Swinging around up high in his 02 level cabin, he had to be miserable at times, but captains don't get seasick. Let me rephrase that. Captains are not seasick in public. Several times in rough weather, the skipper missed a meal or would be absent from the wardroom for a seemingly long period of time, to appear later with a pale, exhausted face. Even seafaring men get seasick.

Turkeys from the Sky

We barely wet the anchor the next day at Campbell Island. Captain Penny set a record, slightly over an hour in the harbor before we were underway for ocean station. Seven-foot seas and overcast skies accompanied the *Vance* as we neared ocean station. There was nervousness on the bridge concerning the low ceiling. We were expecting Thanksgiving turkeys to drop from the heavens and feared we could easily miss them in the cloud cover and choppy seas. "Turkeys off the port bow," bellowed the lookout. Yes, there they were dropping from the heavens.

Several beautifully prepared turkeys, donated by a Dunedin businessman, floated down from the sky for our Thanksgiving dinner. Arrangements had been made to have a navy aircraft make the drop on its way to McMurdo Station. Sealed in canisters, the turkeys were bobbing in and out of sight on the surface as we maneuvered to snatch them up with grappling hooks. The crew and wardroom enjoyed a great Thanksgiving feast. This kindness only increased our awareness of how much we missed New Zealand and the wonderful people of Dunedin.

Picking floating items from the sea could be difficult both

because of the turbulent seas and our ship's characteristics. Turkeys in canisters attached to parachutes were easy because urgency was absent. People were another matter. Under the best sea conditions, the *Vance* required five minutes to pluck a person from the sea. In the cold Antarctic waters, often in the 30°F range, five minutes is not quick enough unless the man in the water is wearing special survival gear, which we didn't have. Falling overboard meant drowning or freezing to death in these frigid waters. Fortunately, we never had a man fall overboard.

On occasion, we junior officers were able to practice man-overboard drills. A few of us even had opportunities to conn the ship into and out of port. As unrestricted line officers, we were expected to acquire a broad knowledge of the ship, and Captain Penny appeared interested in bringing us along this path, although the demanding schedule limited these opportunities. Ship handling and navigation interested me. At times Larry Hanson and I would trudge up to the bridge, grab a sextant, and attempt taking sun lines and, sometimes when we could find one, shoot a star. Results were mixed at best.

I'm not certain why I took an interest in these nautical skills. I had no intention of ever being on another ship. The experience had similarities to riding a camel in the desert, an uncomfortable ride with nothingness in all directions, only you could get off the camel whereas the ship rolled and bucked day and night, seemingly forever. This camel ride continued for twenty-five long days until our return to Dunedin on December 14.

CHAPTER 6

Land of the Snipes

Only the guy who isn't rowing has time to rock the boat.
—Richard Saunders*
*One of the pseudonyms used by Benjamin Franklin (1709–1790)

A Poor Casting Job

In my brief years on the *Vance*, the term "snipe" was used most often in a derogatory manner by the deckhands and the operations department sailors. Snipes worked mainly belowdecks in the engine rooms, an environment of noise, grease, and oil. Theirs was a different world. These noisy holes were the source of the *Vance*'s basic services, including propulsion, potable water, electricity, heat, and air-conditioning. Should the electrical load fluctuate or fail, the sailors maintaining the electronics systems cursed the snipes for the resulting damage to their sensitive radars and communications equipments. Should there be a water shortage, the snipes were universally cursed. Should the engine exhaust bellow soot from the stack onto the open decks or should there be traces of grease spots topside, the deck apes blamed the snipes.

The label "snipe" was also used in a competitive sense, usually by deckhands with a sense of humor. You would rarely find a deckhand or an electronics technician visiting the engine rooms, while the snipes had to emerge from their holes to eat, sleep, and breathe fresh air. Once out of their protective environment, not unlike groundhogs and other burrowing mammals, they were vulnerable to mild abuse, especially from the deck force. Perhaps the deck force just couldn't forget that once upon a time, when ships depended on sails, they were the masters of propulsion. Today the deck force still holds the steering wheel and gas pedal, but they don't know what is under the hood.

The Snipe Saga*

Until the early 1800s, there were no engines and no snipes. About 1812, the US Navy obtained their first paddle-wheel steamer, the USS *Fulton*. To run the boiler and engine, men of steam were also acquired. They were not sailors but engineers from early land-based steam engines. The sailors did not like or appreciate these landsmen and their foul, smoky plants. They were treated with contempt.

Yet the steam engine prevailed, resulting in a split crew, the engineers and the deck force. Soon, an engineer officer was appointed to each ship. He was on equal footing with the ship's master, who still had the upper hand because he controlled berthing and rations. At the time of the Civil War, when steam propulsion was rapidly replacing sails, the navy needed a solution to this divided control.

Their solution was to first make the senior master a captain responsible for the overall command, with the engineer officer reporting to him. Because the engineer officer sometimes outranked the captain, something had to be done to keep the engineer from becoming the captain. To solve the problem, two separate officer branches were instituted, staff and line. Only line officers could command ships. Staff officers, which included supply, surgeons, and engineers, would always be subservient to line officers at sea. At the time, this included all engineers being junior to the deck rates. Engineering petty officers were junior to the lowly deck seaman.

About this time, an engineer officer by the name of John Snipes demanded sleeping accommodations and food equal to that of the deck gang. He also declared that there would be no more harassment for his gang. When the ship's captain laughed at him, Snipes simply had his men put out the fires in the boiler. Snipes brought about changes in the system that in time extended to the entire fleet. The engineers became strictly "hands off" for the deck gang. They became known as Snipes's men and over the years as just snipes.

*No one remembers precisely how the term "snipe" came to be adopted in the US Navy. The above story, by Tom Thomas, is a hypothesis based on the historical evolution of naval steam propulsion. I took the liberty to paraphrase and shorten the above from "The Snipe's Beginnings" on Mr. Thomas's website, www.oldsnipe. com/SnipeBegin.html.

Vance's snipes were rarely seen on the open deck while underway. When out of their holes and mixing with the rest of the crew, they were conspicuous. The grease under their fingernails and on their work clothes made them stand out from the spiffy clean appearance of the radiomen, electronics technicians, or quartermasters, who worked in clean environments. The snipes were natural targets for universal abuse because they were responsible for all basic services. Water shortages or electricity outages affected everyone. Yet never a nasty word was spoken if the radars were down or the forward gun mount didn't work. Neither event personally inconvenienced anyone. All divisions on board were territorial. Each had its own work spaces and storerooms, most of which were readily accessible. The remote exclusiveness and discomfort of the engine rooms, mostly the heat and noise, isolated the snipes. Their world was little understood and their contribution rarely appreciated.

As a new ensign, I too lacked an appreciation for the snipes. Yet here I was, the main propulsion assistant, responsible for twenty-seven snipes who worked to keep the lights on and the ship moving. How the hell did BUPERS pick me for this job? Looking back, I suspect they noticed I had a bachelor of science degree. Why not put the young new officer in an engineering billet where the US Navy will most benefit from his technical training and he will be happy working in an engineering field? Wrong, wrong, wrong. BUPERS should have looked more closely at my record and discovered that after trying my best for one and a half years at the world's premier geological engineering college, I flunked out. I learned the hard way that engineering and science were not for me.

Eventually, at a small liberal arts college, I earned a bachelor's degree in geology because of the family's limited resources. Dad was a clothes presser with three children in college before student loans were invented. The quickest and most practical way to a degree was to complete college in four years, and that meant utilizing my previously accumulated science credits. I didn't have the luxury of following my interests and changing to a liberal arts course of study. The navy probably saw the science degree in my record and deemed me engineering material. Or did my name and the available billet just appear on the BUPERS detailer's desk at the same time? Was it serendipity?

Regardless of how I was chosen, I cursed the gods over the result. Mechanical devices never interested me. That first week aboard, I was stupefied descending into my engine rooms, being confronted by a jumble of piping, ducts, monstrous propulsion engines, and generators. Both impressed and scared, I crawled up the ladder out from this alien world. My eyes were glazed over. I knew I would never master this beast, nor ever feel comfortable in these strange rooms. I had never before experienced towering layers of machinery in confined spaces.

Previous to the navy, most of my work experience was outdoors, with the exception of six months underground in a Colorado coal mine. The high-paying mining job was a necessity for this guilt-ridden kid who wasted the family's limited resources in that first difficult year of college. The coal mine and the engine rooms had much in common: both were alien and confining, one quiet, dangerous, and eerie, the other loud, vibrating, and odoriferous. One was a steel cocoon, the other a rock shell, both unnatural, man-made environments. They were equally depressing, except I could leave the mine after my eight-hour shift and quit if it suited me. Although my time in the engine rooms was limited, I could not escape the ship or the responsibility. I was trapped in this rolling steel shell for the duration, a three-year residency as an officer snipe. God, what lousy casting.

In the British navy and most other navies, engineering officers were trained specialists separate from the line officers who managed most of the other shipboard functions. A similar system was in place on US Navy ships, but restricted to larger, more complex ships than the *Vance*. The wardrooms of the *Vance* and other small American warships were staffed by young officers, all unrestricted line officers, Renaissance men, being groomed for command, and therefore theoretically capable of filling any billet on board other than supply officer. This system depended on the senior enlisted ranks for the necessary technical expertise and the assumption that two or three months of classroom training specific to their jobs was sufficient training for junior officers to function competently as engineers.

Before deploying on Operation Deep Freeze, Captain Penny needed engineering officers. Only one of the three engineering billets was filled. With orders to the *Vance,* I normally would have attended three months of main propulsion engineering school in San Diego. The captain could not wait. I was ordered to report directly to the ship. My task was to learn on the job, an immense challenge made more difficult for me by the newness and rigors of shipboard life, especially the seasickness.

At first, I worked doggedly, going over what system diagrams and equipment manuals were available, soon abandoning this fragmented approach. I was getting nowhere in the limited study time available, and the complexity of the multiple interdependent systems left me frustrated. Trying to wade through equipment repair manuals to understand the workings of the main propulsion plant was impossible. I faced a new vocabulary of rings, pistons, fuel injectors, Dutch boilers, evaporators, micrometers, upper and lower crankshafts, cylinder liners, and more. Where do you start? I questioned the value of the bits and pieces of specific information I could glean from the material. I needed a structured course of study addressing management of a ship's propulsion system, not a service manual for individual pieces of equipment.

There was the nagging question: where did all this effort lead? I could never master the system during my one year on the job before rotating to manage the repair division. And once my three years were complete, I would never go near an engine room again. So what was the value of busting my ass studying during my limited free time? A major reason for abandoning the self-study effort was that the material bored me. I lacked an interest in machinery.

I was tempted to ask EN1 Engles to tutor me, but out of pride and fairness to the man, I steered clear of this idea. Engles already had more than he could handle. We were sadly lacking in senior petty officers. If I worked in the spaces, helped overhaul the machinery, and stood engine-room watches, I would have better understood the main propulsion plant and perhaps been a better division officer. This was not within the scope of work for a Renaissance man.

As I continued to blunder along as the manager of the division, I realized that among the officers, mine was the least desirable job on board. Lucky Fred Levin had reported aboard, fresh from several months of specialized CIC schooling, to lead a small section of clean-cut highly trained radarmen with a mature CPO to manage them. Although Jim Kunz came aboard as the first lieutenant without additional schooling, he had two major advantages. The required technical skills for the job were minimal, and he had Boats Oldervick to run the division. A new officer could readily oversee chipping and painting the decks, launching, and dropping the anchor without formal schooling. The real plum was having the capable Oldervick to look after the deck apes. Jim would huddle with Boats after morning quarters, go over the day's work plan, and walk away confident, knowing Boats would get the work done and handle potential people problems internally. Fred, Jim, and I, the new ensigns, had the three junior billets on board. By popular acclaim, no one wanted my job.

My Fellow Snipe Officers

Fortunately, BUPERS was capable of good casting. They got it right by sending a real engineer to the *Vance* as my boss. LTJG Don Dunn reported aboard the night before we deployed from Pearl Harbor to the Antarctic. Don came from an engineering billet on a San Diego–based destroyer. He probably received a hurried last-minute set of orders. His wife and infant son would eventually follow him to Hawaii to await our return. What interested me was the ease with which Don settled in. He reported to the captain, found his stateroom, tried out his bunk, and asked what was for dinner. Just another ship, another temporary home much like the last one, and ready to depart in the morning on a nine-month voyage. Quite a contrast to my wandering around lost in this strange setting.

Don was a six-footer with a touch of extra flesh on his two-hundred-pound frame, topped with a crewcut and carrying a happy-go-lucky smile. I liked him immediately, probably because he was both friendly and new to the *Vance*'s wardroom, as was I. Unlike me, he had more than two years' experience at sea and appeared to thrive on sea duty. Don was an enigma to most of us because he was a Naval Academy graduate, popularly called a "ring knocker" in the fleet. As the story goes, they tended to wear Academy rings and gently knock them against the table to draw attention to the fact that they were Annapolis graduates. What was an Academy graduate doing aboard the *Vance*? A skipper might be Academy, understandable because command of a DER was a first stepping-stone to the eventual command of a real destroyer and more.

A junior officer Annapolis graduate on this little rust bucket? Never. The Academy boys had high-profile billets in the fleet task forces, aboard sleek destroyers and frigates, prepared to operate in harm's way or better still, rapidly advance. They did not cut their teeth serving on independent steaming weather ships sitting on ocean station for two or three years with the *gooney* birds (albatrosses) for company. We speculated that Don must have screwed up his career somewhere along the line. Years later, I learned that he was actually sent to the *Vance* because of his engineering expertise. After the *Vance* tour of duty, Don was farmed out to a civilian agency to help outfit civilian boats for classified missions. Apparently, the navy was aware of his unique capabilities, which were soon demonstrated to us.

The *Vance* was on the verge of a long deployment to a remote ocean known for some of the worst weather conditions on earth. Preparation for the cruise had been in the hands of an engineering officer who transferred off the ship at about the time I arrived. We put to sea with a department head who had yet to unpack his duffel bag, an ensign who had been aboard for a year, and me. We rated two chief petty officers and had none. We had two competent first-class engineman and rated four. Such was the staffing.

Chuck Laipply, who I had relieved as main propulsion assistant, had been aboard for a year. He now took charge of R division. Chuck, like me, didn't appear the dashing military man. He too was an OCS graduate and a geology major. Chuck appeared easygoing, got along well in the wardroom, and was liked by the crew. In time, he would feel alienated from Don and, by association, me. Don and I were new aboard, and Don had both the knowledge and energy to get the department running his way. I supported Don from the first because he was my boss and I yearned for guidance. Eventually I was drawn even closer because the man was supportive, efficient, and fair.

The working and social relationship with Chuck never improved. He may have resented the new regime. Today I better understand his response to us newcomers. After a year of experience on board, Chuck was now confronted with Don's strong and perhaps intrusive management style and my puppy-dog allegiance to Don. I too would have been disgruntled under these circumstances. Chuck preferred a more passive approach to managing. Neither Chuck nor I were brilliant officers, but I probably showed more enthusiasm, believing we could improve the department. Whether I accomplished anything that first year is debatable.

What probably drove Chuck to despair was Don Dunn's drive and demand that the job be done his way. Don was both opinionated and a dynamo. I gladly followed his lead because I knew nothing about the job and his was the only guidance available. Besides, Don was a good man, easy to be with once you realized and accepted that he had strong views on most things and that underlying these views was a rigid moral code. The man was honest and willing to present the captain with an unpopular opinion regardless of the consequences. He was a by-the-book naval officer, who presented his opinion and rationale, then saluted and did what he was told. If the captain made a bad decision, Don would carry it out. In time, I realized that this level of adherence to the system was not in my makeup. I would fight or sulk. Our relationship was one of student and teacher. Socially, we went our separate ways. He was about four years older than me, married with a child, and had a lot of sea time under his belt. Our paths rarely crossed when ashore. I hung out with the other single junior ensigns, while Don was purely a tourist ashore when on deployment.

As we steamed to Tahiti, Don discovered that no provision was made to take on extra lubricating oil for the deployment. We quickly made arrangements to buy a thousand gallons of lube oil in Tahiti. The problem was how to get twenty fifty-gallon barrels of oil on board in a port that had no equipment capable of lifting the barrels onto the ship. We were Mediterranean-moored, that is moored stern to the pier, rendering our winch, mounted amidships on the port side, useless for lifting the heavy barrels of oil from the pier. Don figured that since oil was lighter than water, we might float the barrels to the portside winch. We rolled a few of the heavy barrels off the pier and watched them plunge into the harbor and sink, disappearing from sight. After several long, tense minutes, they leisurely bobbed to the surface, were floated to the ship, and were winched onto the main deck one at a time. If this had been my responsibility, I would have peed my pants waiting for the barrels to float to the surface.

A more telling event was Don's ability to deal with an ongoing boiler problem that should have been recognized long before deploying. I may be a bit harsh in my criticism. All DERs had problems with their two auxiliary boilers. The boilers were critical to the operation of the ship, for laundry, galley, space heating, steam to flush the ice buildup from the engine-room seawater intakes, and above all, making potable water. Shortly after deploying, we were plagued with boiler problems. A lack of potable water would force us to eventually leave ocean station early, thereby shutting down the critical supply flights to the Antarctic.

Our first major boiler problem was that the fire tubes sprung a leak. There appeared to be no solution short of receiving new tubes and a trained boiler welder from Hawaii to install them. This takes time. We were at sea in the Antarctic. No one aboard had any idea how to solve the problem. Sailors were trained to operate and maintain the machinery. A unique problem that required the technical expertise of the shipyard was normally beyond our expertise. Don personally took charge, squeezing his bulk down behind the boiler in search of a solution. He loved hands-on situations and managed to keep the boiler operating with a Rube Goldberg contraption that temporarily sealed the leaky tube until the squadron command in Hawaii was able to repair the boiler.

Later on the cruise, the boiler feedwater supply was accidentally contaminated and the potable water storage tanks were empty. Without fresh feedwater, we could not operate the boiler. Without the boiler, the evaporators were useless. We could not make potable water. In short, we needed freshwater to make more freshwater, and we didn't have any. Don reasoned that contaminated salty feedwater could be neutralized with an acid. The only acid available was powdered lemonade from the galley. We dumped

Don Dunn (on left) and Doc Gersenfish, Dunedin, New Zealand. (Photo from author's collection.)

several pounds into the feedwater, and it worked. Soon we were producing potable water again.

Don was a can-do man, a trait promoted and admired in the US Navy so long as the solution worked. We were fortunate to have him aboard. I was especially fortunate because most of these problems were in my area of responsibility. As department head, Don handled all interaction with the captain. I reported to Don, and he dealt with the captain. This was how the chain of responsibility worked. If he were less competent or less involved with the ship's engineering plant, he might have had me more involved in explaining the problems to the captain, a chore I didn't relish.

My Snipes

Don was not the only person who helped me along the way that first year. It was serendipity that accounted for EN1 Engles being the senior petty officer of M division. As the *Vance's* largest division, we rated at least one seasoned, older, mature CPO with years of engine-room experience, a man who had seen it all coming up through the ranks. These men were the backbone of the US Navy. But there was neither an engineman nor electrician chief aboard. I couldn't understand how this oversight happened. I felt shortchanged. Generally a new ensign had a CPO to hold his hand. Instead, I had a petty officer who was as new to his position as I was to mine. Engles was on his maiden voyage as the leading engineman aboard. Of the two of us, he had the greater task. He was expected to know his profession, and I was not. I knew how I, unwittingly, was deposited here. I was fortunate that Engles was placed in this critical position. Seniority determined everything, and Engles was perhaps six months senior to the other two first-class enginemen, Varn and Ramirez.

EN1 Varn, a fat, older man with the washed-out face of a heavy drinker, was incapable of leading anyone. Perhaps in his youth, the man was effective. There remained but the shell of a man, doing his best to avoid responsibility. Initiative and self-confidence had long departed this prematurely old man. In contrast, the other EN1, Ramirez, was a clean-cut Mexican American with a wonderful sense of pride in his work. Ramirez I liked. He was smart, honest, and dependable. It is amazing how neat and clean he kept himself in the engine-room environment of grease and diesel oil. Somehow his shirts, even work shirts, were clean and pressed. I later learned that in the evenings, he would iron his clothes in the ship's laundry, a reflection of the pride he exhibited in his responsibilities. Regardless of his qualities, Ramirez was not the best man for the top job because he was Mexican American. The division had a number of rednecks, a few of whom were problem sailors from the South and Southwest. In the 1960s, Ramirez had his hands full managing them. He knew it, Engles knew it, and within the first month I knew it.

I relied on Engles to keep the engines running and me out of trouble. My technical knowledge and my ability to rapidly master new technical information so important to this position were horribly inadequate. I had the potential to spend three years in the department and still not understand the ship's engineering systems. In fact, I managed to achieve this dubious distinction. I'm not proud of it, but I knew enough about myself to be aware of it happening. I had no desire to understand how machinery works. My lack of patience and time worked against me. The real culprit, though, was my lack of interest. How the systems worked held no interest. At best, I could speak intelligently about the main propulsion plant on a superficial level.

When a detailed equipment problem surfaced, I was at a distinct disadvantage and hard-pressed to bullshit my way through it. Always a poor showman and poorer salesman, I did not try to lie or deceive, not for moral reasons, but because I knew I could not pull it off. At times, this relegated me to being a mere messenger when responding to Don Dunn's or the captain's questions. I ran to Engles for the answer. Still, there was some benefit to my gross ignorance. There had to be ways to be competent at the job without being an engineer. Other dumb ensigns must have gone before me and survived. I knew I was not dumb, just the victim of poor casting. Besides, I too was a Renaissance man.

While machinery held no interest for me, people did. Lacking technical capabilities, I survived and eventually prospered due to my ability to take an interest in and understand people. I knew I needed Engles the moment I met him. These were his engine rooms and his men. There was no way I could change this, nor did I want to. I was just passing through, a new ensign in a new uniform here for the ride. The challenge was to establish a good working relationship with Engles, an interesting and subtle task.

Captain Penny inspecting M Division, Dunedin, New Zealand, 1961.
(Photo from author's collection.)

Here was a quiet, soft-spoken man who chose his words carefully, especially with officers. Not unusual, since officers wielded the power and lived in a different world. Engles didn't know the new ensign. Could he and his twenty-seven sailors depend on me for fair treatment and my support as their conduit in dealing with the wardroom? My course seemed obvious. I backed Engles's leadership role in the division, fought for fair treatment of our men, and respected what little privacy and freedom they had. In turn, they were expected to perform and follow the rules.

Engles, by necessity, played our relationship carefully, a cool formal rapport, which screamed out that we were from different worlds. By nature a quiet man, he was careful to minimize our interaction. As a first-class petty officer, Engles

berthed and dined with his men. Were he a CPO, his relationship with officers would have been less guarded, more relaxed.
CPOs were a group unto themselves, sleeping and dining in
their own quarters and wearing the officer-type uniform. They
were separate from the sailors. Engles was not. He was still one
of the engine-room sailors. To do his job, he needed to ensure
the respect of the men, which included not sucking up to officers. He needed to remain one of the engine-room gang. Our
relationship was formal and low-key, with touches of humor
and the deportment of careful poker players. The man was
warily feeling his way in his new leadership position, just as I
was with mine.

Twenty-seven snipes, Engles, and I operated this floating
electric utility and ocean trucking operation. Generally the
condition of the space reflected the personality of the petty
officer in charge. You could eat off the deck plates in EN1
Ramirez's engine room. The same could not be said for the
spaces managed by EN2 Shewry and EN1 Varn. The after engine room, B4, was the responsibility of Shewry, a heavyset
Californian with a cheerful disposition. I came to appreciate
Shewry for his Midas touch. Often, what he touched broke, and
he was a master of jury-rigged solutions. Careless or just in a
hurry, who could tell? Yet there were moments of brilliance,
when the big fellow came through when we really needed him.

The least challenging engine room, B-2, was EN1 Varn's
territory, where he could vegetate and pretend to be busy. Poor
old Varn had drifted into incompetence before reaching retirement age, or perhaps he just wanted to stay forever because
the navy was his home. In short, he was asleep in a leadership
billet. In his engine room were two colorful characters, BT3
(boiler technician third class) Jenkins and his striker Woodie,
whose world revolved around the cantankerous boilers and
evaporator. A wiry dark-skinned man with a friendly smile and
a great sense of humor, Jenkins, a family man, was popular
with the crew. He was from Hawaii; the tan complexion and
dark curly hair supported his claim to Hawaiian ancestry. The

man was easygoing and fun-loving enough to be caught making booze on board, costing him a stripe. It never diminished his apparent joy in life. Woodie was a darker character, with a chiseled nose and square-chin handsome. He proved capable of staying drunk for long periods ashore. Jenkins was dependable when focused on the job. Woodie needed supervision and was destined to return to his native North Carolina following his four-year enlistment.

B-3, the only engine room without a screaming ship service generator, belonged to EN2 Pedro Cantu, a short, quiet, chubby-cheeked Mexican American from Southern California. An industrious, career-minded sailor, Pedro was shy and reserved. He probably had little interaction with Anglos before joining the navy. He was smart enough, just not assertive—a troublesome characteristic when managing snipes, but seniority prevailed and we were short of experienced, rated enginemen. The solution was to avoid assigning troublemakers to his charge because Pedro needed a few more years to confidently manage sailors. The management of an engine room usually was assigned to a senior EN1 with considerably more experience. We lacked senior petty officers.

To compensate for Cantu's lack of leadership experience, we assigned EN3 Jimmie Parkman, EN3 Reuben Taylor, FN Joe Hildreth, and FN Hugh Brennen to his team. All were dependable or new sailors. Taylor, a lean five-foot-seven, well-tattooed Mississippi lad, interested me because he was serious about the job and kept to himself. That's no small feat when squeezed into a steel box with 160 other souls. Hildreth, an eighteen-year-old from Idaho, and Brennen, a twenty-year-old Southern Californian, were new to the navy. At this point, both were willing to go along with the program. Cantu probably was a good influence for them, at least not a bad one, and they were green enough for Pedro to manage without troubles.

A sailor who stood out was EN3 Jimmie Parkman, an older black man, with thick glasses and a long, tired face, a quiet Georgian with an easygoing personality who kept to himself, a dependable snipe. This was the early 1960s, when regional and racial prejudices ran deep. The nine blacks aboard did not hang out together. There were no visible signs of black solidarity. They drew no attention to themselves, worked in a quiet manner, and got along with their Anglo shipmates, though rarely socializing with them. All the black sailors were snipes or deck apes with two exceptions, the head steward for the wardroom and a radioman. My two black sailors, Parkman, a career sailor, and ENFN Melvin Johnson, a quiet young man also from rural Georgia, were excellent sailors. I wished I had ten more like them. The navy was a step up from the Jim Crow environment they had left behind.

The Mexican American situation was similar. Both EN1 Ramirez and EN2 Cantu were good sailors. Correction: Ramirez was an outstanding sailor. Their effectiveness was hampered by racial prejudice, especially from the sailors from the south and southwestern states. Having attended college in Colorado in the 1950s, I was sensitive to how white college boys from both rural and urban backgrounds treated Mexican Americans and Native Americans as second-class citizens. My previous experience with blacks was almost nonexistent, having been brought up in an ethnic neighborhood populated with pockets of Italians, Slovenians, and Irish. Yes, we feared the Southern blacks pouring into the city after World War II because they were different and their encroachment affected property values. I never knew any blacks, except for the four or five in high school, and they too kept to themselves.

I was missing the protest marches in the South. Martin Luther King's famous "I Have a Dream" speech on the steps of the Lincoln Memorial was a year and a half away. During my years on the *Vance*, I was sensitive to the importance of racial equality and realized that this was a long uphill battle. While the blacks in my command were model sailors who kept to themselves, others proved more difficult to manage. The snipes were a mix of backgrounds from hillbillies to farm boys to cowboys to city boys, all different, most young and impressionable.

The Bad Boys

As always, there were the bad boys who had difficulty accepting authority, were too easily influenced, or were just amoral. Keeping the bad boys separated in their work and watch assignments, spreading them out rather than letting them concentrate, was our strategy to minimize their ability to feed off each other's discontent. Separation was a difficult tactic on a 306-foot ship.

EN2 Smitty, a five-foot-eight, weight-lifting, short-haired, blond muscle boy from rural Oklahoma, was the ringleader of the problem snipes. He was smart, defiant in the face of authority, and manipulative. Smitty was a walking problem as he swaggered about the ship squeezing a small rubber ball to display his biceps.

Dark hair and dark eyes on a five-foot-ten slouchy frame, Herbert Key appeared to be everything the navy didn't want in a sailor. Sloppy in appearance, untidy from his bushy eyebrows to his scruffy shoes, this sailor appeared to have brought rural Mississippi with him to the navy. I doubt he was happy aboard. In the wardroom, Key was the poster boy for what a sailor shouldn't be.

Another memorable sailor in the Smitty gang was little Johnny Chance, a small-town Texas boy, pug-nosed, short and muscular at at five foot five. Chance was a tough little bulldog when at Smitty's side, snarling and barking. Without his leader, Chance was an adequate sailor. Unable to stand alone, Chance could usually be found in Smitty's shadow. We made an effort to keep their work and watch stations separate. There appeared to be little hope of reforming Smitty, Key, or Chance. They were what they were. The opportunity to be rid of them was almost nonexistent. The challenge was to restrict their influence.

There was hope for EN2 Sparks and FN Little, fringe members of Smitty's entourage. Sparks, a tall skinny Californian who took pride in his work, was just immature enough to seek the company of the bad-boy group. He existed on the periphery, occasionally getting into trouble because of this association, followed by periods of withdrawal from the gang. Sparks probably wanted to be one of the boys, but realized that he could get burned, having come close to losing a stripe by hanging out with the bad boys. He went on to a successful navy career. FN Little was not so lucky. Here was another small-town Texas sailor, easygoing and surprisingly independent to be a member of Smitty's bad-boy group. Slim, pale complexion, with long features and a casualness that told you that he was from the Lone Star State, Little was his own man but

The bad boys. (Drawing by EN3 Gastil in USS Vance [DER 387] Deep Freeze 1962 Cruise Book.)

sometimes hung out with the bad boys. Little survived, and I'm guessing was in good standing when he left the navy. The man was not meant to be part of a team effort.

My cross to bear was these three bad boys and a few marginal problem sailors. This is not to imply that the others were all model sailors. After twenty or more days at sea, even the best sailors could find trouble ashore. Many of the young snipes joined the navy for the adventure or because they realized that the alternative was the draft, which promised two years in a muddy army foxhole. A few of my charges chose the navy in preference to a court conviction at home: volunteer for the service, or face local prosecution and incarceration. We provided an environment that emphasized working together and not letting down your shipmates. The daily challenge for the senior petty officers, chiefs, and officers was to keep everyone reasonably content and rowing together in the same direction.

In this first year aboard and well into my second year, I came to believe that these few problem snipes would never change. I envisioned having to put up with the troublemakers and discontents until their enlistment periods ended. You tried for a while and then just gave up, assuming that there was nothing more one could do to change attitudes. The job, the quarters, the restrictions, and the structure of a military organization were things beyond my control. In my last year aboard, I was proven wrong. Attitudes could change, and they did. I was just another small player in this transition. There was more to experience with my snipes and the command before I finally witnessed all the oars pulling together. A beautiful experience it was to be, and one I had never expected to witness.

Record Keeping and Relationships

There was more to the division than the engine rooms. On the main deck was the division's log room, a six-by-six-foot closet with a Dutch door, a desk, and two file cabinets, where the engine maintenance records were kept. ENFN Robert Wurm, recognized only as "Grub Worm" by the crew, was the log-room yeoman responsible for maintaining the records. A Kansas boy, Wurm was a lovable little character, five foot four, a muscular body covered with tattoos and a friendly smile for everyone. Wurm was just a nice guy, good-natured, rarely upset or negative. He got along with everyone, taking the typical sailor abuse with a disarming smile. Wurm would be at the desk with two fingers at work tapping out engine log entries on an old mechanical typewriter bolted to the desk. Here Wurm pecked away transferring engine exhaust temperature logs and micrometer readings from greasy dog-eared engine-room log sheets to greasy dog-eared maintenance forms, then filed them in greasy three-ring notebooks and shoved them into the dented file cabinet.

If Wurm wasn't available, log sheets and notes piled up on the desk, some to be lost, others unintelligible entries.

Everyone and anyone had access to the log room; thus Wurm wasn't the only person with his fingers on the records. The system, or lack of one, was haphazard at best, the measurements often carelessly taken, and the entries of questionable value because rarely were they reviewed. Record keeping was approached as a requirement to satisfy the annual administrative inspection rather than as a useful tool for maintenance and repair. Snipes and record keeping mated like oil and water. My snipes were the engine people of the 1950s and 1960s, the guys who grew up working on a 1950 Ford Fairlane V8 in the backyard, with greasy hands, dirty coveralls, and the joy of hearing the engine purr and the dual exhausts roar. Penmanship and spelling were unknown arts, ignored in youth so as to focus on what was under the hood. A year and a half would pass before I had a log room that benefited the operation of the ship, but that's another story.

Engles and I worked well together, probably because I didn't interfere with how he ran the division. We were careful in dealing with each other. Only once in our first year together did Engles actually pay me a compliment, a real rarity. We had a young Navajo Indian sailor, Toglena, with whom I occasionally conversed while he stood at the throttles in the secondary engine-room control station when at general quarters. To a Navajo raised on the reservation, adapting to the abrupt cultural change and especially to the regimentation and confinement of shipboard life must have been difficult. Engles revealed to me how impressed he was that Toglena actually enjoyed talking with me, an officer.

Of course, it did not last. The fence between enlisted and officer was high, especially in the traditional deck and engine-room ratings. It was not a fence I wanted to straddle. The job required me to act in the best interest of the ship, based on how the commanding officer determined this to be accomplished. From time to time, I passed on a bitter unpopular order to my snipes as if the orders were my own. Blaming the order on someone else would only diminish my authority in the eyes of the men, leaving me a mere messenger. It was not long before the young Navajo stopped talking to me.

I cannot recall any other compliments from Engles that first year. At times officers were exposed to sailors' ingratiating behavior, both sincere and mocking. This was not Engles, who was uncomfortable blowing smoke. So why the Navajo compliment? Looking back, my guess is that in those first few months aboard, Engles was trying to say something positive to me because of the obvious difficult time I was having with seasickness and adjusting to shipboard life. Engles and I spent three years together on the *Vance*. When I left, he was still there, keeping the engines and generators operating. After two years together, I helped secure for him a letter of accommodation, and I vigorously supported his successful promotion to CPO, a highly competitive goal and well-deserved promotion. Yet after three years together, I knew almost nothing about the man, except that he was married and had a family, which I never met and which was never mentioned in our many conversations over the years. I did not know where he lived, what he enjoyed doing away from the ship, if he had hobbies, or for that matter, anything about his personal life. I never had a beer with him. Still, we understood and in time respected each other. I wish there could have been more, but what we had seemed to work for us.

Early on it was apparent to me that the *Vance* was a more subtle modern form of an ancient galley, with four Fairbanks-Morse diesel engines rather than two banks of oars. The sailors rowed, the senior petty officers beat the cadence, and the officers navigated. I generated my share of unpopular orders and enforced punishment for infractions of the rules. Befriending the same men you must use for the common good only led to problems. To be liked might be possible, while respect was essential. I was probably too intense and guarded to be popular, and hopefully fair and caring enough to be respected.

My epitaph for those first nine months was recorded in the *Vance* Deep Freeze Cruise Book, a little gem of a book, written and published by the crew. In the M division section, there exists a small cartoon in the lower right corner of the page inspired by the famous three monkeys depicting "hear no evil, see no evil, and speak no evil."

My epitaph. (*Drawing by EN3 Gastil in USS* Vance *[DER 387] Deep Freeze 1962 Cruise Book.*)

In place of the monkeys were cartoon figures, with the caption "see nothing, hear nothing, and know nothing." The "know nothing" figure was a naval officer. Initially, it hurt a bit, but I couldn't deny that the cartoon was clever and there was truth in the message.

CHAPTER 7

The New Regime

December 14, 1961–January 17, 1962

There is nothing wrong with change, if it is in the right direction.
—Winston Churchill

A New Captain

The third patrol ended as we glided up to the Victoria Pier in Dunedin at ten o'clock on December 14, a warm sunny morning. Summer had arrived in New Zealand. Most of us were ignoring the fine weather and the imminent change-of-command ceremony. Instead we focused on liberty and hopefully Christmas in Dunedin. We knew Captain Penny was leaving and little else as we observed his replacement, a medium-height lieutenant commander in dress blues standing on the pier smoking a pipe. On that first day ashore, an introduction and handshake in the wardroom was all we saw of our soon-to-be-skipper, Hank Beyer.

Passing off the baton to the new captain was a hurried affair. After all, how much could one really learn about the condition of the ship in two days? Accountable items were signed for, inspections were organized, and briefings were held. For my part, I simply escorted the new captain through the engine rooms. The engines were all there; at best he could check the tidiness of the spaces, with no idea of the condition of the equipment. The deck plates and ladders had a fresh coat of red paint that contrasted beautifully with big gray Fairbanks-Morse engines. The forward two engines, which drove the port shaft, had elegantly painted on each a beautiful picture of the Road Runner from the Looney Tunes cartoons, labeled Road Runner #1 and #2. Behind them in the after engine room, each of the two Fairbanks-Morse engines that drove the starboard shaft sported a picture of Wile E. Coyote, labeled Coyote #3 and #4. They and the cruise-book art were the work of a very talented snipe, EN3 Gastil.

Smooth polished-brass levers on the control panels provided the crowning touch. The engine rooms could be impressive, and this day they were. Captain Beyer went through rapidly and was probably as overwhelmed with the setting as I was my first time through. He gave no indication of being curious or interested in the machinery. Foolishly, I was pleased that he didn't ask questions and seemed satisfied with a superficial inspection. He appeared as happy to climb out of the engine rooms as was I to see him go. What I didn't realize and should have was that Captain Beyer showed little interest in engineering and that in time this would be equivalent to taking half the oars from the rowers while demanding no change in the galley's performance.

No time was wasted. The next day we formed up on the pier in dress whites for inspection and to hear Commander Penny's heartfelt farewell, followed by Lieutenant Commander Beyer reading his orders as the new commanding officer of the *Vance*. We knew nothing about the new captain, only that his word would be law for the next year and a half. The wardroom atmosphere was reserved. There was none of the usual flippant remarks or jokes among the officers. All was quiet. If Hank Beyer had any serious opinions about the ship or us, he was not passing them on. He was friendly and exceedingly social in the wardroom, giving us hope that life on board would continue as usual. There was a lot for this man to absorb quickly, ranging from evaluating his officers and chiefs to learning the state of the crew and the physical plant.

What we did learn was that Hank Beyer enlisted in the US Navy during World War II, spent two years in an officers' training program, and was commissioned in 1946. He came to us with seventeen years of service, much of it sea duty on destroyer-type ships. He had previously commanded a small landing ship and later a destroyer escort naval reserve ship on the Great Lakes. We assumed the man was well prepared to command our little floating palace or BUPERS would not have selected him. Command at sea was a serious responsibility.

Captain Beyer had an agenda. Seventeen hours after he took command, the *Vance* was underway for a shakedown cruise, a round trip to Campbell Island. I understood that the man must familiarize himself with the ship and the crew and that new captains usually begin with a tough stance. From my perspective, as one who joined the US Navy to see lands and peoples of the world, I resented the time away from port. Why the extra time at sea when our schedule left so little time ashore? This was our hard-earned liberty. Of course, if I had my way, we would never go to sea. Once in the open ocean, the drills started: general quarters, man overboard, repel boarders, and more, over and over again, not an easy five days. The officers were tiptoeing about the wardroom. Casual interaction and humor remained on hold until the new captain revealed his likes and dislikes.

On the fourth day in rough seas, on a hard roll to starboard, a hundred-pound duplex proportioner bounced out of its wall rack and dropped twelve feet through the B-2 engine-room hatch, just missing EN1 Ramirez's head and ripping through his left shoe to cut off his big toe. We hauled Ramirez up the ladder through the hatch and aft to sick bay. Doc calmly proceeded to sew his toe back on while the corpsman, Don Dunn, and I held Ramirez down. The ship was rolling violently as Doc sewed away. We braced ourselves as best we could, trying to hold Ramirez steady until unflappable Doc tied the last knot. I then retired to the open deck and heaved. Doc was not far behind me.

We continued on to Campbell Island for a brief stop and then returned to Dunedin. Ramirez was taken ashore and flown to Christchurch and then back to Tripler Army Hospital in Hawaii. Now we were down to one competent senior engineman, Engles. The normal manning level called for four. We bid farewell to Ramirez, a great sailor. I felt responsible because the duplex proportioner that chopped his toe off was located in one of my spaces. Used to mix foam for fighting engine-room fires, the heavy proportioner had not been secured again after a fire drill. Five months later when we returned to Pearl Harbor, Ramirez was on the pier to greet us with a smile on his face and ten good toes. Seeing Ramirez with all his toes was a personal moment of joy. Engles and I laughed and joked with him on the pier. Unfortunately, Ramirez had been assigned to another DER. We had no chance of getting him back. Doc had already been detached from the *Vance*. Forty-eight years later at our first wardroom reunion, I had my first opportunity to tell Doc that the toe was saved and to thank him personally.

Back in Dunedin after our shakedown cruise with the new skipper, we were invited as a group to the wardroom. Captain Beyer commenced imparting his impression of each officer and of the condition of the ship. He was obviously playing at being the tough guy, a common strategy practiced by new captains. We expected him to come down hard on us and in time lighten up once the officers and crew knew what was expected of them and fell in line with the program. I was too junior to be a serious target, although I expected to be harassed over having lost the electrical load two days before. Instead, he gave my boss, Don Dunn, the negative jabs and moved to the next victim. Either the new captain was indifferent to engineering or just didn't know much about our department because there were few questions for us snipes.

The theme of the meeting was that the *Vance* needed to be squared away and he, Hank Beyer, was the man to do it. The position of ship's captain was too powerful to take lightly. A week or two more were needed before the wardroom atmosphere returned to the new normal. Fortunately I could retreat to the junior officers' bunk room and avoid the wardroom except for meals. I was too busy reacting to daily events to think about the long-term implications of serving under this new captain. I saw this hard-nosed posturing as just a wake-up call, a performance to announce who was boss. Life would return to normal once the new captain settled in. What I should have noticed and didn't was that Captain Beyer focused on the gunnery department and the ship's appearance, almost totally ignoring the engineering plant.

Ashore in New Zealand

The new captain was the last thing on my mind as I looked forward to a glorious ten days in Dunedin over the Christmas holiday. Bless you HMNZS *Rotoiti* for being on ocean station for the holidays. My Christmas Eve was spent in the hotel lobby with Miriam, who was working at the reception desk until midnight. I sat in the lobby with Miriam's mother, a pleasant lady, and her ten-year-old brother. They had driven down from Christchurch for the Christmas holidays. I was certain Mum had been briefed on the nice naval officer. We got along well. After all, her daughter was dating a dashing American naval officer. Waiting for Miriam's shift to end, we spent a pleasant evening with a small crowd of hotel residents and people posing as residents. By law, at eleven in the evening, all Dunedin pubs closed, with the exception of hotel pubs serving their residents—thus, the pretend residents. The good cheer and quaintness of this warm evening of Christmas carols and dancing in the hotel lobby and pub left me both happy and a bit homesick.

The next day, taking advantage of the balmy summer weather, the four of us squeezed into Mum's Morris Minor for a picnic on the peninsula near Taiaroa Head. After Mum and little brother were made comfortable at the picnic spot, Miriam and I allegedly searched on foot for penguins along the cliffs. Here was an opportunity for some privacy. Among the albatross and penguins on the rocky bluffs, Miriam and I found a quiet secluded spot to lie down and embrace. The bra came off while the long legs, those gates to paradise, remained tightly closed. As we began to devour each other, a faint human call mingled with the sound of the wind and the albatross overhead. Little brother was searching for us, and the voice was getting nearer. Chalk this up as another frustrating day in Dunedin. No privacy ashore or afloat.

I began to understand that the answer to the leg problem was that Miriam wanted something I could not consider: a commitment. The relationship was doomed, and we both knew it. Perhaps it was the isolation of New Zealand in the 1960s that raised our little ship of horny sailors to celebrity status. Marriage to a Yankee sailor was a ticket to the outside world, especially to the dubious glamour of America, so artfully sold worldwide by Hollywood. She didn't give up. A month later, I saw her in Dunedin with a *Vance* sailor, and it bothered me. The last thing I wanted was a story floating throughout the ship about a sailor dating an officer's girlfriend. If there was a story, I never heard it, but that doesn't mean a tale didn't make the rounds.

My New Zealand experience was not solely about women. There were interesting day trips into the hills behind the city visiting hydroelectric dams, beautiful countryside, breweries, sheep farms, and private homes. Travel beyond a day trip was not possible because there was no way I would be allowed any of the annual leave I had accumulated. Just after Christmas, the *Vance* organized a trip to Milford Sound for the crew. Two officers were needed to chaperone the twenty-five interested sailors. Jim Kunz and I jumped at the chance. Off we went in an old bus with a nice older farmer, turned bus driver and tour director. The delightful man smiled the whole two days, fixing flat tires and hauling sailors. He readily accepted this interesting combination of sailors in civilian clothes, a bunch of sharp young men with their cameras and a handful of drunks who saw the South Island through a bottle.

The trip was amazing: a jet-boat ride on Lake Te Anau to see the glowworm caves, then to Fiordland National Park, taking a boat down Milford Fiord to the open sea. Several of us paid a crazy Dutchman for a hair-raising flight in his small plane, between the mountains over the Milford Track and Sutherland Falls. What I would have given to be on the

Track, one of the great hikes on this earth. We spent the night in a youth hostel at the terminus of the Milford Track, feasting on local lobster and beer. Several pretty coeds with backpacks tramped in from hiking the Track, a distance of 53.5 km, over three days. Unfortunately I was too busy playing mother hen to several drunken sailors to get better acquainted with the girls.

On the return trip, our usually upbeat bus driver was in a sorrowful state. At the hostel, someone had taken his electric razor, apparently an item close to his heart and difficult to replace. Jim and I were certain one of our sailors had it, but no one came forth and the old farmer was too much of a gentleman to even imply that a Yank stole it. Quietly, we asked the men to chip in to buy him a new high-end electric shaver from the ship's store. The man was near tears as we presented it to him. The following day, Woodie, one of my boilermen, sheepishly brought forth the missing razor. In his drunken state at the hostel, he mistakenly took the razor, thinking it was his own. Drunk for the entire trip, Woodie didn't realize he hadn't taken his razor on the trip until our return, and now he had two. Jim and I decided to bury the issue. Our guide was happy with his new razor; there was no need to open the subject again. For the next two years, the recovered razor slid back and forth in my desk drawer every eight and a half seconds until I finally chucked it over the side. Jim and I had earned our passage to Milford Sound.

Nonjudicial Punishment
Captain's mast was almost a weekly affair while deployed on Operation Deep Freeze and I was usually in attendance. A large percentage of the sailors hauled before the captain was my snipes. Most infractions were AWOL, absent without leave, especially here where the ports of call tempted a sailor to linger. If you were not aboard in uniform for the morning call to quarters, you were AWOL and a formal charge was automatic. A few of the more reckless sailors willingly gambled that the extra time ashore was worth the risk, although most

were AWOL because of a night of drinking. Other violations at captain's mast—such as sleeping on watch, failure to obey an order, provoking speech, and assault—were rare. The chiefs and senior petty officers preferred to handle infractions informally within their divisions. Only as a last resort did they file charges. Formal charges were most frequent for infractions committed outside the division.

We officers never knew half of what transpired on board or the informal steps taken by the senior enlisted personnel to manage their men. How many times must an engine-room watch stander be caught sleeping before being brought up on charges? I never knew the answer to that one. I am certain the first-time offender was never brought up on formal charges. In port, I observed passed-out sailors sleeping in their own urine, saturating their mattresses on the stretched canvas bunk, and fouling the air in the compartment. Nothing to be concerned over, because that sailor would be dumped into a shower, sobered up, and put to work scrubbing down the bunk and a lot more. Dirtying their own nest or fouling the work space was not tolerated. On occasion someone would shit in the bilges. My guess was that a watch stander didn't plan ahead. With a sense of urgency and alone in the engine room, he unscrewed a lower-platform deck plate for access to the bilges and let go. Someone had to clean the mess, and if the "phantom shitter" were discovered, his shipmates sought retribution. The point is that life on board was largely self-regulating. The chiefs and other senior enlisted maintained order. Excessive reliance on formal charges reflected poorly on the division's leadership, both enlisted and officer.

I did my best to avoid placing sailors on report, the act of filing charges against someone. If my lead petty officer placed a man on report, the justification was usually valid and I supported him because I knew this was a last resort. Where the use of this power became tricky was when a sailor showed his disrespect for an officer. For example, once I walked down a passageway and found it blocked by a couple of my bad-boy snipes pretending to be busy talking and not seeing me. As a rule and a courtesy, sailors cleared a space for officers to pass in the ship's narrow passageways. The bad boys intentionally stood fast, leaving barely enough room for me to squeeze by. The intent was to embarrass me and advertise to their audience just how tough they were.

I had the option to squeeze by or order them to stand aside and threaten to put them on report. Both options advertised that I was admitting publicly to being successfully harassed, overreacting, or hiding behind my rank. I would lose face and thereby erode my authority. Instead, I stopped and stared down the leader, the subliminal message being, *"You are on the brink of disaster. Move aside or I'll throw the book at you."* The sailor knew that if he didn't move very soon, this would be an open act of defiance against an officer, punishable by court-martial. He made room for me to pass without a word being spoken. There were no winners here. I let the senior petty officer follow up as he saw fit to ensure this was a one-time event. I maintained my position of authority and saved the silver bullets for when I really needed them. Still, the bad boys' leader could later claim to his followers that he had thumbed his nose at the system.

Captain's mast was interesting from the perspective of the division officer, the senior petty officer of the accused, and the accused. We all three had something in common. None of us wanted to be there. I attended a number of these affairs because M division had a nest of bad boys and some easily influenced young sailors. Engles and I stood with the accused and usually were compelled to say something positive on his behalf. The psychology was that if you provided a damning recommendation, the man's attitude would only worsen. A supportive word or two, even if you wished the man were in prison, might influence him to be a better sailor or at least feel that he owed you something for saving his ass. If the man had a record of infractions, there was no need to say anything. Another option was to pass on your true feelings to the XO prior to the captain's mast, although this rarely influenced the captain's decision. We put up with problem sailors because there was no recourse when deployed to Deep Freeze.

The punishment usually doled out at captain's mast included restriction to the ship when we were scheduled for a good liberty port, extra duty on board, reduction in rating, forfeiture of pay, or just a warning. The number of sailors hauled up before the captain appeared to be about the same under both Captains Beyer and Penny, and a disproportionately high number of these were my snipes. Should the captain think the charges warranted more consideration or potentially greater punishment than he could legally dole out, a court-martial convened. We officers shuddered whenever one was assigned because of the deluge of paperwork and the hours of preparation that came with it. Most cases were disposed of at captain's mast.

Captain's mast was held in the crew's mess. The props were a podium and American flag positioned in front of the ice cream–making machine. The mess deck was cleared of sailors, and the cooks told to take a break from the galley. In attendance were the skipper, the XO, a yeoman who recorded the proceedings, and the chief master-at-arms. The accused, with hat in hand, stepped forward in front of the podium, accompanied by his division chief, division officer, and department head. Rarely did the accused deny the charge, although mitigating circumstances could and usually were introduced. Having been briefed earlier, the captain usually was able to quickly dispose of the case. Captain Penny used his deep voice and sizable presence to impress and awe the accused, a controlled response. I think he was acting. In contrast, Captain Beyer, with his face reddened and the turkey nobble on his neck vibrating, would get angry. His emotions were too involved in the decisions. Very different approaches.

While in port before the New Year, Captain Beyer held his first captain's mast. Six sailors had been brought up on charges, five of them my snipes. We hoped finally to break up the bad-boy gang in M division. It didn't happen. The skipper let the ringleader, EN2 Smitty, off with two weeks restricted to the ship. Don and I were surprised and frustrated at Smitty's light punishment. Here was the ringleader we needed to tame; instead, he returned to the division claiming to have beaten the system. He strutted about as if invincible, a man incapable of being controlled, perhaps a superman and we had no krypton on board. His sidekick, Herbert Key, a frequent offender, was awarded a court-martial. This was the first of several court-martials over the next few months. They consumed considerable time and were major headaches for the officers who had to conduct them.

Demotion and Coronation

At one in the afternoon on the second day of 1962, we again singled up all lines and waved good-bye to the small crowd on the pier as the lines were taken in, and the *Vance* headed up the channel for my fourth patrol. After a day and a half of drills, we dropped anchor at Campbell Island once again. This time we spent several hours visiting because Captain Beyer wanted his chance to see the island or at least visit the weather station. Few officers cared to go ashore, and thus I was able to finally go ashore and explore a few coves, spot penguins, walk by resting seals while looking out for the more aggressive sea lions, and run among the enormous sea elephants. Reaching to sixteen feet in length and weighing up to eleven thousand pounds, these snorting, farting sea elephants had difficulty maneuvering on dry land. How I would have enjoyed a month exploring the island; still, these few hours were more than I expected. I enjoyed them.

At sea again heading for ocean station, one of my proud accomplishments, that of being a qualified OOD underway for independent steaming, was taken away from me and the other junior officers. Captain Beyer decreed that we junior officers could only be trusted alone on the bridge when the *Vance* was on ocean station, a thousand miles from the nearest landfall and thousands of miles from shipping lanes. At all other times, we were relegated to a training position as JOOD under the supervision of more senior officers on the bridge. I had been standing OOD bridge watches for four months, Frank Collins for twelve months, and Larry Hanson for fourteen months. We now stood exactly the same watch, but in a training status. Only when we reached ocean station were we entrusted with the responsibility for the ship. We took this move as a lack of trust in our capabilities, a slap in the face.

There was some logic in having the most senior experienced officers on the bridge. Putting the most qualified person in charge of the ship when underway made sense if we were in a static world. But we weren't. Every year, new officers were arriving and experienced ones departing. The CO was responsible for training his junior officers, and that meant providing opportunities to learn and to load us down with responsibilities. Captain Penny's position had been that junior officers should shoulder as much responsibility as they could handle. Milligan was the ship's navigator as an ensign. Junior officers conned the ship in and out of port under Penny's tutorage. He willingly gave us the opportunity to learn. The new policy was a real ego buster, a complete reversal of what we thought we had achieved.

There was a positive side to this fourth patrol. It lasted but thirteen days, the shortest patrol on record. We were back in Dunedin on January 15. To this day I do not know for certain why the short patrol. Being an engineer and hiding out in the bunk room, I either missed or forgot the reason for our quick return to Dunedin. We doubled up the lines at seven in the morning, rushing to prepare for the Miss USS *Vance* Coronation Ball, a beauty contest sponsored by the ship and to be held that evening. This may have been the reason for the short patrol. Could the ball have been that important? I am uncertain how the event was conceived and approved. My guess was that some of the crew had the idea, a selfless undertaking, a charitable event for the British Sailors' Society. Captain Penny probably said okay to please the crew and scheduled the ball for late January after he departed the *Vance,* or perhaps Captain Beyer had approved the idea shortly after taking command. Because of changes in our operating schedule, the ball had to be held immediately upon arrival. The *Vance* was to return to sea in two days.

The city and port officials, in fact all Kiwis, were tolerant and hospitable folks. We were about to test the limits of the town fathers' tolerance and hospitality by hosting the Miss USS *Vance* Coronation Ball. The Dunedin Town Hall was made available for the evening. Ticket sales, at twenty shillings a couple for the worthy cause, were adequate. Dunedin's dignitaries obligingly attended. I had the impression that Captain Beyer was a strong supporter of the event, perhaps because once committed, it had to come off successfully. Attendance was mandatory for us officers. Why couldn't this have been my duty day on board? In uniform, Kunz, Hanson, and I sat in the very last row of the hall, embarrassed, hoping we would not be recognized and that the bloody event would end quickly. In attendance were local dignitaries, distinguished older gentlemen, including the Lord Mayor and the President of the Port Authority. Of course, the press corps was there with flashbulbs popping documenting the fiasco.

I use the term *fiasco* because the ball was the brainchild of and executed by young Yankee sailors for a conservative New Zealand middle-aged audience. The sailors understandably fashioned the ball based on their personal experiences, the conventional American high school prom of the 1950s. To pull the event off successfully would have been a difficult task for a professional social planner. The Coronation Ball was in the hands of the crew. Perhaps the fatal element was that the event was planned and carried out by the crew and for the crew, a crew from a hard-driving, seagoing ship with few liberty days in port. The distinguished audience, the Who's Who of Dunedin, was an afterthought. The town fathers and the press were to witness a sailor's night in port.

Poor Larry Hanson, the *Vance*'s public affairs officer, was responsible for the event. The master of ceremonies, a likable outgoing young sailor, had volunteered for the job. Larry had every confidence in the man until just before the opening curtain. We were sitting in the back of the hall when a sailor tapped Larry on the shoulder and anxiously whispered, "Mr. Hanson, what are we going to do? The master of ceremonies is backstage staggering drunk." Larry hurried backstage and drafted another sailor to take over the MC duties. The poor guy, without a script and with a bad case of stage fright, was a disaster, but then again so was the pageant.

The most charitable observer would consider the Coronation Ball a wasted evening. The event might have been amusing had it not been officially sponsored by the visiting US Navy ship. The Coronation Ball had the sophistication of a high school prom and the purity of Quinn's Bar in Tahiti. Many of the crewmembers in attendance were drunk and of course loud, providing a great photo opportunity for the local reporters and a tolerance test for the official guests as they glanced at their watches without betraying their despair over enduring such a distasteful exhibition. It was a real test of the famous British stiff upper lip.

Obviously the sailors' girlfriends were the beauty queen candidates. Some were nice girls, and some were known to be less nice. A month later at sea, the rumor was that the sailor whose girlfriend was crowned Miss *Vance*, showed up in sick bay with a case of the clap. Now Doc would only divulge to the XO the finding of his VD cultures, but the *Vance* was a small ship, where secrets perished quickly. Regardless of whether the rumor was true or not, Miss Clap *Vance* jokes were popular with the crew for months, all the way back to Pearl Harbor.

The Coronation Ball was probably our low point in New Zealand. Was the event salvageable? Some think the urbane Captain Penny could have pulled it off. The man was an amazing diplomat, but I believe it unlikely that even he could have saved the event. I felt sorry for the new skipper, who was left with this inherited time bomb. Public relations was not one of his strengths. Of course, this is all part of being in command—total power and full responsibility. Some of us were embarrassed and eager to put the event behind us. Little did we realize that the welcome mat was about to be removed. For the first time, I was not unhappy leaving Dunedin. The past two days in port were enough. We were underway once again for ocean station and then to Tasmania.

with this material if the bomb. Public relations was "overrun" and his smoothly run machine efficiently managed publicity and wanted public relations and publicity control as much as were major manufacturers to "sell" ... which it is little ... manufacturers involved. Some of these very existing media ... include some, some of these very existing media ... They were out there to tell ... that everyone needed good public relations if a ... bomb told ...

CHAPTER 8

Life at Sea

If the world was perfect, it wouldn't be.
—Yogi Berra

Bunk Room and Fart Sack

When the *Vance* was converted to a DER in the 1950s, the crew realized better living conditions. The newly enclosed space on the main deck amidships provided new crew living quarters and the crew's mess, including a more spacious chiefs' quarters. Although we all felt cramped for space, the World War II sailor had been truly squeezed aboard the old *Vance*. The most important addition was air-conditioning, a critical requirement for the electronic equipment and a blessing for the crew, especially when operating in the tropics.

With the ship reconfigured as a sophisticated radar and communications platform, the number of officers aboard increased. Faced with inadequate space for all the officers, we junior officers had to be shoehorned in somewhere. I deified the ship designers for their solution to this problem. I prefer to believe that the designers had themselves at one time been junior naval officers afloat and therefore did us the favor of isolating the bunk room. My beloved bunk room was the result. Thank you, ship designers!

The beauty of the bunk room was its isolation. Except for the weekly space inspections, I never saw the CO or XO, or for that matter, any department head venture aft into the bunk room. The location was an inconvenient journey from officers' country forward, requiring a trek through the crew's mess, crossing over to the port side through a passageway/crew bunk area, back to the starboard side, down a ladder to the second deck into the snipes' sleeping area, and then an immediate left to the bunk-room door. Why make the journey when we were always reachable by phone?

Most sensible junior officers, myself at the top of the list, believed passionately in the saying "Out of sight, out of mind." My hero was Ensign Pulver, from Thomas Heggen's novel *Mr. Roberts*, who managed many months aboard before the captain knew he was there. In the Ensign Pulver tradition, I hung out in the bunk room. Mealtimes and the nightly movie were the only occasions I voluntarily appeared in the wardroom.

Our meeting place and survival shelter was the bunk room. The captain, XO, and department heads had staterooms forward. The rest of us, usually six to seven junior officers plus the occasional guest, lived here. The furnishings included: a toilet, two sinks, shower, three desks, wardrobes, bookshelves, eight wall safes, and nine bunks.

The jewels in this crown were the bunks, or fart sacks, where an intelligent officer would spend his free time, especially when the ship was severely rolling or pitching. All lounging was horizontal, the bunks being the only comfortable refuge. I spent my most enjoyable hours there. These beauties were configured in three stacks of three, with twenty-four inches between bunks, the lowest bunk being four inches off the deck. All bunks faced fore and aft, the preferred body motion being side to side rather than having your blood flowing from head to toe and back again every eight and a half seconds. The ideal bunks were in the middle; the uppers required an inconvenient climb and tended to be hot, while the lower bunks hugged the deck and were colder. Freshwater tanks beneath the bunk room ensured that the deck remained cold. Five-inch-thick mattresses sat on a flat surface of stretched springs, a reasonably comfortable fart sack, a luxury compared with the crew's flimsy two-inch-thick mattresses on stretched canvas. Our bed frames had sides that held the mattresses in place. In very rough seas, I would wedge a board or large book between the mattress and the open side of the bed frame or tie a line across the frame to assure that I remained in the bunk. Rarely was this necessary because we quickly learned to sleep glued to the mattress, similar to a squirrel hugging a tree trunk.

When not sleeping, I read by the small indispensable bunk light. Two mail-order reading clubs kept me supplied with books. I lived in the bunk, this refuge that turned into a time-and-space capsule. I fled the ship by burying myself in books: common fiction, historical novels, classics, history, current affairs, anything other than ship's business and our little world just outside the bunk-room door. Here in isolation, I developed an insatiable need to know what was happening in the world. What was I missing while locked in this rolling metal chamber at the ends of the earth?

Jim Kunz and I shared a desk, bookshelf, drawer space, and a wardrobe, all facing amidships, their contents moving back and forth with the ship's roll. Masking tape was indispensable for holding in place pencils, paper, toothbrushes, plus any and every loose item. I learned the hard way that clothes on hangers could be a problem on this rolling platform. Upon our return to Hawaii the next year, I discovered that the cuff of my beautiful civilian summer suit had worn through from rubbing against the wardrobe door every eight and a half seconds for the past nine months. Everything I owned moved unless tied or taped down.

We had more privacy than anyone except for the captain, who had a private stateroom with a bathroom on the 02 level. The

Junior officers' bunk room.
(Photo courtesy of Tom Milligan.)

staterooms of the XO and department heads adjoined the wardroom, a busy spot. There was no hiding in the forward staterooms.

A Rigid Planned Existence

The great truth, which has been known to seafaring captains since the cooling of the earth, is that a busy crew is a good crew. Translation: Don't let the crew have time to think about their restrictive lives and what they are missing ashore. A ship's routine was designed to ensure minimum free time. The tool was watch standing for both officers and crew. For five and a half days a week at sea, a daily work schedule was observed, equivalent to a forty-hour-per-week job ashore with a bit of unpaid overtime, such as four hours on Saturday. We started with morning quarters, took a break for lunch, and ended at dinnertime. The crew also stood a three-section watch seven days a week and officers a four-section watch. I thought I would never get used to one unbroken night of sleep in four, but I did. The schedule left a bit of time for meals, a movie, and little else.

Seven days a week, six hours a day, I was on the bridge. There was no escaping the routine and the accompanying boredom. Floating in this far corner of the world, boredom gradually crept in and took hold. The real work was to keep boredom in check. At least the sailors on the bridge watch had some variation. They could talk among themselves in the pilothouse and rotate positions. Lookouts came inside every half hour, and the helmsman switched off with the engine order telegraph operator. The petty officer of the watch could bullshit with the quartermaster and everyone else, until before long they all knew each other's stories and they too became bored. Perhaps these conditions were responsible for the origin of sea stories, events repeated, reconfigured, and embellished over and over again, all to pass the time on watch.

The lone officer on the open bridge had largely himself for company. Boredom readily crept in, particularly at night when the captain and crew slept. Alone on the open bridge, I had my pipe, tobacco and lighter to fiddle with, a mug of coffee, and memories to occupy me. A part of me was always on edge, alert to the course being steered, the level of chatter and movement in the pilothouse, and the off chance that the captain might venture onto the bridge. In the first six months, I became comfortable with this routine. Getting along with the watch section was key. At first they took pity on the new OOD and were cooperative. In time, we got to know each other, and I was comfortable on the bridge. You had to be insensitive and a bit of a fool not to run a squared-away bridge watch. Everybody knew their job and how to do it. I enjoyed these deck apes and got to know them better than my division of snipes, if only because I spent so much time on the bridge.

Officers didn't stand engine-room watches. What little I saw of my snipes was at quarters each morning. Engles and some of the more senior snipes I saw more frequently, usually in the log room or on the mess decks where they stopped for coffee. Much of my workday was pushing paper and carrying out additional chores that, on a small ship like the *Vance*, the navy managed to provide in abundance. They were called collateral duties. I liked to think of them as mosquitoes or black flies, irritants, not life-threatening but annoying just the same, and ever present. The best one could hope for was to avoid the most repugnant of the collateral duty assignments. The list was long.

Some collateral duties were naturals for certain division officers. Larry Hanson, the communications officer, was the registered publications custodian because he was the user of most of these publications. He also was the perfect man for public affairs officer. Both were miserable jobs, and they belonged to Larry.

There was no avoiding being assigned one of the more miserable communications assignments, membership to the crypto board. The job called for decoding incoming messages every fourth day after normal work hours. Classified messages arrived encrypted, and depending on the classification, required decryption by an officer. Rarely was I called upon to decrypt, but when I was, the exercise was pure torture. The crypto equipment was in a locked closet in the communications center. Squeezed in this small steel mausoleum was a desk-mounted crypto machine, a chair, and me. Here I sat, in this tight closet with the door shut, no ventilation and the room in constant motion, wedged between the bulkhead and the desk, two fingers slowly and methodically typing. Decryption was complex and tedious. One small mistake, and the text printed out garbled. I would begin over and over again, claustrophobic and ready to barf. I hated crypto duty.

After a few of these experiences, I got wise. The radiomen on watch, knowing I was taking forever fumbling through the decryption process, ignored my plight. I was saved by Plumb, a gregarious good-natured radioman who offered to help. With six years' experience, he could knock off a decryption in a matter of minutes, while I required an hour or two with barf bucket in hand. With Plumb's help, the decryption was done quickly. I would offer to buy him a beer in port. We both knew we wouldn't be drinking together ashore. Still, this was the only way I could say thanks.

Another dreaded collateral duty was that of religious lay leader. The assignment called for leading a prayer group each Sunday in the mess decks. Fred was handed the job of Jewish lay leader, responsible for the religious needs of all four Jews aboard. I think Hank Fox led the Protestant service, and I was a contender for Catholic lay leader. When joining the navy, I had to fill in the blank space on the application asking my religious preference. I was concerned that "no preference" would reflect poorly on my application, the US Navy being a God-fearing organization. I was brought up Roman Catholic, so Catholic it was in my record and the letter "C" on my dog tags.

I had embraced Catholicism at the early age of six, when my mother's sudden death from leukemia during World War II resulted in my brother and me spending the next three years in a Roman Catholic orphanage, until Dad remarried and we were all together again. Although our family had always been mildly religious, the intense dose of orphanage Catholicism followed by four more years of browbeating, intense social pressure on the family from the dictatorial parish priests, and the realization that the religious leadership didn't practice what they preached caused me to walk away from St. Jerome's Parish after the seventh grade to attend public school. Six more years were required before I was able to shed the crippling guilt that the church had harnessed me with. I was then a new man, at peace with myself.

With "C" stamped on my dog tags and service record, there was an attempt to name me Catholic lay leader. I strongly stated that I had no religious preference and was not suited for the job, realizing at the same time that this was the military. The XO could stick me with the job regardless of personal objections. Jim Kunz saved the day by volunteering for the job. Catholic lay leader suited his Jesuit background, and he must have realized that I was the least fit person for the job. It pays to have friends who are very different from you.

The other big duty to avoid was mess treasurer, a difficult high-visibility job critiqued daily at wardroom meals. The job was a natural for the supply officer, who already was responsible for provisioning the ship and feeding the crew. I was lucky. I had avoided the most miserable collateral duties, mess treasurer and religious lay leader, while getting help on the crypto board. I managed also to avoid legal officer, recreation officer, charity fund campaign coordinator, educational services officer, movie officer, voting assistance officer, and athletic officer, and was too new to be crowned career counselor.

I had fewer collateral duty assignments than most, probably because engineering officers were perceived as having a greater workload. Apparently there was a consensus that engineers were able to count. I found myself with collateral duties requiring accountability for funds and goods. Monthly, I could be found huddled with old QM2 Beeman, our postmaster, counting the money and inventorying postage stamps in his little post office. I went on to inventory everything from candy bars to condoms, anything and everything having to do with money or supplies, recreation funds, mess funds, and the goods in the ship's store. Despite my complaining, I was fortunate in having accumulated so few collateral duties. They all consumed time. I guess this was part of the intent.

Servants

In the 1960s, officer comforts and minorities could be addressed together because aboard the *Vance,* and perhaps all US Navy ships, minorities provided all cleaning and dining services for officers. Never having been waited on, at first I was uncomfortable with being served each meal by a steward in a white jacket and having someone make up my bed each day. I didn't mind the cleaning. Each division assigned junior sailors to clear the crew's head, mess decks, and sleeping compartments. I just was unaccustomed to personal services. Yet for over three years, I accepted the system and probably still would today, knowing the use of minorities for these jobs is long past. I have come to realize that my discomfort stemmed from realizing that there was an invisible barrier between me and the African American or Filipino waiting on me. He had an agenda and set of guiding principles that I was not privy to. I liked to understand the people I dealt with.

In my years on the *Vance,* I came into contact with three minority groups: African Americans, Mexican Americans, and Filipinos, plus a lone Navajo. The Filipinos were on board to be servants for the officers, with one exception. Our wiry black wardroom cook, Singleton, was a throwback to World War II, when almost all career African American sailors were stewards, the US Navy rating that cooked, cleaned, and waited on officers. Singleton was comfortable in the navy as the senior steward on board, with twenty-three years of service and no plans for retirement. For this quiet loner, the navy was home and a way of life.

Filipinos were a whole different matter. The average young Filipino sailor was alien to American society. The navy began actively recruiting Filipinos as stewards and mess boys as early as 1898. Most were assigned as stewards, performing the work of domestics, serving as cooks, and doing menial jobs, such as cleaning the galley, the wardroom, and living quarters of officers. I was not comfortable with servants, but the navy liked this out-of-date gentleman's luxury. In fact, it was prized and came to be expected. The career Academy officers appeared the most afflicted, because they were taught to adhere to the many customs and traditions of the US Navy, rooted in the eighteenth and nineteenth centuries, including being waited on by servants. Historically, the middle-class naval officer corps, in their insulated world, emulated the old moneyed upper classes. The trappings and ritual were many, from wardroom silver serving sets to calling cards. Silver trays were placed in the captain's foyer for the junior officer to leave his calling card when paying the obligatory courtesy house visit to his commanding officer. Calling cards were also a must for the poor junior officer's young wife. She too was obliged to leave her card. There was even a large publication dedicated to defining the social requirements expected of the officer's wife. This was a must-read for both the ambitious and the frail-hearted who wanted to avoid embarrassment.

Five Filipinos served on the *Vance*. One, Zaida, was an exception. He was a career disbursing clerk second-class. This short pleasant man, with a huge smile on his face, handled the cash on board. Zaida planned one day to retire in America and seek a career as a bookkeeper. He probably joined the navy as a steward and eventually managed to change ratings. Unlike the other Filipinos aboard, Zaida was emancipated, no longer a steward but a regular member of the crew. His fellow workers and friends were American sailors.

The other four Filipinos were stewards, who formed a tight little group dictated by the job and common culture and language. They stuck together. All communication among them was in Tagalog. Jose and Atilano were career sailors, their English adequate for the job. The other two, Labasan and Averilla, were newer Filipino recruits, who claimed not to understand English when convenient. I knew Averilla better than the others because he was assigned to the junior officers' bunk room, cleaning, making the beds, hauling the laundry, and helping to serve the wardroom meals.

The opportunity to be a US Navy steward was highly competitive in the Philippines. I assumed that these were high-caliber men in their native country, who were literate and intelligent. Navy pay was great by Philippine standards and an opportunity for US citizenship was inviting, while the job was demeaning. Averilla was an unhappy sailor. Being the junior steward, he was assigned to the bunk room because shit flows downhill for all of us. We were just in different valleys. Looking into Averilla's eyes, I saw hatred for the job, for being a servant, and for us pampered officers. He was never openly defiant. He understood the power and benefits of the system and that he was a captive of it until able to amass enough money to open his own little business in the Philippines. For now, the navy was better than zero opportunities in the Philippines, but he was not happy. He understood that his fellow shipmates had real jobs, while the steward was a servant. Admittedly, I grew used to the system and the conveniences over time.

Meals and Entertainment

Despite my strong attachment to the bunk room, the arena where we officers congregated was the wardroom, a large space forward on the main deck stretching a full twenty-eight feet amidships. Here we took our meals, held meetings, and relaxed after the workday. Left untouched by the major modification of the *Vance* to a radar picket ship, the wardroom and furnishings were unchanged from the time when the ship was chasing U-boats during World War II, except for the small black-and-white TV bolted to the overhead in a far corner of the space. No, we didn't watch TV. Reception, via a rabbit-ears antenna, was only available when moored to the Pearl Harbor pier.

The major luxury was wall-to-wall carpeting, nothing elegant, just a heavy-duty grayish short-napped carpet that snaked around the few welded-in-place pieces of metal furniture, a couch with end tables, a small corner table, a sideboard, and a dining table that seated ten. Directly above the table, nested in the usual bundles of cable and air ducts winding through the overhead, were operating lights and battle lanterns. The wardroom was the ship's medical station during wartime conditions; our dining table serving as the operating table. Bon appetit!

Ten heavy-duty metal chairs framed the table. In difficult seas, a line threaded through the chair legs and tied in a circle around the table prevented flying chairs. They just happily banged about. Next to the couch was a freestanding easy chair, which also had to be tied down in rough seas. The chair was a throne of sorts. We always stood up whenever the captain entered the room, and the chair was immediately vacated for his use.

As my seasickness faded after the first few days at sea, I would show up for breakfast, an informal affair, served between six thirty and seven forty-five, with officers placing their individual orders, eating quickly, and then dashing off to meet their divisions at eight. Rarely were there more than five of us at breakfast at any one time, and never the captain, who took breakfast in his cabin. On Sunday, some of us never made it to breakfast, preferring to sleep in. I quickly learned what Singleton prepared well and the limits of the larder. The breakfast favorite was Singleton's cheese omelet, powdered eggs double-folded with cheddar cheese inside. Eventually, I embraced this more hardy breakfast. Long weeks at sea, tension, boredom, and the lack of exercise led to overeating. I came aboard at 135 pounds and departed the *Vance* three years later twenty pounds heavier.

Lunch and dinner were more formal mandatory affairs, with the captain always in attendance. Usually there was a white tablecloth, unless the seas were acting up, and then the fiddle boards were installed. Fiddle boards, the two-inch-high aluminum frames that attached to the tabletop, provided an individual corral for each place setting, ensuring the dishes and food stayed within your own sector of the table. I didn't find them practical. They might prevent flying dishes, but not spills. In foul weather, we normally ate each man braced at the table, our rear ends on the edge of the chair, legs spread wide, elbows on the table, with a hand on the cup and the plate wedged against the fiddle boards. When the seas were totally out of control, the galley could not operate. Crew and wardroom both lived on cold sandwiches and coffee.

The captain presided over the meal at the head of the table. Even in an empty wardroom, rarely would anyone sit in his spot. Mealtime seating was by seniority, the XO on the captain's right, the next senior officer on his left, and so forth, filling the ten seats with the mess treasurer seated at the foot. Not a bad position being far away from the captain, considering that the mess treasurer took the heat if the meal didn't measure up.

With two of the fourteen officers on watch, the table for ten left the two most junior officers to eat alone at a second sitting. Filipino stewards in white jackets served the captain first and then commenced serving where the "buck" was placed. I liked the concept of the buck; a small miniature eighteenth-century deck cannon was rotated from place to place each dinner, ensuring that everyone had the opportunity to be served second to the skipper. This may have been a Naval Academy tradition. When Captain Penny departed the *Vance*, so did the tradition. The little cannon remained in a drawer with the napkins for the next two and a half years. As time passed, fewer if any people knew its function. It may still be in that drawer.

The egalitarian buck was more a symbolic gesture than a gastronomic benefit, except when something special was being served. For example, Captain Penny craved baked Alaska, a dessert perfected by Singleton for the captain's pleasure. About once a month following the main dinner course, Singleton, who normally didn't serve, would emerge from his galley with a big grin on his face, carrying forth a tray with a huge sculptured baked Alaska squatting on it. There was a sense of urgency in the air because buried beneath in this mound of meringue rested a gallon of the ship's homemade dirty-beige-colored powdered ice cream sitting on a sponge cake.

The captain licked his chops at the glorious treat as he scooped a manly portion for himself. The other officers carefully took small portions, knowing the skipper would want seconds by the time the rest of us were served. Singleton stood proud as the captain praised his creation, with we officers echoing his compliments like Elvis's backup singers. Now, this was not great baked Alaska, but aboard ship in the middle of the ocean, it was a marvel. Singleton, constrained by the size of his oven, coordinated the use of the larger oven in the crew's galley and overcame the challenges of a rolling ship, the lack of fresh eggs and cream, and the questionable navy ice cream, a cold mushy substance made from a powder and water mixture harboring a strange taste reminiscent of the oily guts of the large gray World War II ice cream machine bolted to the deck in the crew's mess. Singleton's baked Alaska was a true achievement, a real treat for the wardroom, at least for the officers at the first sitting. At the second sitting, little remained but a beige lukewarm puddle. We never saw baked Alaska again once Captain Penny departed the *Vance*. The ritual was the same for Captain Beyer, only fresh king crab legs replaced the baked Alaska.

Following dinner each and every night, there was a movie, or rather three movies, one in the mess deck for the crew, one in the chiefs' quarters, and one in the wardroom. The most junior officer not on watch lashed a 16 mm projector to the wardroom table and threaded the first of three reels, being careful to ensure that the movie and not the numeral countdown started at precisely the moment the project was turned on. If the countdown numbers appeared, the projectionist was booed and harassed. If the film broke or the reels were not changed quickly enough, the harassment began again. In these endearing moments, I couldn't wait to gain some seniority.

Once the nightly movie was over, the game boards and playing cards appeared. The skipper's pleasure determined the game. Backgammon was extremely popular in the navy. Captain Penny, a backgammon fanatic, had little trouble finding an opponent. As a non–watch stander, Robbie was generally the chosen one, whether he wanted to play or not. Once Doc Gersenfish came aboard, he was drafted as a third for bridge, with Tom Milligan, the navigator, as the fourth. All three non–watch standers were logical choices for the evening bridge game.

Bridge was also Captain Beyer's favorite game. Rounding up three willing officers was more difficult after Deep Freeze, when Milligan and Doc were transferred. More than one officer regretted having acknowledged that he knew how to play the game. If the skipper wanted to play, an emissary might ask, "Will you be a fourth for bridge?" knowing you had the midwatch and should be sleeping. The captain never personally searched for players. Someone, often the XO, would do his bidding, another excellent reason for living in the bunk room. There was never a formal order to play, just a request that a rational person could not ignore. Life was easier if the captain liked you.

Links to the World

When at sea, we were isolated from what was happening in the world. The limitations of communications technology in the early 1960s dictated the postal service as the primary personal link with family and friends. The mailbags were hauled aboard each time we entered port, the married men being the most anxious recipients. I enjoyed receiving mail from home, despite the contents being as repetitive as my letters home. I existed in a different world, a world that could not be adequately described or explained in a letter. The best I could do was write that I was fine and tick off the countries and tourist sites I visited. News from home was equally bland. Nothing earth-shattering was happening, and though we all said we missed each other, I rarely thought about home and family. I was on my big adventure, having long since left Cleveland behind me. The postal service served me best by providing books and news magazines. I would read every scrap of information in a weekly news magazine, while back in the States, the same periodical would merit only a brief glance. News was always late, but I liked receiving it in large doses, articles covering events that tended to include thoughtful analysis as opposed to daily news feeds.

The evening movie was the most popular and important link to the outside world. The nightly movie was a staple. Both the crew and wardroom were addicted to movies. Unless you were an avid reader, the movies were the primary vehicle of escape from the boredom of long periods at sea. Before the days of Hollywood and recorded sound, sailors sang shanties in the fo'c'sle, and soldiers sang around the campfire. Many of their songs are still with us, frozen in time, but we no longer sing for recreation. Radio, television, and movies replaced singing. Movies were the new focal point of every evening at sea. We depended on the navy's system for distributing and trading these reels throughout the fleet, always hoping to secure newer, popular flicks. For each patrol, the movie officer, another collateral duty, ensured that we had on board a different movie for each day at sea. We started the deployment with a good selection from Hawaii. As the months passed in the southern oceans, the selections became more limited, at times downright lousy. On one patrol, we had twenty-four straight days of the 1950s and 1960s *Perry Mason* television detective series. In the boredom and hunger for a normal existence, wardroom officers fell in love with the correct and homely Della Street, the fictional secretary to Perry Mason, played by the forty-two-year-old Barbara Hale.

The silver screen distracted us from being at sea by promoting dreams of different worlds. In desperate moments, when nothing else was available, we were reduced to watching the *Victory at Sea* TV series, an unreal experience. Stretched out on the wardroom carpet with the *Vance* and the movie screen rolling back and forth, I would watch images of destroyers in the North Atlantic battling the waves. Two different ocean motions at the same time? No, thank you. I fled to read a book in my bunk.

On rare occasions, our ham radio station would find a single-sideband link with another ham operator in the continental United States who would be willing to dial up our family members on a collect call, permitting voice communication. The 1MC would announce that we had a connection to the States. Crewmembers would provide home phone numbers, then wait their turn for a few minutes' conversation with their families and loved ones. The link was tenuous, often garbled or disrupted by atmospherics, but the minutes were precious and appreciated.

Only once did I submit my home phone number, thinking how nice it would be to say hello to my parents in Cleveland. I waited my turn in the communications space with fifteen sailors, all of us standing around or sitting on the deck listening to the phone conversations over a speaker system. There was no privacy. All conversations blared out over the loudspeaker for those of us in the room to be the audience for intimate family conversations. I understood the need for the monitoring: the chief and radiomen had to manage the tenuous single-sideband link. Unfortunately, the people on the other end weren't aware of their conversation being listened to by a roomful of sailors.

I felt like an intruder. I didn't want to listen in on private conversations, especially between husband and wife. As I was about to make a quick exit, the chief announced, "Mr. Jaras, I have your mother on the line." A single-sideband transmission reminds me of World War II aviation movies. The pilot receives the message, presses his transmit button, and says, "Roger, over and out." I greeted my parents, and they were astounded to actually be speaking directly to me in the Antarctic. Then my stepmother, to whom I was very close, became emotional. She said, "Tommy, we miss you so much." On and on it went until finally, she realized she must get off the line before I could respond. I was uncomfortable letting the crew into my private life and having them witness the emotional attachment between this naval officer and his mother. Apparently I wasn't so different or interesting, because nothing echoed back to me from the crew. As I noted earlier, there are few secrets on a small ship. Without privacy, I couldn't enjoy calling home. I never again called.

CHAPTER 9

Tasmania

January 17–March 3, 1962

Don't be an art critic. Paint. There lies salvation.
—Paul Cézanne

Beware lest you lose the substance by grasping at the shadow.
—Aesop

Disappointed with My Leaders

Once again we cast off all lines, backed from the Dunedin pier, and headed into the channel, bound for open water and our fifth patrol. The date was January 17, the weather typical: sunny, breezy, and cool until we passed Taiaroa Head and entered the open sea. I looked forward to the patrol because after our time on ocean station, we were scheduled to attend the Royal Hobart Regatta in Tasmania. Little did I realize that the pleasure of visiting Tasmania would be overshadowed by the realization that the *Vance* had a problem. For the first time, I seriously questioned the skipper's decisions.

As a green ensign, I was hesitant to draw conclusions and make sweeping observations. I had only the few months under Captain Penny from which to make comparisons. New skippers make new demands. Who was I to complain because the drills continued? The *Vance* was a naval ship of war. We naturally would grumble at the inconvenience of scrambling out of our bunks to go to general quarters at midnight. Unhappy about the drills? Yes, I was. I understood the need for a well-trained crew. I just wasn't used to living this way. Perhaps in his last months aboard, Captain Penny had been lenient, and I had accepted minimal drills as the standard. I had no reference points by which to judge the new captain's actions.

149

I took a less tolerant stance concerning the plight of us junior officers, who were demoted to JOOD on bridge watches after having been qualified as OOD by Captain Penny. This was the captain's prerogative. He was responsible for the ship and had every right to place only the most experienced officers on the bridge when underway. I didn't like being demoted, but I understood the captain's logic behind the move. I might disagree with some of Captain Beyer's decisions; still, he carried the burden of responsibility for the ship and crew. He had more experience than the rest of us. His style was less engaging when compared to that of the debonair and confident Captain Penny. Captain Beyer seemed bent on flexing his muscles to ensure that we understood he was the boss. Again, I assumed this to be the standard approach for new captains. Be tough at first and then in time lighten up.

While I believed the new skipper's actions were what might be expected, the XO, second-in-command, earned little respect from the day he reported aboard. Mel Huffman, a congenial man perched on a light five-eight frame, was so different from our expectations that it was difficult to take the man seriously. On his first patrol, Mel was in the ship's galley cooking a large kettle of stew for the crew while posturing and joking with the cooks and anyone passing by. This may appear to be normal behavior to the man on the street, but on a warship, such behavior detracts from the XO's effectiveness. What a contrast to Tom Jewell, the man he relieved.

Mel's job was important because the XO ran the ship day-to-day. The CO owned the ranch. The XO was his foreman. He functioned as the bad guy, the enforcer, the whip who carried out the wishes of the captain. He was the one man aboard whom a captain could confide in. We had had a good team on the *Vance*, with the handsome, charismatic Penny balanced by a quiet, serious Tom Jewell, who appeared at ease and very much in control of the day-to-day operation of the *Vance*. Jewell was ten years my senior, a graduate of Heidelberg University, one of those fine, small, private, liberal arts colleges hidden away in the hills of rural Ohio. He came through OCS, and I assume he was sufficiently enamored with sea duty to make the navy a career. He was icy in expressing his wishes, so I received the message loud and clear that a friendship was not to be attempted. To be effective, he kept some distance between himself and the other officers. Nevertheless, he was liked and respected in the wardroom. I assumed there was excellent rapport between Penny and Jewell because the ship seemed to function smoothly. I hardly knew these two men. In fact, I rarely saw or spoke to either man. Yet I sensed that all was well.

Mel Huffman could not have been more different, overly friendly, accessible, glib, and a showman. He did not demand or expect respect. Rather, Mel wanted to be liked. I was not privy to Captain Beyer's working relationship with his second-in-command. My gut feeling was that with Beyer their communication was in one direction. Mel's attempt to be the tough, hard-driving ranch foreman was an act. He would stick out his angular, less-than-prominent jaw to emphasize a point, relying on the thin veneer of age difference to awe. The subliminal message was, "I've been around and seen it all."

Throughout this fifth patrol, I just accepted the changes and assumed that in time all would be well. Ocean station didn't disappoint us. The sea rose to twenty-five feet, and the winds blew at thirty to thirty-five knots. The resupply season to the ice was rapidly coming to an end. On the morning of February 5, the bridge watch was unusually alert and chatty. In the passageways, sailors seemed upbeat, and there was an abnormal buzz of conversation in the crew's mess. The boredom of ocean station gave way to anticipation of liberty in Hobart. We were underway for Hobart, Tasmania, and the Royal Hobart Regatta. Across the Tasman Sea and the international date line we steamed, sighting land after four days.

I admit to having been excited at the prospect of visiting this charming out-of-the-way port and attending the Royal Hobart Regatta. We had just completed another difficult patrol.

After twenty-four days at sea, the crew looked forward to five well-earned days of liberty in Hobart. We were to be the official US representatives to the Royal Hobart Regatta. As usual, I researched the subject, devouring a couple of books on nineteenth-century Tasmania and the infamous penal colony at Port Arthur. I was ready to go ashore.

We made landfall and were steaming toward Hobart when the skipper guided the ship into an isolated bay and dropped the anchor. Captain Beyer was also looking forward to the Royal Hobart Regatta, but with a twist. He envisioned a glittering warship, the *Vance*, gliding into Hobart Harbor, not a tired workhorse weather ship supporting Operation Deep Freeze. To this end, he decided to waste one of our five liberty days in isolation painting the ship before proceeding the last few miles to Hobart and the Regatta. I couldn't believe it. Here we sat in Adventure Bay, Tasmania, after twenty-four difficult days at sea, trying to make the ship superficially pretty in the next twenty-four hours. Christ! We were a working ship doing an important job. Wasn't that enough? The Aussies would understand this.

Painting the Vance *in Adventure Bay, Tasmania. (Photo from author's collection.)*

We were a working ship fresh from the Screaming Sixties, with five Antarctic patrols in the last six months. Many crazy things happened in my three years aboard, but I cannot remember being more frustrated than at that moment. My surprise at this order left an indelible mark on my brain. From this time on, I would never again be surprised by stupid orders. Angry perhaps, but never surprised.

The entire crew was ordered to turn out to paint the ship. Snipes, radarmen, sonarmen, electronic technicians, mess cooks, stewards, aerographers, anyone who could hold a paintbrush joined the deck force in slapping gray paint over the sea salt–encrusted hull. Dangling over the side on lines were sailors painting down to the waterline, careful only not to smudge gray over the black waterline and our hull numbers. Others were high on the main mast and funnel with brushes. Sailors were everywhere painting and polishing brass, making a holiday of an event they had no control over.

There was no surface preparation. We were painting over the rust and salt! I looked at Boats Oldervick, who was busy handing out cans of paint. He glanced over at me with his "no message" stoic pose, no smile on this face today, and in a flat tone said, "Captain's orders, Mr. Jaras." I hadn't the heart to kid him that day. Slop the paint on thick! In the engine rooms we were always short of funds, but I knew at that moment, there would always be funds available for paint, brass fittings, and anything else that made the *Vance* look pretty.

Here I stood on the open deck, anchored in Adventure Bay, Tasmania, looking at the barren hills and wondering if this bay had ever witnessed anything so ridiculous. Tobias Fureaux probably hadn't. He was an Englishman who was the first to anchor here in 1773. Four years later, Captain Cook landed here with the young William Bligh aboard. He was probably too busy mapping the region to teach Bligh how to manage a crew. Eleven years later, the now Captain Bligh was briefly here again, this time with the HMS *Bounty*. He was probably preoccupied with getting to Tahiti and harvesting breadfruit. Little did he know what awaited him the next year in Tahiti, 1789, when the crew mutinied. If Bligh were commanding the

Vance, I wonder if he too would have broken out the paint in Adventure Bay.

Was I reading the Adventure Bay fiasco correctly? Why didn't I see more disappointment on the faces of the crew? Was I the only one motivated to get ashore in Tasmania? We had a once-in-a-lifetime opportunity here, something to truly cherish, exploring this island at the ends of the earth and its colorful past. Granted, some of the crew were indifferent to the ports we entered, and others had a fatalistic view of their leaders' decisions. Stupid ideas were not new in the armed forces. Why get excited when we had no recourse? Perhaps others just reined in their anguish, as I had to. I realized that my disappointment and anger were rooted in a deep-felt sense of injustice being inflicted on me. I chose the US Navy and sea duty, believing here were opportunities to see some of the world. So I was stuck on the *Vance*. Well, I worked hard and made the most of my situation. Our bosses in Christchurch and Hawaii believed we had earned this R&R or they wouldn't have scheduled it. Should poor weather, equipment failure, or schedule changes have interfered with the duration of our visit at the Royal Hobart Regatta, I would have been disappointed but not upset and angry, which was the way I now felt. Apparently I was serving under a captain who was as passionate over making superficial impressions as I was about seeing the world.

I had been willing to grant Captain Beyer the benefit of the doubt regarding the changes he brought and the hoops he had us jump through. After all, he was the captain, older and more experienced and deemed qualified by BUPERS for command. Besides, I liked the man. He was approachable. Yet this day had me questioning the man's judgment. I could not get past the fact that he was willing to paint over the entire salt-caked ship—a paint job he knew was superficial—believing he would be making a favorable impression. Apparently, showing the flag at the regatta and the fact that it happened to be the queen's birthday proved too perfect a stage for the skipper to ignore. Perhaps this was a standard public relations operating procedure for navy ships showing the flag abroad. Regardless, I believe you fool no one. I subscribed to an honest representation of who and what we were. My guess was that while I dreamed away my youth about the Wild West and foreign lands, the skipper probably spent his youth dreaming of seafaring men and naval heroes on freshly painted ships. You might say we had different interests.

Tasmania

Tasmania, an Australian state, is an island separated from the Australian mainland by the Bass Strait and surrounded by the Indian and Pacific Oceans. The Derwent River reaches the coast at Hobart, the state capital and largest city in Tasmania. In 1646, the Dutch explorer Abel Tasman was the first European to discover Tasmania. The first permanent settlement was established in 1803 by the British in the Derwent estuary. The early settlers were mostly convicts. About 75,000 were shipped there by 1853 to develop agriculture and minor industries. Two of the more infamous penal colonies were Port Arthur and Macquarie Harbour. The British Colonie of Tasmania became the Australian state of Tasmania in 1901.

Royal Hobart Regatta

The Royal Hobart Regatta is the oldest continuous public holiday in Australia. In 1838, the governor of Tasmania, Sir John Franklin, declared a public holiday during which members of the merchant navy and local sailors would hold a friendly competition, with free food and beer for the settlers. Today the regatta encompasses the entire Derwent River for three days and is supported by the warships of the Royal Australian Navy. Events include sailing, rowing, swimming, and other competitions.

I shelved my thoughts the next day as the newly painted *Vance* doubled up her lines at the Hobart piers. The festivities had begun. But first the captain rolled out the ship's honor guard. Yes, our little ship had an honor guard, which formed up for visits by dignitaries in New Zealand and now in Tasmania. I have no idea if honor guards exist on all US Navy ships or how large a ship must be to support such a unit. Our volunteer unit of fourteen sailors was comprised primarily of my snipes. This was one of the great mysteries of life. Why did my semi-disciplined engine-room gang seek membership in the voluntary honor guard? Was it the adornment? The white helmets, white spats, and white belts supporting bayonets in white scabbards, or the standing at attention with shiny World War I–vintage Springfield rifles? For some mystifying reason, the snipes were drawn to this activity like mosquitoes to blood. I hardly recognized my normally grease-smudged snipes smartly decked out as a disciplined honor guard. Captain Beyer showed unusually strong interest in the group, more than he ever showed when they worked as engine-room snipes. He ensured that the honor guard lacked nothing. Once again, the honor guard snapped to attention as the visiting dignitaries arrived to welcome the *Vance* to Hobart.

The Governor of Tasmania and I

Invitations were pouring in. Each officer not on watch was assigned to attend several parties and official events each day. During the round of parties, Jim Kunz and I hooked up with a couple of young officers from the Aussie aircraft carrier HMAS *Melbourne*. Part of the Australian Fleet was in town with the carrier and several destroyers and auxiliary ships. The Aussies showed us the town, and we met and socialized with local families. The hospitality was amazing. We made a shabby attempt to repay their kindness by having the Aussie officers and a few civilians aboard the *Vance*. Unfortunately, our Puritan-inspired navy, unchanged since Prohibition, deems there should be no spirits on board American warships. What a contrast! The Aussies supported a great bar on the *Melbourne,* and in return we served our guests American coffee and gave them a tour of a working ship. I had a similar experience with the French navy in Tahiti. American coffee and a tour of our ugly little ship in exchange for a steak and fries dinner with a bottle of red wine. Still, we were able to hold our heads high, knowing that the *Vance* was a working ship and they warships without a war.

USS Vance *honor guard at Hobart, Tasmania,*
February 1, 1962. (Photo from author's collection.)

Nevertheless, there were times I thought I had joined the wrong navy. The *Vance* was a workhorse with a tight schedule, much sea time, and few days in port. The Aussie and French naval ships we met spent considerable time in port showing the flag. Neither navy had a major worldwide Cold War commitment. In contrast, the *Vance* either patrolled on the DEW Line in the North Pacific or supported Deep Freeze. Without these missions, the *Vance* would have been in mothballs or turned into razor blades. My point is that these foreign naval units served as symbols of a national presence, whereas the *Vance* was just one of many small service ships in a very large navy. Like penniless kids with noses pressed against the candy-store window, we accepted reality, but couldn't ignore how well the others lived. We had our pride, knowing the *Vance*'s mission was essential and that we proved our worth enduring some of the worst seas in the world. We took some comfort in seeing other navies as cruise ships with weapons.

*Government House, Hobart, Tasmania. (Photo
courtesy of Government House, Tasmania.)*

In Tasmania, we had an opportunity to play at being am-
bassadors, if only for four days. During these four days, I volunteered, in response to an inquiry if there might be an officer aboard who would like to play tennis with the governor's
daughter. This appealed to me. I had played varsity tennis in
college, had my racket aboard, and had never met a governor's daughter. The governor of Tasmania resided in Government House, an early Victorian country house in neo-Gothic
style with seventy-three rooms. Lord Rowallan's daughter, who
was about my age, was very pleasant, while the private tennis
court was a new experience. She noted that I had an unusual
forehand stroke. *How could I explain that growing up playing on
Cleveland's public courts, I was self-taught, never having had a
tennis lesson?* We batted the ball around, played a set, and quit
early to prepare for the Regatta Ball at Government House
that evening.

The *Vance* officers were invited to the event as the official
representatives of America, and frankly, I was excited at the
prospect of dancing the night away to the music of a naval orchestra in the huge ballroom at Government House. The invitation stated formal attire. All we possessed were dress blue

uniforms; they would have to do. Here I was the blue-collar immigrant's son spending an evening in a Gothic mansion, dancing to a full naval orchestra, sipping champagne, meeting some of the more important people in Australia, and just having a grand time as an official representative of my country. My Cinderella evening had me decked out in smart navy blues, the uniform I bought secondhand from a guy who flunked out of the Coast Guard Academy. A tailor changed the "coastie" buttons to navy buttons, and presto, a beautiful navy dress blue uniform worn by a proud young ensign.

I quickly realized that the governor's daughter, a pleasant, attractive girl, had little time for me. She was busy as the hostess for the younger set, the junior naval officers, and the local girls. The hall was flooded with young Australian naval officers and a shortage of girls. Despite my dapper appearance, I did not impress anyone but the governor. Unfortunately, I met the governor of Tasmania, Lord Rowallan, under less-than-ideal circumstances. Tapped on the shoulder, I turned to face an irate governor, who pointed to a snubbed-out cigarette butt on the floor near my foot. He loudly proceeded to scold me over putting out cigarettes on the rare Huon-pine ballroom floor. In a quiet, humble voice, I pointed out to him that I was innocent because I did not smoke cigarettes. Lord Rowallan was too worked up to let the matter rest. I am not certain he was listening to my meek response, and if he were, I'm not certain he believed me. He neither apologized nor kept quiet. The angry and excited lord stopped the orchestra in midtune and firmly announced to the three hundred people in the room to refrain from putting out cigarettes on the rare Huon-pine floor. Standing next to the governor during this public reprimand, I appeared guilty by association.

Recently, I discovered that the governor, Thomas Godfrey Polson Corbett, 2nd Baron Rowallan, passed away two years later at his ancestral home in Scotland. Lord Rowallan had an impressive career of public service and happened to be the head of scouting in the British Empire. Had I know this at the time, I'd have pleaded that, as an Eagle Scout, I could never have done such a dastardly deed as put out a cigarette on a Huon-pine floor. I also discovered that Huon pine is a slow-growing tree, some being found to be over two thousand years old. The tree is native to Tasmania, extremely rare, and the wood is highly prized for its golden-yellow color, fine grain, and natural oils that resist rotting. Today, I better understand the governor's concern. The story continues. Three years later, as a naval courier in Spain, I was in the British army's officers' mess on Gibraltar having a drink with several young British and Commonwealth officers. While swapping stories of our travels, an Australian naval officer stationed on the Rock began to tell a story about the governor of Tasmania and how he stopped the Royal Hobart Regatta Ball to lecture the crowd and some poor American ensign concerning cigarette burns on the Huon-pine ballroom floor. Small world.

Unfortunately, the four days passed swiftly. On Wednesday, February 14, we cast off in the early morning for the trip back to ocean station. Our sixth patrol was much like the others with some rough weather and a few calm days, the same daily routine, and the same long spells of boredom standing the bridge watch. I couldn't get the Adventure Bay paint-job fiasco out of my head. My window of experience was narrow. All I had were a few personal observations to mull over. I tried to dismiss even thinking about the captain, but the Adventure Bay fiasco wouldn't let go of me until we doubled up the lines and slid the gangway onto the pier in Dunedin after seventeen days at sea. This was to be our final visit to New Zealand.

CHAPTER 10

Heading Home

March 3–April 6, 1962

Don't cry because it's over. Smile because it happened.
—Dr. Seuss

Farewell to Dunedin

After a brief and final visit to Campbell Island, we arrived in Dunedin at noon on March 3, looking forward to a merry time in this grand old town. It never happened. We departed three days later, heading for Melbourne, Australia, and eventually home. The abrupt departure appeared strange. Why hadn't we just steamed from ocean station directly to Australia instead of steaming two days in the opposite direction for a brief stop in New Zealand? This didn't make sense. I had understood that we would be in Dunedin for nine days, enough time for a proper farewell to this hospitable city.

I admit that I was probably the last person in the wardroom to learn our operational orders. Perhaps the schedule was changed to ensure that we arrived in Melbourne for the Moomba Festival, or maybe there never was a schedule change; perhaps three days in Dunedin was always in the plan. Recently I quizzed several of my shipmates for an answer. There was some agreement that we had overstayed our welcome and perhaps the Miss *Vance* Coronation Ball hurried our departure. I will never know for certain if we were asked to leave. The vulgar Miss *Vance* event and perhaps one or more other events that I was not privy to were sufficient justification for the Deep Freeze command in Christchurch to order us to weigh anchor. Today, the events and speculation are nothing more than entertaining gossip. At the time, I was not happy missing out on several more days in Dunedin.

161

I wished we could have stayed another month, or better yet, a year in Dunedin. Under the circumstances, perhaps it was for the best that we departed quickly. Our infrequent time in port was frustrating, so little time to fully appreciate this wonderful town and its generous people, and always knowing that everyone and everything here was temporary. We always knew the time would come to return to the northern hemisphere. I suspect that some in Dunedin were not unhappy to see us depart. The population was generous and forgiving, but even the most gracious host has limits. The timing was right for us to say thank you and depart. I say this because our interaction with the locals was not always acceptable or appreciated.

Most of our sailors were model citizens, and I was proud of them and the impressions they left behind. The *Vance* baseball team played a number of New Zealand teams and even beat their national champions. Sailors were invited on hunting and sightseeing trips and to private parties. Local families adopted some. A few married Dunedin girls, and at least one moved permanently to New Zealand.

All was not rosy, however. Overstressed and immature sailors long at sea tended to be a problem, especially in this small insular community. Unfortunately, I had more than my share of problems to contend with ashore. In dress blue uniform, hat in hand, I waited with one of my snipes, a married man with a family, in the office of the dean of women at the University of Otago. I was there to apologize for his behavior, hoping the dean would not press charges for his drunken lewd conduct in front of the girls' dorm. The little beady-eyed snipe, a pleasant but weak man, recently sober in a clean blue uniform, with head bowed as if in church, stood next to me while I apologized for his conduct, for the *Vance*'s existence, for my having been born, and for everything but the United States' foreign policy. Maybe I apologized for that too, anything to keep our indiscretions out of the newspapers. Disciplinary problems were a specialty with this college dean, a woman who probably grew up and learned her trade in the nineteenth-century Victorian environment of this more-British-than-the-British society at the bottom of the globe. I took a verbal beating that day.

Another memorable moment was when the police called the ship to forward a complaint from a mother that her sixteen-year-old daughter, who hung out with *Vance* sailors, hadn't been home for a few days. Of course, the sailors in question were my snipes, and I was deputized to find the girl. With a shore-patrol sailor, I conducted a search of known hangouts. Thinking we had the right house, I burst into the bedroom to find her in bed with one of my snipes. I ordered the man back to the ship and the teenaged girl to dress and get home to her mother. I had the wrong girl. In the meantime, the mother reported that the girl had come home, probably having learned that a search was underway. Other division officers may have had similar, though far less frequent, experiences. Thankfully the local police were understanding and worked closely with us, always letting the *Vance* handle her own problems.

At times I envied the sailors who lived a carefree life ashore. I couldn't. I had no private life ashore, no private hangout, and no girlfriend bestowing favors. We were leaving New Zealand, heading home. A few sailors left girlfriends behind and we all left new friends behind, yet most of the crew looked forward to returning home. I didn't want to leave. There was nothing in Hawaii for me. I cared little about returning to the United States. Had I met the right girl, I would have served my time and still be in New Zealand today. The country was that appealing.

Here I was walking the streets with Jim Kunz on my last few days in Dunedin. Time was running out, and I had been without a girlfriend the last few times in port. Our celebrity status had come to an end. The parties were over. By chance on the last night ashore, I happened to meet a charming, fun-loving, strong-willed Irish girl, who was spending a year in Dunedin visiting her brother. Rosemarie was from County Down in North Ireland. Such torture, my meeting this beautiful eighteen-year-old redhead the last night in Dunedin. The positive spin on this relationship was that we corresponded by mail over the next two years. Lonely and just marking time until my days on the *Vance* were over, I spent quiet nights on the bridge watches dreaming of her. Here was something to look forward to, a beautiful Irish girl I hoped to revisit one day. Perhaps this was only a dream. A dream would have to do for now.

The morning of March 6, the *Vance* was ready to get underway, our final departure from New Zealand. I watched from the fantail as the captain ordered all lines singled up. Boats Old-ervick and his deck apes on the fo'c'sle were scratching their heads. There was no one to cast off the last lines. The pier was empty except for a few of our sailors' girlfriends. Boats had to ask their assistance, explaining what to do as captain and crew waited tethered to the pier. Eventually with Boats directing, the girls lifted the heavy lines off the bollard, and the *Vance* pivoted on #1 line. The girls then cast it off and we were clear, never again to be a part of New Zealand. A sad moment indeed.

Hundreds had greeted our triumphant entry seven months earlier. Few noticed our final departure as we steamed up the fourteen-mile-long channel. The cars didn't honk their horns. The old ladies didn't flash their mirrors. No schoolchildren were visible. The newness and excitement of the visiting weather ship had run its course. Rounding Taiaroa Head, the old salt by the lighthouse remembered and respected we fellow sailors. He dipped the New Zealand flag to us this one last time, and we reciprocated as we set a course for Melbourne, Australia. Muddled affairs ashore had no bearing on the brotherhood of seafaring men.

Moomba in Melbourne

After four days steaming back across the Tasman Sea, then through the Bass Straits, we entered the Melbourne Harbor. No longer the darling of small ports, the *Vance* was assigned to a commercial pier, #6 North Wharf, hidden away in the massive port complex of this second-largest city in Australia. We were a small fish in a very large pond. The Aussies had not forgotten us, though. As with the Kiwis, the Aussies remember World War II. They genuinely liked Americans, and we received a warm welcome. Quickly the wardroom had multiple invitations to parties and beach homes. Our reward for the arduous Deep Freeze deployment was seven days of rest and relaxation in Melbourne. Despite the parties, waterskiing, and sightseeing, I found Melbourne the least rewarding port of call, perhaps because in this major metropolitan area, we lost our celebrity status.

The city was in the throes of the Moomba Festival, named for an Aborigines' word supposedly meaning "let's get together and have fun." Apparently the original organizers didn't realize that the Aborigine definition tilted more toward having sexual fun. There may be something to this definition. After watching the Moomba Parade, Jim Kunz and I approached a couple of girls in a restaurant, who were most receptive to us sterling young naval officers decked out in white uniforms. My girl, a nice-looking twenty-two-year-old blond, was rubbing the inside of my leg under the table and invited us over to their apartment later in the day.

Not wanting to insult them, we accepted the invitation and hurried back to the *Vance* to change into civvies and buy some condoms from the ship's store. Jim's righteous Jesuit training kicked in. He decided to forego this adventure. I was not deterred in the least. Unable to find anyone to open the ship's store, I took a cab into town and found the stores closed for the local holiday. I abandoned the condom search, and then found that the bars had closed early, a futile government effort to cut back on Aussie drinking. The cabbie pulled into an alley. I held the money out the window, and two large bottles of beer were passed in. One couldn't arrive empty-handed.

The apartment was quite nice. The beer put aside, we sipped white wine as I explained Jim's absence as a military necessity, possibly a true statement if you accept the Jesuits as a military organization. The roommate retired to the bedroom for the evening, suggesting an established routine. My long-haired blond, whose name escapes me, made me comfortable on the couch with a glass of wine and herself. Shortly the heat rose, and we called time-out so she could retrieve a mattress from the bedroom. This was to be my big moment in the southern hemisphere, the two of us breathing hard, naked on the mattress on the living-room floor. The doorbell rang. Hurriedly, she put on a robe on the way to the door. A male voice on the other side sounded dejected when my Aussie blond said, "No, not tonight, I'm busy," and locked the door.

Here I was on the verge of entering paradise when my mind shifted into high gear, all the alert buttons flashing in my head as she lay there. *Here I am without a condom, with a very experienced and sexually active woman, whom I picked up in a bar a few hours ago, in a country I've been in for only two days.* My willie made the decision for me by shrinking. A beautiful female body was under me, yet I knew the evening was over. Embarrassed, I weakly explained that the cruise had been demanding and I was tired. What hogwash! And we both knew it. Yet she

Jim Kunz and Tom Milligan waterskiing off Melbourne, March 1962. (Photo from author's collection.)

mothered me, suggesting we rest for a bit. Not possible. I was too embarrassed. I dressed, apologized, and beat a hasty retreat to find a taxi. I wasn't proud of my performance, or rather lack of. I had craved sex for as long as I could remember, and yet ran from the opportunity. I had much to learn about what it was I wanted.

Instead of a cold shower, the next day I went waterskiing with Jim Kunz and Tom Milligan. A hosting family loaned us their boat and skis. With Milligan at the helm, Jim laughing, and me on the skis, we raced out into the ocean at full throttle. The laughter had to do with the warnings and lively talk about shark attacks and how these waters were infested with them. I saw myself as one big fishing lure. Milligan was laughing while trying his best to whip me off the skis. Frantically I fought to stay upright, periodically glancing behind me looking for the telltale fin. My ride over, I quickly climbed into the boat. "Who's next?" No takers.

On March 17, a warm Saturday morning, we set the special sea detail, split the electrical load, and had all four engines warmed up, ready to get underway. A small crowd gathered to see us off, none of whom I recognized. I guess others were more successful than I was at making friends in Melbourne. The visit was fine. I just had trouble letting go of my near sexual experience. *What the hell was wrong with me? Best just to look ahead and quit kicking myself.*

Tahiti and the Equator Again

Underway once more, we had before us a long voyage in tropical waters from Australia heading north, crossing the international date line again, a second visit to Tahiti, across the equator into the northern hemisphere, and on to the Hawaiian Islands and our home base, Pearl Harbor. The tropical waters were a treat after Deep Freeze. Still, the nine days of steaming to Tahiti was anything but smooth. The first day after leaving port usually began with captain's mast, to deal with infractions accumulated in port, mostly AWOL cases. This time four of my snipes were brought up on charges. All were AWOL, the usual problem, a drunken night in Melbourne and not enough sense to get back to the ship before liberty expired. I was concerned because my snipes continued to account for almost half the disciplinary cases brought before the captain. I had no real strategy for squaring away the division. At best, I was reacting to problems as they surfaced. I believed there were a few troublemakers who had to be removed, and I had no power to remove them. *Had Engles and I both failed? Was there more we could have done to reduce the infractions? Or were these repeat offenders unmanageable?* I blamed it all on the individuals. In time, I learned I was wrong.

We were heading home, a tired ship and crew, led by a skipper who was not tired. Captain Beyer wanted a squared-away ship right now, and he drilled us continually to this end: man-overboard drills, antisubmarine exercises, darkened-ship drills, general quarters drills, repel-boarders drills, and everything over again and again, to get it right, to do it faster, to do it better. He was concerned over what lay ahead when we rejoined the squadron in Pearl Harbor. An administrative inspection and a repair-and-training period were scheduled before reassignment to the northern Pacific Barrier patrols. As a new skipper, understandably, he was sensitive to the first impressions of the squadron commander.

I am certain that Captain Beyer envisioned the *Vance* as a sleek warship smartly streaming into Pearl Harbor. This didn't seem realistic after a difficult nine-month deployment, with the engineering plant having taken a beating and the crew's mood that of ending a saga, not a rebirth. On the twenty-second, five days out of Melbourne, there was a fire in the forward engine room. The timing chain on #2 engine parted, causing an explosion in a cylinder. Rarely would a timing chain wear out and break, but one did on this occasion.

Shipboard fires were serious business, especially engine-room fires, with fuel and lube oil catching fire and the resulting ventilation hazard. We put out the fire, cleared the smoke from the space, and assessed the damage. Number-two engine was disabled, with two cracked cylinder liners, one destroyed piston, and a broken spring pack. Replacing a liner at sea took a gang of snipes working around the clock about twenty-four hours in decent weather. The huge upper crankshaft must be hoisted up and secured suspended overhead, the piston rod assembly pulled, and the liner replaced. Fortunately, we were in tropical waters, and the seas were cooperative. With all four big Fairbanks-Morse diesels back online, we surged on to Tahiti.

Four days later, guided by the harbor pilot, the *Vance* slipped through the opening in the reef into Papeete Harbor. We were here because, given a choice, the crew voted for R&R in Tahiti again rather than American Samoa on the return voyage. Remembering their wild visit to Papeete the previous August, they didn't think American Samoa could top Tahiti. They were probably right, except for me the second time around could never match the first experience. This time the French navy was not in port, and the *Mutiny on the Bounty* film crew and their ship, the *Bounty*, were gone. Remembering us, the Chinese owner of the motor scooter rental was more careful with whom he did business. The very social Captain Penny was no longer here to produce special entries into Tahitian society. The beautiful native girls with whom I had danced the Tahitian war dance had disappeared, and we didn't know how to conjure them up. We had no parties to attend; we were not snubbed, just unnoticed.

On motor scooters, Kunz, Milligan, DeMott, and I circled the island, exploring the countryside and the hidden beaches. Although the visit was enjoyable, the fascination and delight of our first encounter with Tahiti could not be repeated. I was ready to leave and beginning to look forward to Hawaii. The last day of March, we were underway for home. A new level of excitement was in the air, emanating from the married men and those expecting orders, as the *Vance* began the final leg of the voyage.

After four hours of steaming from Papeete, a sailor was reported missing. Fortunately, he was not one of mine. Prior to departure, each division officer reported the results of a head count to the bridge. The senior petty officer took the count but the division officer was responsible for its accuracy. R division was missing a snipe. We radioed Papeete, learned the sailor was there, and requested he be put on a commercial flight to Hawaii. The French authorities replied negative and said, "Come and get him." Eight hours after departing Tahiti the first time, we returned to find a shabby sailor, who had spent the previous night drunk under a table at Quinn's Bar. He climbed up the *Vance*'s rope ladder from the pilot boat waiting just outside the coral reef of Papeete Harbor. I felt sorry for the poor bastard. On the fantail, half the crew silently watched, with the captain staring down at him from the 01 level. Captain Beyer was pissed. The court-martial would wait until we were home again.

A special court-martial seemed a harsh punishment. I knew the kid had been AWOL in Melbourne and now again in Tahiti, but the fault for missing the ship rested with the false roll-call report. The captain acted from anger. I figured that the eight wasted hours at sea was what set him off. I didn't realize that the squadron commander was aware of the ship's movements and that this would be a major embarrassment for the skipper. Although I knew fuel wasn't charged to our budget, I wondered at the cost of diesel fuel for eight hours underway at fifteen knots.

To reach Hawaii, we again crossed the equator with a visit from King Neptune. This time we were all shellbacks, except for the few crewmembers who had met the ship in New Zealand. Jim Kunz, Fred Levin, Doc Gersenfish, and such old seagoing men as Boats Oldervick and Captain Beyer were candidates for initiation. We had some fun. I can still visualize Doc Gersenfish standing lookout on the bridge with two rolls of toilet paper for binoculars. The crew, especially the deck apes, enjoyed initiating their popular leader, Boats Oldervick. Otherwise, the ceremony was restrained when compared to the wild and fun-loving ceremonial crossing on the way to New Zealand. One problem was the difficulty of initiating your captain. Sure, King Neptune could take over the ship for a day, and in the spirit of the event, run the skipper through the mill with the rest of the pollywogs. Tomorrow he would be the captain once again, so we had to proceed carefully. There was no way we were going to shave Captain Beyer's head or subject him to other severe indignities. The ceremony followed the usual ritual, with an unspoken self-imposed limit on abuses. Still, it wasn't a bad ceremony. The skipper took his licks like everyone else, crawling around the hot deck and kissing the greasy belly of the Royal Baby. He seemed very pleased to finally be a shell-back after seventeen years in the navy. If the ceremony was less lively this time, the reason was we were heading home. The big adventure was about over. Enthusiasm was in short supply.

Seven days out from Tahiti, we made landfall on the Hawaiian Islands, then headed for Oahu and the entrance to Pearl Harbor. I had experienced little of Hawaii before our deployment. It had been more like a two-week tourist visit. Now I would have two years to get to know the islands, and I was looking forward to learning more about this tourist haven. Unlike our Antarctic voyage, I did not expect Hawaii to be an adventure.

CHAPTER 11

Back with the Squadron

April 6–July 6, 1962

> There is nothing like returning to a place that remains unchanged
> to find the ways in which you yourself have altered.
> —Nelson Mandela

Wardroom Changes

At one o'clock in the afternoon, Friday, April 6, a tired *Vance* steamed into the Pearl Harbor channel. Sailors in dress whites lined her rails, and as usual, my head poked out from the fantail hatch to take in the event. We moored at the Bravo Piers, the very best berth for destroyers because of the convenient parking and access to the Navy Exchange and Officers' Club. Here was our moment of glory, the return of the conquering heroes, about as close as we could come to fame in the Cold War navy of the early 1960s. The navy band struck up "Anchors Aweigh," and the families of the crew waved.

As the deck apes doubled up the lines, the squadron commander was first aboard to welcome us home. Then the 1MC shouted out liberty call. The married men rushed ashore to embrace their families, a few unlucky ones hoping their letters home had satisfactorily explained their innocence in response to rumors of unfaithfulness. Ambitious single sailors were already planning their transfer requests to the next Deep Freeze ship. We single officers wandered over to the Pearl Harbor Officers' Club for a cheap drink. We had no transportation to Waikiki, and besides, half the day was gone. This was no Dunedin, where we moored in the heart of the city, where we were celebrities, and where we had people reaching out to help us. Here on beautiful Oahu, we single men were strangers—no wives, no families, no cars, and no links to anyone ashore after a nine-month absence. Still, it was terra firma, and that was enough for me.

Our return brought considerable change. The *Vance* was in a new operating environment. At Pearl Harbor, we were just another ship on the major US naval base in the Pacific Ocean. The *Vance* was one little ugly destroyer escort in a harbor chock-full of submarines, other ugly DERs, sleek destroyers, a frigate or two, oilers, tugs, repair ships, and visiting carriers and cruisers, plus, lest I forget, the daily visit of a giant catamaran with loudspeaker blaring and filled with tourists snapping pictures of the Arizona Memorial. No longer were we the darlings of every port of call.

The important changes were in the wardroom. Over the next few months, half of the officers were new faces. I was learning that job assignments for line officers, we Renaissance men, were good for one year before moving on to a new responsibility. The chiefs and senior petty officers provided the continuity. They remained within the boundaries of their expertise. We officers fluttered from flower to flower, gathering experience in a broad range of jobs. Hopefully, enough experience to one day command a ship. What made this possible was the turnover in the wardroom.

I guess we were all growing in some manner. New bodies in the wardroom elevated Fred, Jim, and me to positions of self-importance. We were, after all, experienced seagoing men who had braved the Antarctic seas. Our golden eagle hat insignias and golden shirt collar ensign bars showed touches of green from oxidation and months in the salty ocean environment. We were careful not to polish away the green hue, this subtle advertisement that we were seafaring men. Perhaps subconsciously, we were aping the salty, manly images of World War II German U-boat naval officers, those sea wolves in their casual garb of battered hats, beards, white scarves, and leather coats. We were poor imitations—no scarves, beards, or leather permitted. Battered hats were tolerated.

If the audience missed the subtle insignia oxidation, they

couldn't miss the blue Antarctic Service Ribbon we now displayed above our left shirt pocket. Rarely did a junior officer have a medal. Ours drew the attention and sometimes the envy of our peers. God, we were salty, real seagoing men. Nine months before, I had been a frightened little ensign, cautiously finding my way in Pearl Harbor. Now, with a crusty hat and in my scuffed Wellington seaboots, I confidently swaggered down the pier, a seasoned mariner. I accepted shipboard life and understood seasickness as a given. The initial terror I had experienced was long gone. I had learned to tough out my seasickness, accepting that there would be a couple of seasick days each time we got underway. That's life, and there was nothing I could do about it. Grin and bear it.

The Deep Freeze deployment completed, we no longer rated a doctor. Doc Gersenfish, my partner in seasickness, was the first to go, immediately transferred to another ship. The operations department quickly changed hands. Ray DeMott joyfully returned to civilian life, with Larry Hanson stepping into the department-head job. I was sorry to see Doc and Ray depart. Both were easygoing shipmates. Doc was a favorite with the crew, and Ray was a quiet, reflective individual, devoid of the macho cockiness prevalent in many junior officers. Hank Fox, the electronics officer, transferred to another duty station. Foxie was a career officer whom I would miss, a generous easygoing shipmate we all took advantage of. I felt a bit guilty having not been more of a friend. His replacement, LTJG Harvey Payne, an OCS graduate like myself, came to us from a reserve fleet destroyer on the West Coast. This easygoing, handsome man was the least inhibited person I have ever met. In time, Harvey became a close friend.

Two new ensigns, both recent OCS graduates, reported aboard. The first, Bruce Young, filled the communications officer billet vacated by Larry Hanson. Bruce, ever outgoing and energetic, took to the job like a duck to water. He was a natural for navy life. It was a pleasure serving with him. The guy was an optimist and could be relied upon to give a positive spin to life in the wardroom. I believe it was Bruce who came up with the name "Green Jeans" for the XO. I liked Bruce. Fred Levin remained CIC officer, rounding out the operations department with four officers, all of whom I enjoyed serving with.

The gunnery department also underwent major changes. Tom Milligan extended for an additional year for orders to a new and real destroyer, just as I was beginning to know him better. The guy was smart and due for a bigger challenge than the *Vance* had to offer. Our Texan, Frank Collins, packed up his family and, I think, transferred to another duty station on the mainland. I never was close to Frank. The married officers rarely hung out with us. Fox division went to Jim Kunz upon his return from six weeks at the Antisubmarine Warfare School in San Diego. The now-vacant first division slot went to Ken Wood, the other new ensign reporting aboard. Ken, an athlete who loved rugby, was well-suited for the romantic role of boss of the deck apes. He had the "Ernest Hemingway obsession," a common condition of the 1960s, when Hemingway's literature was extremely popular. The paramount Hemingway personality trait was physical manliness, accompanied by an intellectual superiority acted out in an adventure setting, an ideal stage being a combat zone or a foreign country.

The Administrative Inspection

Engineering remained the fiefdom of Don Dunn, with me as his trusty assistant. Chuck Laipply remained in the department until the new officer, on whom we had orders, arrived in a few months to take over my job in main propulsion. In preparation for my next assignment, that of damage control assistant (DCA), I needed an eight-week Fleet DCA School in San Francisco. Don supported my request, and I received temporary orders to the school shortly after our return to Pearl. I had a busy month and a half before escaping to school in San Francisco.

The squadron commander's welcome home included a schedule for a week of repairs while moored alongside the tender at Ford Island, training days off the coast, and an administrative inspection. The inspection was an annual event, a form of torture that was designed to make a statement about the ship's readiness. Captain Beyer kept up the barrage of shipboard drills, knowing the inspection was coming. The squadron staff was equally anxious to determine the operational readiness of the *Vance* after our difficult months deployed to the Antarctic. Between the captain's demands and the squadron's inspection, we, the returning heroes, were run ragged. The administrative inspection, scheduled for early May, was conducted by the squadron staff, assisted by officers from another ship in the squadron.

Inspections were conducted to identify problem areas. Eager captains focusing on advancement could lose sight of this. Some sought Band-Aids when surgery was required. I was proud of Don Dunn, who told it like it was. We had 141 engineering department discrepancies, a ridiculously high number. We were honest about our problems. Many pieces of machinery were inoperative or unreliable due to a lack of parts and manpower, including portable firefighting pumps, air-conditioning units, oil pumps, the whaleboat motor, and more.

The engineering department did not fare well with the inspection results. Captain Beyer wasn't happy. We engineers needed more time and adequate funds and received neither. The blame lies in several laps. Commanding officers were expected to do the best they could with what they had. Captains liked to hear the can-do song from their officers, and I suspected squadron commanders also liked to hear it. It was a very popular position, the willingness to meet our operational requirements without asking for additional assistance. My guess was that the squadron staff had their own problems, a tight budget, and a demanding operating schedule. These vintage ships all had problems, and the *Vance*'s engineering problems, while significant, probably didn't appear earth-shattering.

There was probably no one clear answer as to why the engineering plant had to struggle along for another year until our normal shipyard overhaul. We managed, yes, but it was a hell of a ride for the snipes, and in the end for the skipper also. The one most affected by our engineering shortcomings was the captain. His promotion was directly linked to the ship's performance during his brief eighteen months aboard. The captain's tenure aboard relative to the shipyard overhaul cycle seemed important to me. Because the *Vance* had a shipyard overhaul during Captain Penny's tenure, I assumed he commanded a reasonably problem-free hull and engineering plant. Unfortunately, Captain Beyer's eighteen months in command started with the *Vance* a year out of the shipyard and ended as we entered the shipyard. He inherited a well-worn hull and an engineering plant that ran constantly for nine months in the Antarctic. On our return to Hawaii, the skipper had twelve more months before he was transferred and the ship underwent another yard overhaul. Ragged and underfunded, we were no match for other squadron DERs more recently overhauled.

Following the inspection report, Don and I were sitting in his stateroom discussing the 141 discrepancies and how we were going to proceed from here. Naïve me. I figured that by revealing all our problem areas, we would receive the necessary time and funds to correct them. In a perfect world, this might happen. We were allotted a week alongside the tender, never saw any increased funding, and were placed back on the Pacific Barrier patrols. The squadron had commitments to meet and lacked funds. Don looked up from the inspection report and said, "Tom, we may be looking at a green table." In my innocence, I asked, "What's a green table?" Well, a court-martial never occurred. We engineers were never personally blamed for the department's condition, though I doubt the skipper escaped unscathed.

There was a positive result from the administrative inspection, although I didn't realize it at the time. The crusty old squadron engineering officer, Lieutenant Hazard, a leather-faced, older, white-haired officer who came up through the ranks as an engine-room snipe, was touring the ship with Don and me when I mentioned the extra ten thousand gallons of diesel fuel we carried in the bow. "You what?" he yelled, his leathery old face losing its tropical tan. We explained that the *Vance* always carried, in addition to her normal hundred thousand gallons of diesel oil, an extra ten thousand gallons stored in the forward-most void in the very bow of the ship. Void spaces are designated sealed airtight compartments between the keel and the second deck. Sometime prior to Don and my coming aboard, Captain Penny, or perhaps the skipper before him, had the extra diesel oil stored here for use in an emergency. Time on station was important. The longer the ship could stay on station, the better our performance. An extra ten thousand gallons came in handy. We could take chances, knowing if our fuel calculations were wrong, there was always the extra fuel hidden away. Our daily fuel reports never reflected the additional ten thousand gallons.

I recall that we used the extra fuel once on our first Antarctic patrol, our longest time at sea. Because the void was not designed to be a fuel tank, we had to snake a fire hose through the forward compartments on the second deck, access the void by removing the cover plate and gasket, secured by twenty bolts, and using a portable electric pump, transfer the fuel through the fire hose aft to a fuel tank. The procedure was a fire hazard, unsafe, and everyone knew it, but it worked and Captain Penny approved it. I avoided mentioning to the squadron engineer how we transferred the oil, realizing this would only upset the man more and probably get us deeper into trouble. Calming down, he proceeded to lecture us on voids being an integral part of the ship's design and how the weight of ten thousand gallons of fuel in the bow endangered the ship. The hull was not designed to take this additional weight, especially in the forward-most section of the bow. Excessive stress was placed on the normal fore and aft flexing of the hull.

I understood this better the next month at DCA School. Apparently no one thought much about it the previous two years. I suspect, as Renaissance men, the *Vance*'s engineering officers and the previous captains were ignorant of the implications.

I calculated that the void filled with diesel oil added about thirty-six tons of weight in the bow, considerable stress for a 1,680-ton ship. Recently I discovered that we weren't the only ship using this void. The USS *Savage*, having unreliable boilers for making potable water, a design curse all DERs suffered from, stored ten thousand gallons of potable water in their forward void. That was almost forty-three tons of misplaced weight. A shipyard crew was detailed to help us empty and clean the void. The void episode could not have helped the captain's career. With Captain Penny long gone, Captain Beyer took the heat.

Fleet Damage Control School

Following the tense squadron inspection, I escaped the *Vance* and Hawaii for two months on Treasure Island in San Francisco Bay. Nothing could be finer. I was finally to be schooled in my new area of responsibility. I spent a week learning how to fight fires. Since I was the only officer in the firefighting class, the instructor, a crusty old chief, made certain I was the front hose man, especially for the billowing gasoline fires. I lost my eyebrows and forehead hair in the process, but I have never feared fire since.

The course on ship stability was especially meaningful to me. I learned to calculate a ship's *metacentric height*, which gave me the ability to know a warship's stability. It was reassuring to know how far the *Vance* could roll and still recover and what factors affect this number. Theoretically the *Vance* could heel over to 90° and still right herself. Many factors, such as fuel tank levels, deck load, friction, and wave action reduce this number. I knew from experience that the *Vance* could roll 66° and still come back, but could never survive a 90° roll with the mast radar antennas in the water and the fifty tons of iron ingots of ballast in the bilges beginning to shift. I at least had a number that told me we could take one hell of a roll and what I could do so as not to degrade that number.

Damage Control School was a big plus, and San Francisco

a wonderful city. No watch standing and no duty days on the Treasure Island Naval Base, where I lived in the bachelor officers' quarters (BOQ). I needed transportation in the city and upon return to Hawaii. With my savings over the past nine months and a small credit union loan, I bought a two-year-old 1961 MGA roadster from a graduate student at Berkeley for $1,600. Eventually the navy would ship the car to Hawaii. But first I put down the top and drove several hundred miles, the length of California, crossed the border into Mexico, and returned. Oh, what a wonderful feeling! Butt hugging the pavement with the wind blowing in my face, I guided the purring little roadster down US Route 5 in the merry month of May. I was alive, answering to no one, responsible for only myself, and I was on terra firma. After a week at home visiting the family, I was ready for Oahu again.

While on the mainland, I was fortunate to miss the *Vance*'s daily operations off the Oahu coast. The real prize for going to the mainland was my missing the *Vance*'s first patrol to the North Pacific since returning to the squadron. This proved to be the only time I was to miss a patrol in my three years aboard. I am not bragging. I tried every way possible to miss patrols. Leave was granted to officers only while the ship was in port. One had to be on his deathbed to be excused from a deployment.

Oahu Social Life
On return from the mainland and now having my own transportation, I became better acquainted with Hawaii. For us single officers, who knew no one on Oahu, Waikiki was the logical place to hang out, with its tourist traffic, upscale bars, restaurants, hotels, and beaches. Between Pearl Harbor and Waikiki was downtown Honolulu, a run-down area mostly frequented by fleet sailors. Hotel Street, the center of activity, was populated by bars, strip joints, and tattoo parlors. The sailors referred to Hotel Street as Shit Street. Closer to Pearl Harbor were a number of bars, most frequented by the spillover from

the naval base. Typical was the Monkey Bar, where the large glass wall behind the bar was home to live monkeys eating, screwing, or just swinging on limbs, looking as hopeless as the observers on the barstools. Waikiki was definitely the epicenter of the tourist trade and single women, the prey of horny young naval officers.

Waikiki was expensive for junior officers existing on $222 a month. The standard liberty run was to Fort DeRussy, a prime beachfront property on Waikiki that happened to serve cheap drinks and meals, exclusively for the military. We roamed the beaches and bars, restricting most of our eating and drinking to the affordable O Club at DeRussy. The club was an open-air World War II collection of unimpressive single-story buildings; the prices were right and the beach identical to the Royal Hawaiian Hotel's beach close-by. Actually the social life sucked on Oahu. Meeting young ladies was difficult given our brief forays into Waikiki and the transient nature of the tourist trade. With limited time in port and unable to afford an apartment, we too were tourists, the difference being our commute was shorter and spending money tight.

Occasionally, a private party was in the offering. Early after my return from school on the mainland, Larry Hanson and I attended a house party in Waikiki. I never did learn who the hosts were. A few other *Vance* officers were there, some with dates. Chuck Laipply's blind date, a willowy twenty-two-year-old *haole* (Hawaiian for white person or foreigner) gone native, loved to dance native style, and I obliged her. We were all drinking heavily, and I was letting go, dancing the Tahitian war dance with this girl. She could really dance. Chuck just sat there with his thumb up his ass, and we ignored him. This gone-native girl and I were hitting it off rather well, to the point that we were necking up a storm in a quiet hallway, when I was sucker punched in the jaw by an irate Laipply. She screamed; I recovered quickly and lunged for him. Larry Hanson grabbed me, someone held Chuck, and we were pulled apart. I made noises, but really I was not interested in fighting. I would if I had to, but fighting never made sense to me. I could and did put on a show of anger. I was secretly tickled that I cut out Chuck and potentially found myself an interesting girlfriend. Chuck, understandably, was pissed, his manhood made a mockery of. Besides, he already harbored a dislike for Don Dunn and me, the newcomers to the engineering department. This anger had been brewing for several months, and my little escapade with his date proved too much to endure. I certainly deserved the punch in the jaw for my behavior. At the time, we were all just cocky young men concerned with appearances. Fortunately for both of us, Chuck was transferring a few months later. Quietly, I endured a sore jaw for a few days. I never hit it off with the young lady, who found the native dancing exciting, but the conflict too unnerving.

Losing the dancing girl I never had seemed unimportant as the deck apes were singling up all lines, preparing to get underway. July 6 was a hot sunny day. Weren't they all in Hawaii? We backed from the Bravo Piers, turned, and headed toward the channel and the sea for another patrol, to be my first on ocean station in the North Pacific.

CHAPTER 12

North Pacific Station

July 6–September 26, 1962

There was a grandeur in everything around, which gave almost a solemnity to the scene; a silence and solitariness which affected everything. Not a human being but ourselves for miles; and no sound heard but the pulsations of the great pacific.
—Richard Henry Dana*

*Author of the American classic *Two Years before the Mast*, based on his experience as a merchant seaman on the brig *Pilgrim* bound from Boston to California in 1834

Vance *and the Pacific Barrier*

As the *Vance* steamed out of the channel, in some ways I was happy to get away from Pearl Harbor. After having operated independently over the past year in New Zealand, I was sensitive to our role and status in the naval establishment. Quiet, whale-shaped, well-maintained nuclear-powered submarines manned by competent volunteer crews glided in and out of the submarine base. Real destroyers, sleek-hulled, bristling with five-inch guns and capable of cutting through the seas at thirty-three knots, occupied the better berths at the Bravo Piers. They always appeared to be going to or returning from some interesting mission, a Far East cruise or as part of an aircraft carrier task force. They chased down submarines and provided air defense for the task force. The submarines returned from long secretive missions on the front lines of the Cold War. Everyone had an active role except the barrier patrol ships.

In the middle of this busy harbor sat the short, slow, pregnant-looking DERs, usually four ships at most. One was deployed to New Zealand, one on ocean station on the DEW Line, one in transit to or returning from ocean station, and probably one in for a shipyard overhaul. Our ships were three-legged

185

greyhounds, slow and clumsy and usually in need of repair because we spent an inordinate amount of time at sea manning
the DEW Line. When in port, we were required to pretend we
were warships by training with submarines and aircraft. The
DER was really a floating fixture, a kind of floating lighthouse
bristling with radar rather than a lantern. Apparently the navy
wanted us to be both a warship and a lighthouse. We did a passable job as a radar lighthouse.

The Pacific Barrier

The USS *Vance* (DER 387), a destroyer escort radar picket ship, and other
DERs existed because of the need for an ocean-based missile defense system
in the late 1950s and early 1960s. The key words were "escort" and "radar."
Escorts were small, inexpensive warships mothballed as leftovers from World
War II. They were the remains of the hundreds of destroyer escorts built during
World War II. In 1955, these direct-drive diesel or *Edsall*-class DERs were
taken out of mothballs and modified in support of a missile defense system for
the continental United States.

   After a year of alterations, including the addition of improved air-
search radar and extensive communications equipment, the *Vance* was
recommissioned as a DER, an ugly duckling of a ship but suitable for its
mission. The recommissioned *Vance* was one small response to the threat of
nuclear war. The North American Air Defense (NORAD) early warning system
was built in the 1950s because of the growing Soviet bomber and missile
threat. A large part of the system was the Distant Early Warning (DEW) Line in
the Pacific. In 1961, US Navy radar aircraft were departing every two and a half
hours from Midway Island to fly a loop to Adak, Alaska, and back. The *Vance*,
and the six other ships of Escort Squadron Five, supported this extension of
the DEW Line by keeping two DERs on station along the route in the North
Pacific Ocean. By 1962, the number of ships on station was reduced to one.
The ships provided navigational aid to the aircraft and radar coverage. This
translated to long, year-round independent patrols on the midocean picket
lines in the North Pacific. They and the Atlantic barrier DERs were the only navy
ships that performed their mission on a round-the-clock basis. I doubt the duty
was any better in the Atlantic. I can only testify to the boredom and difficulties
of two years on the Pacific DEW Line.

As we steamed along at fifteen knots following the Oahu
coastline, I was not looking forward to two more years of patrols, although I was optimistic that the engineering problems
would be manageable. At least logistics would be easier and
the squadron would take care of our needs. Not until years
later could I put our situation in perspective. First, the navy

never wanted the static Atlantic and Pacific Barrier mission. This was a drain of resources from the navy's primary mission, control of the seas and the projection of power, the mission of all the other naval assets in Pearl Harbor. We, the DER squadron, received minimal logistical support, and rightfully so, because we never were very important in the grand scheme of national defense.

The DEW Line, as we knew it, was technology-dependent. By 1961, when I first reported aboard for duty, the navy already knew that technological advances in the pipeline, over-the-horizon radar and satellites, would soon end the navy's role on the barrier. This was not common knowledge. In 1965, one year after I left the *Vance,* the navy shut down the mission. For those of us busy keeping the ships together with bailing wire, an official statement would have been necessary to attract our attention. I am happy we never knew we were

> **Johnston Island**
> The Island, located 860 miles west of Hawaii in the North Pacific, is an uninhabited atoll that was mined for guano in the mid to late 1800s. In the twentieth century, the island first was a wildlife refuge, and then, just prior to World War II, a naval air station. In the 1950s and 1960s, the island was used as a nuclear weapons test site. Occasionally the *Vance* and other DERs participated in these tests by trailing Soviet trawlers in the test area. In 1963, the Limited Test Ban Treaty placed a hold on nuclear tests at the site. The island then served as a chemical weapons storage and destruction site. By 2004, Johnston Island was completely deserted. Today, the island is part of the Pacific Remote Islands National Monument. Now and then, a ship may stop there.

obsolete. Being uninformed, we continued to care about the mission, believing we were holding back the horde of Soviet Bear aircraft from dropping their nuclear payloads on the continental United States. We took our mission seriously, as we were meant to.

On the second day, steaming on course 355° at sixteen knots, we braced ourselves to observe a hydrogen bomb test at eleven that night. The nuclear bomb test was on Johnston Island several hundred miles away. The *Vance* was assigned to observe this test. We lined the rails, uncertain what to expect.

187

A flashing light on the horizon? Maybe. A tidal wave? Certainly some sort of activity was expected even here, hundreds of miles away. We braced ourselves because all bets were on a tidal wave. The wave never came, and the visual show was almost nonexistent. At least the event occupied us for a few days on station.

The next year, we had another H-bomb nonexperience. While moored at Pearl Harbor during a Johnston Island test, we were warned of a possible tidal wave. I had the duty, with a third of the crew aboard, the engines warmed up, gangplank taken up, and the mooring lines singled up, as we waited in vain for a tidal wave. The seriously disappointed people were the surfers who lined the beaches at Waikiki waiting to ride the big one that never appeared. This was the extent of my participation in the now-historic Johnston Island nuclear tests.

Ocean Drifting

Aside from observing the setting off of an H-bomb, ours was a typical summer patrol, which began with two and a half days steaming at fifteen to sixteen knots on a direct course for ocean station to relieve the ship currently on station. In the summer, this was usually a delightful transit: the seas tended to be relatively calm, the sky clear, and sea life abundant. Whales, including killer whales and dolphins, were common. On occasion we would sight a school of tuna, maneuver into the school, and start casting. The fishing rods of twenty sailors on the fantail would suddenly, all at the same moment, bend violently. Excited sailors were yelling as tuna were flipped up and onto the deck, shaking themselves off the baitless hooks and finally quieted by a rap on the head. Two or three casts at most and the school was gone, the fish collected, and the dinner menu changed. I have never tasted better fish than these few opportunities to eat truly fresh tuna.

Often in the calm summer seas en route to ocean station, we had company, generally porpoises playing off the bow, telling us in their amusing way that the lumbering *Vance* was out of its element. Killer whales had a more sober message. A school of them sometimes accompanied the ship for a few hours on a parallel course two hundred yards off our beam, probably curious as to what this big noisy hunk of metal was doing moving along at fifteen knots. As I watched these big guys from the bridge, the sonarmen on watch asked if they could play a killer whale tape over sonar. When the tape played, immediately the school of six huge killer whales turned 90°, heading directly on a collision course with the ship. I thought of Ahab and Moby Dick as they veered off and disappeared. I guess after a closer look, they decided the *Vance* was no killer whale or too big a fish to fool around with.

Despite my extreme preference for terra firma, summer in the North Pacific Ocean could be enjoyable and wondrous. On July 16 we were drifting on station, in mild three-foot seas with the wind at two to three knots. Number-one engine was on standby, meaning fifteen minutes were required before the *Vance* could get underway. A second engine was on thirty-minute standby in case we needed to move beyond a crawl. Just a lazy day, except for the drills, especially scrambling to the general quarters drill, again and again, always too slow until about the third time.

For abandon-ship drills, the crew lined up suited out in life preservers and stood by their assigned life rafts. This particular drill was always carried out in a festive mood. The weather was usually mild when the crew was required to stop work and assemble on the open decks. All that was required was showing up at your assigned raft for a head count. I had read a number of historical accounts of Shackleton, Bligh, and others, who had barely survived in lifeboats in open seas. I appreciated the inflatable rafts with their emergency kits of Spam, World War II Camel cigarettes, and first-aid equipment. I was particularly fond of them because the life rafts were designed to inflate automatically when under twenty feet of water, and they had a protective roof, which increased the chances of survival in rough seas. I was delighted in the Antarctic when heavy seas flowing over the ship activated the inflation mechanism on a couple of life rafts. They worked!

Summertime meant drifting. The challenge for every skipper was to remain on ocean station as long as possible. Conserving fuel was the only way to ensure a long stay. Daily fuel report messages permitted the squadron to monitor our ability to conserve fuel and schedule the relief ship. To save fuel, we usually operated on one engine at five knots, which provided just enough rudder control to steer a course. In calm seas, the engines were shut down and we drifted, the ultimate fuel-conserving mode.

Drifting brought a change over the ship, an altered environment. The constant cadence of the main propulsion diesels ended. The sound of the remaining working machinery became more distinct, especially the continuous high-pitched whine of a ship service generator online. The constant hum of auxiliary motors and ventilation fans became more individualized, each identifiable at its location, where previously there existed but one collective sound of machinery. No longer was the hull being thrust forward against the seas; the forceful bucking and slamming of steel was replaced by a slow creaking and straining of the ship rolling in concert with the ocean swells. As the ship rolled gently in the trough in harmony with the swells, resistance vanished—no more fighting to enforce our will on the seas. We were a rubber ducky floating in a bathtub. Having lived so long with the ship combating the seas, we forgot that there could be life without this steady din. Now nature ruled. We drifted with the swells, at peace with the mighty Pacific Ocean. We would continue to drift until the ocean deemed otherwise. Anyone who has spent time at sea knows that we mere mortals are the guests of the sea-gods. We do not enforce our will on the seas. Rather, we react to the ocean's demands, always conscious of how puny, how limited we are in its clutches.

When drifting, life aboard ship changed. A mood swing occurred, a transformation so dynamic even the constant humming of our life-support systems went unnoticed. Drifting brought a laxity, a gentle quietness to the *Vance*. Urgent matters no longer appeared so important that they could not be put off to another time. Fart sacks were hauled topside and draped over the rails for airing. Sailors had their fishing lines over the side. Most of the crew spent time on deck. Even snipes were topside. Men chatted good-naturedly with one another. A scarcity of four-letter words was evident, or at least more gently applied. The weather was beautiful: a soft breeze, warmth from the sun, and the horizon sharply visible in all directions. We had become a part of nature, blending with the sea.

Now that we no longer fought the environment, the ocean occasionally granted us a glance into her mysteries. Ocean sunfish, or *mola*, floated to the surface, exposing their huge flat sides, often ten feet or more in diameter, to the warmth of the sun. They tended to just pop up to the surface close to the ship, perhaps lured by curiosity. Why not scrutinize this strange hunk of floating metal while basking in the sun? I watched seabirds landing on sunfish, thinking perhaps they were a resting place, a floating island in a world of water. I was wrong. Through the binoculars, I noticed the birds were pecking parasites from the exposed bodies. Like arrested champagne bubbles, more sunfish floated to the surface. I thought of the Alfred Hitchcock movie *The Birds* and the gradually heightened suspense as a growing number of crows entered the frame. Larger and larger numbers of sunfish arrived, little by little arising from the depths to gently break the surface, then turning sideways to expose their huge flat sides to the sun. One day, for just a few hours, I witnessed thousands of sunfish covering the entire ocean surface as far as the eye could see in all directions. It was as if the sunfish had replaced the water and the *Vance* were floating on a sea of fish.

A less spectacular, but equally exciting, experience was to witness the entire sea covered with Portuguese man-of-war, a reoccurring event to witness if you were willing to float for twenty summer days in the middle of the North Pacific Ocean. We were transformed to become a part of nature, just another form of sea life, large and metallic, yet we blended with the other inhabitants, going nowhere, just enjoying the calm seas and summer sun. Whales migrated north for a summer of feeding. When the whales arrived, they wondered who this big metal brother was. Or did they really care? When we drifted, they might take the opportunity to scrape their backs along the side of the hull. At night once or twice, I could hear them scraping their bodies near my head as I lay in my bunk. It was truly a bizarre sensation in the quiet of night, a thousand miles from land, a whale and me separated by a quarter-inch-thick steel plate and a bit of bulkhead insulation.

In the summer, sea life was more abundant, or perhaps more observable. Sharks were always nearby and especially evident when drifting. The big ten-foot blues enjoyed our chow and the regularity of it. At least twice a day, the galley-mess cooks emptied the trash over the fantail. To this was added the wastewater being constantly pumped overboard from 160 men using sinks and toilets. While the ship was drifting, the garbage floated nearby, attracting sharks. Sailors on the fantail found time to hook the big blues on fishing line, reel them in close enough to be snagged with sharpened grappling hooks, and heave their thrashing bodies onto the deck. Knives in hand, men danced between sharks, avoiding the snapping jaws and dangerous flapping tails. From the bloody deck, decapitated sharks were thrown back to swim away headless, followed by their hungry brothers in search of a meal. Carved out and cleaned, shark jawbones were coveted souvenirs, as were the more disgusting eyeballs. I believe the process was to boil, then varnish the eyeballs. Eventually when the fascination wore off, they were hidden away as souvenirs.

One day three eyeballs stared out at me as I opened a sound-powered phone box in an after passageway. No one stepped forward to claim them, so over the side they went, these foul trophies. The sailors' orgy with the hated sharks was over; the novelty had worn off, and in time not a shark souvenir was to be found. Shark fishing was a tonic, something to do to relieve the monotony. The event was a show, excitement and flirtation with danger, performed by a few exhibitionists. Some enjoyed the hunt and dismembering; others hung onto their fishing poles focusing on the catch, rather than the mutilation. Most found a viewing place on the 01 deck, cameras in hand, laughing and enjoying the circus. This was a break in routine, something different, something to talk and laugh over for a few days.

Drifting in midocean was a temporary condition. The seas rarely cooperated for long. When the surface was smooth as glass, we drifted to the gentle roll of the hull. Gradually swells developed and grew, the roll intensified, and we began experiencing 30° to 40° rolls. Huge rolls played hell with galley food preparation. Eating from a table became near impossible. Playing cards or watching a movie was an effort, desk work impossible, and engine sumps in danger of spilling oil. Every eight and a half seconds, the ship snapped back from a 30° roll, like a child's hollow toy figure with weighted feet. What a strange feeling. No pounding, no vibration, no sound, just a quiet big roll, permitting the mind to focus totally on the motion, whereas when underway, the roll was but one of several motions in play and less noticeable. Life on board became impossible. Time to bring an engine online, get underway, and nose the *Vance* out of the trough at five knots.

My New Division

On July 28 we left ocean station for Hawaii. As we doubled up the lines at the Bravo Piers, my deliverance was at hand. Ensign Lee Cole, fresh from OCS, reported aboard as the new main propulsion assistant. Lee, who was from Kansas wheat country, had an engineering background equal to mine, which was zero. This wiry, medium-height, freckle-faced ensign with a pleasant smile was smart and had the all-important quality that kept us sane on our little floating asylum: a sense of humor. Lee learned fast and proved to be an excellent addition to the department. I appreciated his challenge, having passed on to him the most demanding and difficult division on the ship. Don, Lee, and I had a great working relationship for the year we were snipes together. Once again, a new MPA had been ordered to the *Vance* without the proper schooling. I was adamant, and Don Dunn supported me: Fleet MPA School was a necessity. Lee would be on the next patrol and then off to San Diego for the six-week school, followed by a few days back home to get married and move his bride to Hawaii.

Chuck Laipply, now a career officer, would eventually have orders to another ship. Until then, he became the new gunnery department head, fulfilling his wish to leave the engineering department. In a few months, with Chuck's departure, the new gun boss would be LTJG Bob Baker, a married man who had transferred in from another ship. Bob, a six-foot-six giant, with crew cut and long arms, was a likable guy, easy to get along with. Bob moved into a forward stateroom, and thus I had little contact with him. With Chuck as the gunnery officer, I finally took over the repair division, having anxiously awaited the move since my return from Damage Control School. Why the euphoria? For the first time since reporting aboard, I was responsible for an assignment that I knew something about. I had completed DCA School and knew I could make a meaningful contribution.

The division I left to Lee had undergone several positive personnel changes since our return from Deep Freeze. Deployed for the nine months, EN1 Engles had found himself the only competent experienced engineman aboard the *Vance*. We were hurting, and it showed both in maintenance and leadership. Engles did a great job, but he was only one man. Our allowance called for a chief and three EN1 billets. An engineman chief had reported aboard. I wondered how he and EN1 Engles, who ran the division for the past year, would get along. Chief Ronie A. Mooney was a quiet, sincere man, more focused on engines than management. He wisely let Engles pretty much continue to manage the men, and in turn, Engles deferred to the chief. I liked the chief. I liked his humility. There was no showmanship here, just a highly competent technician interested in doing his best. Loyalty was never a question. Chief Mooney was about five or six years older than me, about my height, with a heavier frame. At first he appeared very reserved, almost shy. In time, I came to appreciate the humor in the man, only revealed by a quiet impish smile and a twinkle in his eyes. The chief had seen his share of diesel-driven ships, and I was certain we needed a man with this level of experience.

He and Engles working together was a good arrangement, which eventually became even better with the addition of two more excellent first-class enginemen, Alex and Mac. We were assigned these experienced enginemen because there were two open EN1 billets. We had lost EN1 Ramirez because of the sliced-off toe, and the older, nonproductive EN1 Varn had been reduced in rate at captain's mast through my urging. I had given up on Varn. Avoiding the problem was unfair to the sailors who did pull their own weight, and I badly needed experienced, competent senior petty officers. I couldn't transfer the man; there was no way another ship would accept Varn. I was stuck with him, but the more senior billet was now available. I didn't like the task of reducing in rate an old sailor, but I bit the bullet and did what was necessary.

The quality of the two new enginemen couldn't have been better. The lanky Mac, a twenty-seven-year-old bachelor, was popular with the men, a good leader, and technically competent. The man was smart, easygoing, and approachable, a combination of traits that by association helped Engles become more relaxed and less guarded. No longer alone, Engles now had a knowledgeable chief and two fellow EN1s to work with. In time, this infusion of quality leaders belowdecks would pay big dividends.

Alexander, always called Alex, the other new first-class engineman, was special in that he possessed skills rarely found in the rate. Good-natured, never without a smile, this tall, slim sailor was a happy optimist, who willingly carried on a dialogue with me over engine maintenance records. Most enginemen deplored paperwork and saw little value in it. Alex took over organizing the log room, with its messy record keeping. I had started the job but was never able to find the right snipe to ensure that the records were maintained properly. The young log-room yeoman Wurm tried, but lacked the horsepower and experience. I may have laid the groundwork, but Alex improved the system and made it work. To his and Lee Cole's credit, the *Vance*'s log room became the jewel in the crown. Even the crusty old squadron engineer was impressed—very impressed. They were really wowed the year after I left the *Vance,* when our record keeping led to identifying an inherent problem with the finicky #1 ship service generator. The generator had always been unreliable. With a documented pattern emerging, further investigation determined the unit had been installed incorrectly in 1943. Accurate record keeping led to the discovery and correction of this twenty-year-old problem.

Rarely was I involved with the personal lives of my snipes. When it did happen, seldom was the experience pleasant. One of my saddest days on the *Vance* was several months after Alex came aboard. I found myself in dress whites standing over the open grave of Alex's infant son as the casket was lowered into the earth. There were four of us—the minister, Alex, his wife, and me—at the cemetery on a hill with the ocean off in the distance. The world of these young parents had shattered. They were lost, having discovered their infant son dead in his crib. The parental grief, guilt, and uncertainty that accompany sudden infant death syndrome rained down on this poor couple. I stood hat in hand, feeling inadequate and unwilling to utter trite platitudes of condolence. Mute, I ventured a touch on Alex's shoulder and endured a polite introduction to his wife. I wanted to flee. What was I doing here causing the wife to politely greet his division officer when the poor woman was being torn apart with grief? I knew they wanted to be done with the ceremony and flee this cemetery hill to share their sorrow together alone.

On the hilltop cemetery or at their home, they were alone. This is all part of military life. I know the navy proudly claims that it takes care of its own. They do try, but there is no substitute for family and familiar surroundings at a time of grief. At best, Alex and his wife would spend the evening at their home, in naval housing on Oahu, Hawaii, thousands of miles from family.

The burial over, I beat a hasty retreat, knowing there was nothing more I could do. No one asked me to be at the burial. Something inside compelled me. My feeble, unspoken message was that I took the time and cared enough to be here at the gravesite. The tears arrived on my drive back to the ship. Two days later, Alex was back aboard, subdued and keeping busy trying to shake off the pain. For this memoir, I dug out a small photo Alex gave me of his family. His pain is still with me. Why the attachment? Probably because this was a good man who unselfishly did his best for both the *Vance* and me.

We didn't forget Engles and the burden he carried for nine months. Within two weeks of our return to Pearl, EN1 Engles was awarded a commendatory mast, an official thank-you from the command for a difficult job well done in keeping the engines operating during the Deep Freeze deployment. Don and I had lobbied the captain for this recognition. A year later, with this accommodation in his record, together with excellent fitness reports and high exam grades, the US Navy promoted Engles to chief petty officer. He deserved it.

I moved on to manage R division. The "R" stood for repair, a meaningless title for this collection of sailors that represented all the engineering responsibilities on board other than the main engines, boilers, and generators. The division had two or three shipfitters, an important skill because ships are all steel and aluminum, interlaced with pipes and valves. Shipfitters welded and machined as necessary to maintain them. They replaced the carpenter when metal ships replaced wooden ships, also assuming the new task of plumber. Ships fear fires, and warships are especially sensitive to flammable materials. Everything is metal. If a metal desk was to be moved or the captain wanted an ashtray next to his bunk, welding was required. Shipfitters repaired valves that didn't seat properly and welded the forever-appearing cracks in the aluminum superstructure. Everyone needed shipfitter services at one time or another. The shipfitter gang operated from an adequately equipped machine shop located amidships on the main deck.

My largest group was the six electricians who were critical to the life of the ship and the scourge of the electronic technicians and everyone else on board when the ship lost power. Electrical power was the lifeblood of the ship, and those responsible, including me, reacted when the lights flickered. When the lights went out, I leaped into my seaboots and dashed to the engine rooms. It all seems silly today, because the electricians and enginemen knew what had to be done and were frantically working to bring a generator online. I could be of no assistance, only a hindrance if I got into the act. At best, I was an observer who would question what happened after the problem was corrected. I was never told to be at the scene of a problem, yet I knew my presence was expected. It was unthinkable to remain in your bunk and handle the problem over the internal phone circuit. The subliminal message was, *this is your responsibility; be there.* Subjected to three years of reacting to power outages, I was transformed into a version of Pavlov's dog. Six months were required after leaving the *Vance* before I no longer became tense when the lights flickered.

The division had five additional electricians specializing in maintaining interior communications systems and the ship's gyroscopes. We also had a few enginemen who maintained the air-conditioning systems and the small portable engines, such as the motor whaleboat and portable firefighting pumps. A couple of the men doubled as the ship's divers should the need arise to go over the side to inspect the hull or to untangle a fishnet fouling the screws. The lone damage-control man aboard also resided in the division, for a total of twenty-one sailors and a chief electrician.

Chief Petty Officers

In my first year aboard, I did not have the luxury of a chief to run the division. In the second year, I lacked a top-notch chief petty officer. I was jealous of those officers who worked with chiefs who totally ran their divisions for them. The US Navy ran on chiefs and senior petty officers, men who came up through the ranks, technically experienced and knowing how to manage other men. They were the backbone of our navy, in contrast with the Soviet navy, which depended on a technically proficient and highly specialized officer corps that managed a smaller, weaker, career-enlisted cadre and a large draft contingent. Our enlisted ranks were considerably more able, permitting us officers to think of ourselves as Renaissance men.

CPOs, with their years of experience and technical expertise, were key to the smooth functioning of the ship. A wise junior officer valued and respected these men, who had achieved the summit of their professions. Chiefs differed widely. I liked to view them as either young or old. The older salty chiefs tended to populate the more traditional naval ratings, such as bo'sun's mate, quartermaster, gunner's mate, and to a lesser extent, engineman. For most of these traditional rates, there was a long, slow advancement ladder to climb, slowed by an excess of candidates and too few positions to fill. Middle-aged, intelligent sailors with distinguished service records took the competitive advancement exams in these rates over and over again, hoping that one day there would be an opening and they might gradually advance to CPO. Younger chiefs with less time in the navy were more prevalent in the newer technology areas where the navy competed with the private sector. Early promotion and incentive pay were the norm in these ratings.

Promotion to chief was a major change in status. The new chief began wearing an officer-type uniform, discarding the traditional bell-bottomed sailor uniform and Dixie hat. He moved into CPO quarters, on the *Vance* a separate compartment from the crew, not unlike the junior officers' quarters. His food was still prepared in the crew's galley, but he was served in the chiefs' quarters, where a sailor was assigned to clean his compartment and fetch his food. The luxury of privacy was his. A courtesy knock was expected before entering the chiefs' quarters. The *Vance*'s CPO quarters housed a fine collection of chiefs, who were crucial to the efficient operation of the ship. In the supply, gunnery, and engineering departments, the chiefs were older men with near twenty or more years of service. They had seen it all, and they knew their technical specialties. Most were excellent leaders.

On one of my rare visits to the CPO quarters, I happened to glance at the open washroom door and noticed a couple of chiefs showering. I tried unsuccessfully not to stare at the tattooed, naked, wrinkled backside of an old sailor. A huge hooded cobra was emerging from the crack in his ass and coiling up around his body. I was viewing a historic document. The colors, once bright greens and reds, were faded. The strong, dark, defining lines were now gray and wandering aimlessly through wrinkled skin. Yet the size and quality of the tattoo were impressive, probably the masterpiece of a Hong Kong or Shanghai artist. The old bo'sun's mate chief probably remembered the pre–World War II days with the Asiatic Fleet.

New on board, the grisly old chief, as the senior man in first division, was wise enough to let Oldervick continue to manage the division, while he sat with his coffee mug telling sea stories to an impressionable audience of young deck apes. His delivery reminded me of a dehydrated, older, featherless version of Foghorn Leghorn, the Looney Tunes rooster with the authoritative rhetoric, "Son, I've worn out more seabags than you have socks." Or when providing his young wards detailed lectures on female anatomy, "Son, do you know the length of a woman's taint?" Having told the tale a hundred times on probably twenty different ships, he would wait for the assured audience response, "What's a taint, chief?" And then launch into a graphic description of the distance between the two private orifices of the female body.

His wife was a female version of him, in a skinny old

rawhide body and possessing a vocabulary equal to that of her husband's. As to the cobra, I didn't know if she also had one and didn't want to know, but I wouldn't bet against there being a second cobra. Actually I liked the old salt. He made no real contribution to the *Vance* because we didn't need him, but we were stuck with him and at least he was not a problem.

Rest and Relaxation

While the old chief drank his coffee on the fantail under the stretched canvas awning, I was busy getting Lee Cole settled in with his new division and working with Engles ordering spare parts. Here in late August, we were on tropical hours, in an attempt to avoid the intense heat on the steel decks. The workday began at seven in the morning and ended at one in the afternoon, without a break. I liked the hours. We avoided the worst of the heat and had enough time to make a weekday liberty trip to Waikiki practical. At nine one morning, the 1MC screamed out, "Mr. Jaras, report to the quarterdeck." I climbed out of the engine room in rumpled khakis, sweating like a pig, and made my way to the quarterdeck to find my college roommate Bob Yohe standing there in Bermuda shorts.

I had lost track of Bob while on Deep Freeze. Bob had entered the navy six months after me, was commissioned via OCS, and then, because the brown-shoe navy needed additional officers, he went on to become a naval aviation navigator. Bob is one of the most likable people I know and perhaps one of the most laid-back. I hesitate to call him lucky because he is both intelligent and precise, and hardworking when cornered. He is not aggressive. While I can shave my face in five minutes, Bob required twenty minutes to ensure that each hair was located and adequately shortened. I would spend weeks preparing for final exams because I'm a habitual planner. Bob would only open the books for the last twenty-four hours with the help of a few pills, and we would both receive passing grades.

Apparently, his precision paid off. Bob graduated second in his class at navigator's school, which increased the likelihood of being granted his first duty choice, the type of air squadron he would fly with. As newly commissioned naval officers, our knowledge of the US Navy was superficial, based on the news media, movies, and posters. At OCS, we ship drivers foolishly wanted destroyer duty, while the new brown-shoe graduates like Bob favored fighter squadrons, both dashing, romantic choices. His first choice was heavy-attack A-6 Intruder aircraft, a new flashy option that eventually took heavy casualties in Vietnam. Bob was lucky. He was given choice number three, a VR squadron. Someone had advised him that the great duty for seeing the world was flying the multiengine aircraft of the VR squadrons, slow, big planes that hauled cargo and passengers. Bob was assigned the VR squadron at Barbers Point Naval Air Station on Oahu. Soon he was the navigator for CINCPACFLT and then for CINCPAC. This last one was the top US military command in the Pacific, Admiral Sharp. Bob traveled the world with CINCPAC, while I, the destroyer sailor, sat in midocean dreaming of terra firma and all the cities of the world yet to visit.

Patiently I explained to Bob that we now lived in different worlds. I was unable to go to Waikiki with him at nine in the morning on a weekday. Nor could I show him around the ship this morning, not during working hours. We met later in the day on the beach and after that when our schedules coincided, over the next two years. It was like old times hanging out together, and for me, learning what I missed when I turned down naval air to be a dashing, salty, black shoe. The differences in our environments were enormous. The officer-enlisted distinction was less rigid for Bob. Lives were interdependent when you flew together, a big difference from my trying to have all the oars rowing together.

We had little time together that August. The *Vance* was scheduled for a four-day R&R trip to Kauai, the Garden Island of the Hawaiian chain. The *Vance*, together with a little fleet oiler and a diesel submarine, was dispatched to Nawiliwili Harbor, Kauai, for the weekend to show the flag by marching in the local Flag Day parade. There was a wardroom discussion over which unlucky junior officer would lead our gung-ho honor guard in the parade. Thankfully, Jim Kunz, who owned a sword and knew how to march and salute with it, volunteered for the parade. Jim, who had served in the Washington, DC, honor guard, was perfect for the task. We reserve officers were not required to own swords, fancy gold-encrusted tools used only for ceremonial purposes. At OCS, where we learned all the niceties of being officers and gentlemen, there wasn't time or swords enough for us to learn what to do with them. Jim knew all about parades and ceremonial presentations, and I think he enjoyed them. Jim, with the *Vance*'s honor guard following, tramped proudly though the unpaved streets of Nawiliwili, avoiding the chickens and dog shit. The rest of us, with cameras in hand, explored the island. Kauai was a nice diversion, with a drink or two at the few pricey resorts on the island, great snorkeling in an isolated cove, and ping-pong battles with Harvey Payne at a luxury hotel. There were few tourists and no women.

Our last night in Kauai, I had the duty on board, which allowed me a better picture of what the crews were up to. We provided a shore patrol unit together with the other two navy ships to ensure that misbehaving sailors were brought back to their respective ships, so as not to burden the local authorities, who could not deal with four hundred sailors in town, and to keep our dirty linen private. A busy night it was herding groups of drunken sailors over the quarterdeck. The shore patrol periodically dumped off a load of exhausted, bruised sailors. Some were happy drunks; others were chewed up from fighting sailors from the other ships. Thankfully, no locals were involved. My guess was that the locals stayed home until this blizzard of white uniformed locusts departed the island.

The petty officer of the watch called me saying, "Mr. Jaras, there's a sailor swimming out to sea. What do you want to do?" We determined that it was an intoxicated submarine sailor, probably egged on by his drinking buddies. He had jumped off the pier and started swimming out to sea. I expected the man to sober up in the cold water and head for the pier, but he didn't. He kept up a determined crawl stroke, with no sign of a course change. Something was driving this guy. I'm not certain what he had in mind; the next landfall was Oahu, a good day's steaming in the open ocean. If he missed Oahu, the west coast of the United States was just another three thousand miles. Oblivious to warning shouts from shore, the swimming sailor tried his best to clear the harbor and head into the open sea, soon to be out of sight. I had no intention of lowering the whaleboat to go after the fool. Besides, we jealous DER sailors claimed that submariners, the navy's privileged elite, could walk on water. We made the submarine's quarterdeck watch aware of the situation, and they reluctantly launched a rubber boat to reel him in. Interesting night. Perhaps the *Vance* didn't have a lock on sailor problems.

Even more interesting, the *Vance* crewmembers hauled back to the ship by the shore patrol had been in drunken fights with sailors from the other two ships. These were the same sailors who bitched continually about being stuck on the lousy *Vance*, the same guys who couldn't wait for a transfer or the end of their enlistment. Apparently bitching about your own ship was acceptable, but don't let them catch someone else, especially a sailor from a different ship, degrading the *Vance*. Strange how this works. I've witnessed the same phenomenon regarding schools, cities, countries, and most everything else that people relate to. There was comfort in knowing the crew identified with the ship. I admit to the same feelings, yet I was eager to transfer to terra firma permanently at the first opportunity.

My Eighth Patrol

To transfer was a dream and nothing more. We were underway September 1 for my second Pacific Barrier patrol, my eighth patrol since reporting aboard. We rounded Oahu, picked up the usual choppy seas on the windward side of the island, and steered a northwesterly course for ocean station. I was into my second year aboard, one of the three salty ensigns. Fred,

Jim, and I were now elevated to OOD underway, no longer understudies on the bridge. As such, we had the newer ensigns standing bridge watches under our tutorage.

Ken Wood, the new first division officer, was on watch with me that first moonlit night as we steered a course for ocean station. The relatively calm sea erupted, and a huge whale broke the surface, twisting and reaching into the air directly in front of the ship. Ken froze. I took control and ordered a turn to port to avoid the whale. For that one moment, Ken was startled by the sudden leap of this huge bleeding mass of whale with sharks clinging to its flesh. The dying whale quickly disappeared into the depths, leaving the surface red with blood. The event was over in a moment. Unusual? Yes. Dangerous? No. It didn't even rate mentioning in the deck log, but the incident ensured that a friendship with Ken would never happen.

Like a fool, I chuckled at his momentary fear, a big mistake on my part that I regretted. My sin was to witness Ken's moment of surprise, and then to stupidly show that I was amused. This cursed knee-jerk reaction of kidding or poking fun at someone's discomfort was a foolish habit I acquired in childhood in a competitive family environment where humor and put-downs were interchangeable and frequent. I meant no harm with my brief chuckle. With someone else, my immature response would be forgotten. Unfortunately, we were young, and for Ken, who harbored an Ernest Hemingway obsession for manliness, I had witnessed a moment of weakness. This was to be the defining moment of our relationship; the opportunity for friendship, if one ever existed, had vanished.

Ken was never a problem; we just didn't hang out together. He was a good officer and a natural leader. I regretted my handling of the event partially because I wanted to be liked and respected by my fellow officers and because we were thirteen men living and working together for long periods of time on a little ship. I am certain that my unimpressive five-foot-six-plus frame, my sometimes biting commentary, and my bookish demeanor didn't fit Ken's idea of a manly man. Still, we got along in this highly structured environment in which your date of rank meant everything. Jim Kunz, Fred Levin, and I, the senior group of ensigns, had established close ties, because together we had endured the trials and tribulations of new officers. Lee Cole, Ken Wood, and Bruce Young, the new batch of ensigns, were to establish similar loyalties and group ties.

On patrol in the North Pacific, unlike the isolation of the Antarctic patrols, we were within reasonable steaming range of the Midway Islands to the south and even closer to Adak, Alaska, to the north. Adak became a regular refueling port over the next few years. After nine days knocking about on ocean station, we were underway for Adak. We arrived just before midnight on September 12 to take on forty-eight thousand gallons of diesel fuel. Adak was always a nasty harbor to approach. We battled either strong winds or blinding fog. Fortunately a harbor tugboat was usually available to assist. The first order of business was to get the fuel lines on board and, if time permitted, hook up to shore power and top off the potable water tanks.

Adak, Alaska

Adak Island is located in the Andreanof Island group of the Aleutian Islands, the string of rugged, volcanic islands curving twelve hundred miles west from the tip of the Alaska Peninsula. The islands separate the Bering Sea from the Pacific Ocean. Adak lies in the maritime climate zone, characterized by overcast skies, moderate temperatures, high winds, and frequent cyclonic storms. Winter squalls produce wind gusts in excess of a hundred knots. Extensive fog forms over the island during the summer.

Historically the Unangas occupied the Aleutian Islands. The once-heavily populated Adak was eventually abandoned in the early 1800s as the Aleutian Island hunters followed the Russian fur trade eastward and famine set in on the Andreanof Island group. However, they continued to actively hunt and fish around the island over the years until World War II broke out. Adak army installations allowed US forces to mount a successful offensive against the Japanese-held islands of Kiska and Attu.

After World War II, Adak was developed as a naval air station, playing an important role during the Cold War as a submarine surveillance center. At its peak, the station housed over six thousand naval and coast guard personnel and their families. In 1994, the base was downsized, and both family housing and schools were closed. The station officially closed on March 31, 1997.

The naval base command understood our situation of long weeks in miserable seas. They opened the chiefs' and officers' clubs when we were in port regardless of the day or time. Adak was not a liberty stop. The crew remained aboard, while the captain, supply officer, and a few other officers and chiefs went to the clubs. Fueling being my responsibility, I had to remain aboard. These brief port visits for refueling always bothered me. The longer we remained moored, the more likely I would lose my sea legs and become seasick once we were underway again. Short visits served me best. This one lasted eight hours. As a result, I suffered through a brief stage of seasickness as we headed back to our ocean station. Two guarantees accompanied each Adak visit: a few hangovers for those officers and chiefs who maximized their time at the bar, and fresh king crab legs for dinner the first day back at sea. When in Adak, the supply officer was under orders to secure a supply of king crab legs from the local fishermen in the harbor. Wardroom and crew always ate well departing Adak.

We stayed on station ten more days. The casual trip from Hawaii to ocean station was always very different from the return journey. After being at sea for almost a month, there was a longing to reach Pearl Harbor without delay. Once in voice radio contact with our relief ship, we moved to the southeasternmost corner of ocean station. Perhaps we even cheated a little, moving a few miles off station, poised as a sprinter in the hundred-yard dash. The electrical load was split between generators #1 and #3; all engines were warmed up and ready. The moment the relief ship arrived, we were already at fifteen or eighteen knots steaming for home. No side trips, no looking for the smoothest ride, we pushed the old *Vance* as fast as she would endure, praying the weather would cooperate and get us home quickly. After three days, the *Vance* arrived in Pearl Harbor the afternoon of September 26.

CHAPTER 13

Winter at Sea

September 26, 1962–April 18, 1963

If the highest aim of a captain were to preserve his ship,
he would keep it in port forever.
—St. Thomas Aquinas

Chastity—you can carry it too far.
—Mark Twain

Command of a Tired Ship

The saga of the *Vance* for 1962 and part of 1963 was rightfully the story of its commanding officer. The captain's power was that of the chessboard queen, the most important and most powerful element, whether stationary or active. Command of a ship is an awesome responsibility, a difficult undertaking for the best of men. And the navy tried its best to pick the best. Yet not every captain's situation was the same. The challenges varied. In the right situation, a less-than-the-best captain might perform adequately, given luck, a sound ship, and a supportive crew that would mask the captain's shortcomings during his brief year and a half aboard.

Captain Beyer was a good man, who inherited a ship and crew that were wearing down during a difficult Antarctic deployment. Moreover, my guess was that the squadron received minimal material support because the Pacific Barrier mission was not a priority. In short, the skipper was truly tested while in command of the *Vance*. I liked the man, especially in a social environment ashore. He just was not the ideal man for the challenges facing the *Vance* at that time.

As the saying goes, "hindsight is 20-20," and I am guilty today of picking away at the man's actions with the benefit of

209

fifty years of hindsight. Looking back, there was a clear pattern of a man trying his best to forge the *Vance* into an excellent ship and earn for himself a promotion to full commander. As a reserve officer looking forward to being a civilian once again, I didn't realize how important the stepping-stone to the next rank was for Lieutenant Commander Beyer. I didn't know or I ignored the news that he was passed over for the next rank while we were deployed on Deep Freeze.

Being twice passed over for the rank of commander was the end of a career. The officer then was forced to retire with twenty years of service. For any man who loved the navy and the sea as much as the skipper did, this would be an unacceptable finish. Civilian employment could never be as fulfilling after having tasted command at sea. Beginning in the second half of 1962, the next

(Left to right) Chief Mooney, the author, Scullion, and Jim Kunz at sea, 1963. (Photo from author's collection.)

twelve months was the last opportunity for the skipper to impress the US Navy with his performance. I was not privy to the fine points of the selection process at BUPERS, although I was certain that the squadron commander's evaluation of his ship captains was critical. Looking back, I believe that the skipper's intensity and anxiety that we witnessed those last twelve months were linked to an urgent need to impress the squadron commander. The condition of the engineering plant did not help his cause.

Are You on Fire?

The afternoon of September 26, the *Vance* limped up the Pearl Harbor channel and into the harbor past the busy shipyard, heading for the Bravo Piers. Tired and beaten up after a long patrol, she chugged along belching heavy black smoke from her stack. As we passed by a nest of ships at the Ford Island tender, the captain of the outboard DER, with tongue in cheek, sent us a message by flashing light, "Are you on fire? Do you require assistance?" Red-faced and tightly gripping his corncob pipe, Captain Beyer was livid. A raw nerve had been touched. I moved to the opposite side of the bridge to be out of harm's way. The clouds of black smoke from the stack might have been caused by Jenkins, our boiler technician, working on a problem boiler, or perhaps by the two cracked cylinder liners on the big Fairbanks-Morse diesels. The importance of looking good entering and leaving port could not be overemphasized. The skipper was absolutely embarrassed and angry that his ship was viewed as something less than a glamorous spit-and-polish ship of the line. That day, the image of a squared-away ship that he worked so hard to promote disappeared in one big belch of black smoke. The *Vance*, with all her warts, was exposed to the world in the middle of Pearl Harbor. On the positive side, we did manage to get home under our own power.

The way to avoid such embarrassment was to solve the engineering problems, get funding, have the time to overhaul the engines, be more considerate of the physical limitation of the plant, and above all, show some interest in the snipes. What we snipes received was enough time and resources to perform halfway fixes. I would never fully learn what problems confronted the captain or what attempts he made to seek assistance from the squadron commander. My guess was that he shied away from publicly admitting that the ship needed help. That was counter to the pervasive can-do philosophy. If there were a solution, he must have believed it was to be found in appearances.

The clouds of black smoke were gone. We were moored at

the Bravo Piers with all services provided. With the generators and main engines secured, the snipes could begin to replace the cracked cylinder liners on a big Fairbanks-Morse diesel. And hopefully we could find out why #1 ship service generator was again running amuck. What could be accomplished must fit in between periodic training exercises. We were usually free from operational exercises for the first week back from a patrol, a window of opportunity to begin tearing into the machinery the moment we hooked up to shore power. Once the training commitments began, the engineering department must ensure that the ship could perform as required. What I would have given for one or two uninterrupted months to overhaul equipment.

An Assistant Secretary of Defense

A whaleboat trip through Pearl Harbor by an assistant secretary of defense confirmed what I already knew about the skipper. For some mysterious reason, he relished appearances. I came to understand this addiction when he had the ship painted from stem to stern and from waterline to masthead in Adventure Bay, Tasmania. Moored at the Bravo Piers, we were advised that an assistant secretary of defense was in town and would be crossing over to Ford Island by whaleboat the next afternoon. Alarm! Alarm! The boat would pass within a quarter mile of the *Vance,* moored at the Bravo Piers.

Captain Beyer stopped work and ordered the outboard side of the ship to be painted immediately. I watched Boats Oldervick as he received the order for his men once again to waste a day and a lot of paint to cover the rust and salt on the hull's unprepared surface. Nothing was more abhorrent to a good bo'sun's mate than slopping paint over an unprepared surface. Old loose paint and rust must be chipped off, the surface washed free of salt, and a primer coat of red lead applied before the finished coat of gray was applied. I waited to see if Boats would lose his cool for once and get pissed off. Boats, solid as a rock, received the order with an unemotional, "Aye,

aye, sir." At the paint locker, he began to break out paint for his deck apes and the others of the crew drafted for the job. He knew I was watching for a reaction. We made eye contact; I received an unreadable, little forced grin, and nothing more. I knew what he was thinking, *Stupid order*, but stupid orders were nothing new to a career sailor. Then the big bo'sun's mate switched smoothly to a big smile, which told me I wouldn't get the satisfaction of seeing him pissed off. Amazing man, that Oldervick.

The next day I made a point of watching the whaleboat carrying an assistant secretary of defense chug across the harbor to Ford Island. As I stood at the rail, I thought of my only other association with an assistant secretary of defense. At OCS, a son of one such species was appointed my company commander. The self-important lad was treated with kid gloves by the OCS staff. I am certain he believed himself a reincarnation of John Paul Jones or Admiral Farragut or perhaps Admiral Arleigh Burke, because the lad was destined for a fast new destroyer of his choice. Here was a lad placed in a position to square away us fellow OCS cadets, and he relished the job. Admittedly he did bring unity to our forty-man company. Thirty-nine of us thought him a worthless pain in the ass, an unfortunate person who had no idea of how to interact successfully with his fellow human beings. Of course the lad, our leader, had carte blanche at OCS. When marching, we so enjoyed following his commands as he proudly led us, sword in hand. If the assistant company commander led us, we would help him out by staying in formation and covering for his faulty commands. For the reincarnated John Paul Jones, we would follow his every command into walls, through other marching companies, wherever his squeaky high-pitched voice commanded. We were a thirty-nine-man marching menace.

So what was behind the captain's need to paint the ship for a passing VIP? My guess is that he viewed the *Vance* as a fighting ship, a greyhound of the seas, a gallant ship of war. To me, she was a stubby, three-legged, miniature greyhound.

He could not see that the *Vance* was a simple, one-dimensional workhorse, built during World War II to protect big, slow convoys from small, slow U-boats, and then fifteen years later, modified to be a radar platform conducting long, physically grueling patrols in isolated oceans. She was not selected for her armament or her speed. The slow, fuel-efficient diesels were the reason the *Edsall*-class DE was chosen. Despite the obvious reality of our mission, the skipper placed emphasis on gunnery and ignored engineering. My guess was that he knew and liked weaponry and had little or no engineering experience or interest in it. Perhaps he dreamed of a fast rakish destroyer the way I dreamed of seeing the world.

The skipper's vision of the *Vance* as a ship of war was consistent with his compelling emphasis on show rather than substance, a coat of paint over rust. He loved the spit and polish of our two little three-inch popguns, but ignored the engineering department. It seemed a minor point that the *Vance* must reach the enemy before releasing its deadly battery. We were an endurance ship. We did not travel with a fleet task force escorting aircraft carriers, the primary mission of the real destroyer squadrons. We could not keep up the pace. The *Vance* chugged along at fifteen to eighteen knots, sat in the open ocean for three weeks, and then chugged home again. First, our engineering plant had to perform. Then our radar and communications systems must function when we arrived on station. The weapons systems were of secondary importance to our mission. Were there no destroyer escorts in mothballs available from World War II and the US Navy had to build new ships for the DEW Line, would they have bothered to arm the ships?

The Single Man's Home

Despite my complaining, I was a happy man. We were on terra firma once again. Once the mooring lines were secure and the 1MC announced, "Liberty commences," all married men, both officer and enlisted, streamed over the gangway, kissed their wives and children on the pier, and headed home. The unlucky few married men who had the duty remained aboard. Unlike the Deep Freeze ports of call, on Oahu the unmarried men, both officer and enlisted, remained aboard. There were few affordable attractions ashore for the typical sailor to rush off to.

For us single officers, getting ashore as often as possible was a serious objective. Unlike the poorly paid, young, single, enlisted man, we had more expendable income—not a lot more, but enough to think we could have a life ashore. Foremost on my mind was to find a way to live ashore, a place to go after work other than the bunk room. Weekdays after the married men hurried home for dinner and an evening with their families, we single officers had dinner in the wardroom with the two duty officers. We rarely left the ship on weekdays, and when we did, it was to wander over to the officers' club for a drink. Driving to Waikiki for the evening was time-consuming, costly, and uneventful without a specific overnight destination. Weekends ashore were a must. The lack of a place to sleep brought me back to the *Vance* each weekend night.

Unfortunately, the *Vance* was the single man's home by necessity. We couldn't afford to rent an apartment on Oahu. Even the rooms in the ratty old wooden World War II bachelor officers' quarters, the Makalapa BOQ, with the community bathroom down the hall, were off-limits to shipboard officers. With a schedule of twenty-six days at sea and twenty-one days in port, an apartment was not practical. In vain, we single officers explored our options, from investing in an old houseboat on the Ala Wai Canal to renting a shared apartment. There were no viable options at our pay level. If married, you received a housing allowance or navy housing. Our home was the ship.

Most of my time in Hawaii was spent aboard the ship in Pearl Harbor. Moored in a nest of ships at Ford Island, I would lean against the rail on the fantail gazing out over the harbor in the early evening. Dinner was over. The crew was either watching the evening movie or sitting around their bunks reading. The harbor was quiet. Close by, the Arizona Memorial was deserted, the tourist boats gone for the day. I could understand the inspiration to name the harbor "pearl." It was once a beautiful place. Perhaps eighty years ago, a pearl could exist here. In 1962, the harbor contained considerable oil and garbage. There was a popular theory that the destroyer tender we were moored alongside at Ford Island, a ship that sat there month after month servicing destroyers, would one day be aground because of the buildup of discarded soda cans flung over the side. I never took much interest in the condition of the harbor until one day looking down over the side, I noticed raw human waste pumping out the side of our ship onto the wood barrier, or camel, floating between the *Vance* and the neighboring ship. All the shit generated by the *Vance*'s crew went straight into Pearl Harbor and every other harbor we visited. As shit piled up two feet deep on the camel, I had the deck force hose it off and vowed never to swim or fall overboard in Pearl Harbor.

The Stormy North Pacific

In addition to contemplating the harbor, I was concerned about my wisdom teeth. The navy dentists at Pearl Harbor claimed I needed three removed, two pulled and the third cut out. So I bit the bullet and let them have at it. With chipmunk cheeks and miserable, I asked if I might miss the next patrol. We were getting underway the next day. Not possible. I was much too valuable to be left ashore. The word came back via the XO, "Don't worry, Tom. Our corpsman will handle any complications." Boy! Did that pick up my morale learning that I was irreplaceable! But then deep down inside, I always knew it. How could the *Vance* get underway without this salty ensign aboard?

Chubby cheeks couldn't eat, so why worry about seasickness on this, my ninth patrol? After only ten days on terra firma, the *Vance* was underway on October 6 for a rough three-day ride to our little thirty-mile radius, designated station in the North Pacific Ocean. I do believe this ocean was misnamed. I can understand how the Portuguese explorer Ferdinand Magellan decided on the name *Mare Pacificum*, "peaceful sea," having found relative tranquility after rounding the harrowing seas at the tip of South America. Had the gentleman traveled north a bit more, say to 50° north latitude, he would have chosen another name, perhaps *Mare Pacificum Sometimum*. Winters up north could be mean, and they usually were. The winters of 1962–63 and 1963–64 in the northern Pacific Ocean seriously beat up the *Vance*.

Approaching ocean station on the tenth, we received an airdrop of critical radar parts that weren't available before departing Pearl. The huge Willy Victor aircraft came in low, dropped the parachute within a half mile of us, and went on its way. Our task was to pick up the parachute and floating canister in five-to-six-foot seas and eighteen to twenty knots of wind. Captain Beyer tried three times to approach the canister from upwind, then drift close enough to snag the parachute with a grappling hook. We tried until the *Vance* sat dead in the water, our air pressure to start the engines expended and the canister still in the water.

The direct-drive diesel engines were dependent on 600 pounds' air pressure to start the engines each time the propellers were stopped and then started again. For example, a maneuver to pivot the ship, "Starboard ahead one-third, port back one-third," required starting air for the two diesel engines on each shaft. The next order would probably be to go forward again, "Port ahead one-third," to match the starboard propeller action. The two diesels powering the port shaft would be stopped, and again 600 pounds of air was required to start the diesels in a forward direction. The orders from the bridge to the engine room were conveyed visually over the engine-order telegraph, accompanied by bells ringing. Thus the term "bells" is used when counting the number of propeller changes ordered from the bridge. The *Vance*'s 600-pound air compressor and storage tank capacity permitted about eleven bells before the air supply was exhausted. A few extra bells were possible from the high-pressure (HP) air compressor in B-3, a World War II leftover from when the deck torpedoes required air for launching. We would warn the bridge that the air supply was exhausted and that HP air was being bled into the system, permitting a few more bells.

In this instance, the captain's excessive maneuvering had exhausted the air supply. We snipes could only report that fifteen minutes were required before sufficient air pressure was available once again to maneuver the ship. All this maneuvering took place with the ship we were relieving, the USS *Brister* (DER 327), standing by. The *Brister* swept in and grabbed the parachute and canister on their first pass. The seas were too rough to launch the whaleboat, so the two ships rigged a highline to transfer the canister. Nothing was said, yet it was obvious on the bridge and to the deck apes on the fo'c'sle that we looked foolish sitting dead in the water as the *Brister* came to our assistance. This was a question of pride in the ship, and by extension, pride in ourselves. As the *Brister* departed for Hawaii, we lost the electrical load. It happens, and when it did, regardless of the reason, I managed a low profile at the dinner table, as did my boss, Don Dunn. Dinner in the wardroom that evening was a quiet affair. The skipper's ship-handling exhibition ensured there would be no criticism about the generator.

By the twenty-second, the weather was getting mean. The sea rose to twenty-five, then thirty feet, and the winds were clocked at thirty to forty knots. After five more days of brutal weather, we started south to refuel at Midway Island. In the late afternoon, the AN/SPE 28 radar antenna, the huge air-search antenna shaped like a giant set of bedsprings, toppled from its mounting and hung precariously from the antenna platform on the port side of the main mast yardarm. On the bridge, we kept looking up, wondering when the antenna would come crashing down and, more importantly, where it would land. With the ship taking major rolls, the seas rising, and the winds at forty-four knots, it was anyone's guess where the bedsprings would end up. Fortunately, after four hours, the huge antenna broke free and toppled into the ocean on the port side.

Without long-range air-search radar, the *Vance* was of little value on the DEW Line. The tranquil ocean at Midway provided five hours of quiet bliss. The ship was moored. I was content to supervise refueling and peer over the side into the beautifully clear blue water, observing the abundant sea life. We happily headed for home after refueling at Midway Island. Lucky Harvey, the electronics officer, flew back to Oahu to co-ordinate the antenna replacement in advance of our arrival at Pearl Harbor. The *Vance* followed, steaming three days back to Hawaii.

Midway Islands

The Midway Islands are an atoll of about two and a half square miles at the very end of the Hawaiian archipelago. The atoll is located in the North Pacific Ocean midway between Japan and the US mainland. The two major land areas, Sand Island and Eastern Island, are inhabited by millions of albatrosses.

Captain Middlebrooks, of the sealing ship *Gambia,* first sighted the atoll in 1859. Eleven years later, the US Navy took possession of the atoll, naming it Midway. In 1903, Midway was on the route of the trans-Pacific submarine cable. A US Navy radio station was established there the same year. Pan-American Airlines flying boats used the island as a stopover on their San Francisco to China service from 1935 until the outbreak of World War II. The most important naval battle of the Pacific Campaign was the Battle of Midway in June 1942, in which the US Navy defeated a Japanese attack against the islands. In the 1950s, Midway was again a naval air station, serving as a refueling stop for ships and planes transiting the Pacific. With the extension of the DEW Line, the navy's "Willy Victor" radar planes based on Midway flew continuously to Adak and back until the late 1960s. During this brief time, the atoll bristled with communications and maintenance facilities and a large military and civilian population.

Following the Vietnam War, Midway's military role was greatly diminished. In 1996, the atoll was transferred to the Fish and Wildlife Service of the Department of the Interior. Ten years later, Midway became part of the Northwestern Hawaiian Islands Marine National Monument. Only the "gooney birds," the albatross, remain.

The Cuban Missile Crisis

I am certain that we, along with our entire armed forces, were on full alert status during part of this October 1962 patrol. Not until our return to Hawaii did we learn of the Cuban Missile Crisis. We didn't know that while riding the heavy sea our fourth day on station, a U-2 aircraft spotted Soviet missile installations in Cuba. The next day, when our AN/SPE 28 radar antenna, the bedsprings, was dangling from the mainmast, President Kennedy addressed the nation, stating that there were missiles in Cuba and that the United States was responding by imposing a blockade of Cuba. Never were we closer to nuclear war than at that moment in history, when the *Vance* lost her radar antenna and thus the capability to detect Soviet aircraft carrying nuclear warheads. The Pacific Barrier could and did function effectively without us. Nevertheless, at the moment of greatest danger to the nation, after years of manning the barrier, the stormy Pacific had our principal air-search radar slowly sinking to the ocean bottom. By the time we reached the Midway Islands to refuel on October 30, the Cuban Missile Crisis was resolved.

Companionship

Hello, Pearl Harbor! We arrived November 2, just in time to allow Fred Levin three days to plan and organize his wedding. Janet, Fred's fiancée, had arrived in Hawaii and was awaiting the *Vance*'s return. Thanks to the lost antenna, the newlyweds would have thirty-eight days together before the next patrol. The simple military ceremony, in the Jewish chapel, a Quonset hut relic left over from World War II, was a major wardroom event, a happy time allowing us to gather as a group to wish the newlyweds well.

We squeezed into over-starched dress white uniforms, laughing at each other's attempt to practice drawing their swords. We had to scramble to scare up enough swords for the ceremony. Swords were only required of career officers, and we were largely three-year wonders. The ceremony came off well in spite of a nervous Fred forgetting his socks. Harvey came to the rescue, donating his socks. I remember the wedding as perhaps the best social gathering of my three years on the *Vance*. The weather was mild, and my fellow officers were happy and in a festive mood. Captain Beyer, who enjoyed a party, was at his best. The ship, the patrols, and the work schedule were forgotten for this one lovely afternoon.

(From left to right) Ken Wood, Salts McKillop, Captain Beyer, Jim Kunz, Mel Huffman, Bruce Young, Gil Gersenfish, Robbie Robinson, Harvey Payne, and the author. (Photo from author's collection.)

While the newlyweds disappeared, the rest of us headed to Waikiki and Fort DeRussy to celebrate. This was my lucky day. At Fort DeRussy, I happened to meet Joan, a special lady who recently arrived in the islands for her first job after graduation from college. Over drinks and a barbeque dinner, we exchanged laughs and stories. Joan was a scientist, a very intelligent one, and a graduate of a good western college. I, of course, decked out in dress whites with the little blue Deep Freeze Medal bouncing around over my heart, was a mid-twentieth-century Hawaiian version of Lieutenant Pinkerton of *Madame Butterfly* fame. We hit it off from the first. This fun-loving, dark-haired, dark-eyed girl had to have a sense of humor. She liked the dashing young naval officer in his dress white uniform, the front covered with barbeque sauce. I drove Joan home that evening to her small, shared apartment, then floated back to the ship, realizing that this could well be the beginning of my happiest time on the *Vance*, which it was.

We made a date for the next weekend, a small dinner party

at Jane's house. Now Jane was Harvey Payne's girlfriend, a midthirties, divorced, Chinese American lady who worked at the naval base. I had no idea how Harvey and Jane met, that lucky man. Jane was an exceptional person, warm, generous, considerate, and fun to be with. At her home up on the hills behind Waikiki, she lived with her nine-year-old son and twelve-year-old daughter. In some social circles the young Harvey, living with the older Asian divorcée with children, was an invitation to whispered disapproval. Easygoing Harvey just ignored the social ramifications and developed a great enduring friendship with this lady. The beauty of Harvey was that social prejudices were never even considered. Here was a very logical and prejudice-free individual. I quietly admired his open relationship with Jane and felt a sense of personal shame because I was too insecure to imagine myself in Harvey's shoes.

Dinner at Jane's was unforgettable. She and Harvey prepared a lovely candlelight meal, and the four of us enjoyed the Hawaiian sunset over the ocean, with the flickering lights of Waikiki along the coast below us. Both the view and the drinks were intoxicating. After dinner, Jane and Harvey were outside on the front lawn enjoying the view, while Joan and I remained at the table. Before long, we were under the table in a passionate embrace. With her dress up, her panties off, and my pants down to the knees, we made love. The pleasure was beyond all expectations. Exhausted, but with emotions under control once again, we joined our hosts on the front lawn. Harvey and Jane greeted us as if nothing had happened. I sat dazed, relaxed as never before, staring off into the Pacific at total peace with the world. To this day, I don't know if Harvey and Jane were just being polite or were unaware of what had transpired. Forty years later, I asked him. He couldn't remember.

I was floating on air, my body free of all tension, a release never before experienced and long overdue. Twenty-four years old, and I finally had my first sexual experience. There was much catching up to do. In high school, it had to be the most beautiful girl in my class or none, and I was shy. So it was none.

Unfortunately in college, I passed up a few opportunities, fearing I was taking advantage of a weeping freshman girlfriend, frightened, but vulnerable to losing her virginity. My early noble gestures were motivated partly by the fear of emotional commitment and marriage. I owed so much to my parents for their personal sacrifices that I dreaded letting them down. Fear of commitment and the Victorian purity of the 1950s had me graduating a virgin. I was born too early. The sex barriers on the college campus came crashing down in the 1960s, a different world from my experience of segregated dorms and strict hours for women. In the navy, living independently, I became liberated from my perceived parental obligations and hopefully was now a bit more mature.

With Joan's assistance, for the next eleven months, we did our best to make up for my years of celibacy. Neither of us could get enough love, but eventually we parted the next year. While the relationship lasted, these were my best days on the *Vance*. When I returned from a long patrol, Joan would be there on the pier, sitting in my MG roadster, waiting for me along with the wives and families of the crew I used to envy. She would be there waving good-bye as the deck apes took in the mooring lines and we headed to sea. The days at sea dragged, yet I was relaxed and tranquil, knowing she would be there on our return.

We explored Oahu together and made love anywhere and everywhere: in her apartment while her roommate slept in the next room, in pineapple groves on the windward side of the island, in hotels, on isolated beaches, and in my MG roadster, a truly contorted experience. Perhaps the most interesting place we made love was aboard the *Vance* in the XO's stateroom. When in charge of the ship in port, as the Command Duty Officer (CDO), I would have Joan over for dinner and a movie in the wardroom. While women were not allowed in the crew's quarters or the junior officers' bunk room, the forward staterooms adjoining the wardroom were accessible. My choice was Green Jeans's bunk.

President Kennedy's Assassination

The navy interrupted my social life at will. We had an under-way-training schedule that also interfered with any serious work on the engines and gave me a daily seasickness problem, sometimes just a nauseous day, sometimes the barf bucket. One sunny afternoon as the *Vance* was returning from daily operations off Oahu, we suddenly went to general quarters. The 1MC blared out, "General quarters! General quarters! This is not a drill." It was November 22, 1963. President John F. Kennedy had been assassinated. The military worldwide was on full alert. Since we were right there, our orders were to patrol the entrance to Pearl Harbor. Sonar actively pinging, we steamed back and forth across the harbor entrance. At my battle station in the after engine room, I was thinking of the December 7, 1941, attack on Pearl Harbor, when the Japanese navy slipped small two-man submarines up this channel and into the harbor. I guess that was what we were there for. Some keen observer once said that the outdated lessons of the last war are always applied in the next war. Later that night, we returned to port, having encountered no Japanese submarines. Too late for Waikiki, several of us stopped at the officers' club for a drink and the news. It was one of those days you remember.

The Sea Anchor

On December 10, we cast off all lines and were underway for my tenth patrol. Now that I had a life ashore, leaving Oahu was difficult, yet the time at sea easier to endure. I had someone waiting for me. The monotonous hours on the bridge passed more rapidly as I daydreamed about Joan. After two and a half days of plowing through difficult seas, we arrived on station.

As usual, by avoiding the wardroom as much as possible, I was not aware of what the skipper was up to. I was caught by surprise when I heard the 1MC announce, "Sea anchor detail to the fo'c'sle." A sea anchor was going to be tested? I had no idea we even had one. The seas had settled somewhat, so I made my way forward to the hedgehog mount just below the bridge to find a good viewing spot for what was taking place on the fo'c'sle. There was Boats Oldervick, with several of his trusty deck apes, lifting a strange contraption, a huge, wooden cross of 4x4 posts, overlaid with stout canvas, a giant kite of sorts. Attached were the kite's strings, stout lines that trailed behind the sailors as they lifted the whole rig up and over the railing and watched it plunge into the sea. Above me on the bridge, I heard Captain Beyer giving commands to back the engines, then bring them to all stop. The lines to the kite or sea anchor tightened. The 4x4 crossed wood braces snapped like toothpicks, and then we knew it was just a kite.

Now a sea anchor was not a new idea. They have been around for centuries and were widely used to stabilize a boat in heavy weather by keeping the bow headed into the seas and out of the trough. Emphasis is on the word *boat*. Anything that floats and acts as a source of drag in the water can function as a sea anchor. Some, as ours did, took the form of a wooden or metal framework supporting a simple kite-shaped canvas. The strength member, a wooden frame, provided enough buoyancy to keep the anchor floating just under the surface. The canvas provided the drag. The sea anchor is dropped over the side, and the line is paid out and then secured to the bow. If all goes well, the resistance of the anchor turns the bow into the seas, keeping the ship from settling broadside in the trough.

Think of the fuel savings if the *Vance*'s bow could ride facing into moderate seas without the need for rudder control. We would be able to avoid having a main propulsion engine online. We would avoid drifting into the trough. We could stay on station longer, much longer. We would have found the Holy Grail!

I honestly didn't know who came up with this idea. I knew that the captain embraced the concept with the ironclad logic of a Catholic theologian. If a small sea anchor worked for a small boat, then a large sea anchor would work for a large ship. There were a few minor points that had to be cleared up. How large and strong must a sea anchor be to hold a 1,680-ton ship in the open ocean? How about considering the forces we were dealing with? The necessary size, materials, and cost of an adequate sea anchor rendered the project totally impractical. I suspect someone with some physics smarts could calculate the forces at work here.

I must admit, the first sea-anchor attempt generated considerable interest among the crew, especially the deck apes, the division tasked to build and deploy the device. Any deck-ape project was Boats Oldervick's baby, and this sea-anchor project was destined to be an albatross around Boats's neck. The splintered remains of the first failure were brushed aside, and a new, larger, stronger anchor was in the planning stages. The next time in port, I observed Boats paging through an old book containing pictures of similar sea anchors. Obviously this design was at least as old as the book. I briefly approached Boats on the feasibility of the idea. By now, the reader realizes that Boats was a cagey guy, never letting on what he was really thinking, especially in this instance, when the skipper had the hots for the sea anchor. I backed off.

For three patrols, Captain Beyer rallied the deck apes, each time to test a new, bigger, stronger sea anchor of wood and canvas. In port, sea-anchor construction was a top priority, the captain personally approving all changes. What the project accomplished was to provide entertainment, a break from the boredom on these long patrols. When the 1MC once again announced the sea-anchor launching, a large audience would gather around the hedgehog mount, signal bridge, and forward gun mount for a view of the fo'c'sle activity. Upon removal of the canvas to expose the huge wooden cross, one might think a passion play were being performed on the fo'c'sle, a reenactment of the crucifixion. Unfortunately this was not the sunbaked Holy Land or Oberammergau, Germany, during Holy Week. There were similarities, especially the agony seen on the faces of the deck apes, but the language differed. They were bitching, harassed by a wet, rolling deck and the cold. High above on the bridge, Captain Beyer oversaw the total submersion of the sea anchor as if this were a NASA space launch.

With a splash, sea anchor number two was dispatched over the bow. Line was paid out as the *Vance* slowly maneuvered to be properly aligned with the anchor. Again we waited for the anchor to do its stuff to keep the ship heading into the seas. Within a few minutes, the wooden braces again snapped like toothpicks and the anchor collapsed on itself. Boats and his crew labored to haul the remains back on deck.

Captain Beyer, in his best navy can-do form, clung to his belief in the anchor, as a guilty man to an alibi. The solution was always bigger, stronger wood braces and some modifications to the canvas. I watched Boats head back to the drawing boards. He knew what I was thinking when I showed a little smile. Never would I refer to the sea-anchor project. Boats looked away, not wanting me to read his thoughts, which were rising perilously close to the surface. No sense kicking the man when he was down. He knew I sympathized with his plight. This second failure was not a good time to joke with him.

For months Boats and his deck apes built and tested at least three sea anchors. Of course, the crew was not as sensitive or understanding as I to Boats's predicament. They had a wonderful time heckling the deck apes. At sea, the passion play was rehearsed yet again, several deck apes dragging another huge wooden cross to the fo'c'sle. Perhaps there was divine intervention at work here because the results were always the same, rapid collapse of the anchor. Each pageant attracted a sizable crowd, with an undercurrent of suppressed laughter and heckling ever-present, but controlled and out of sight of the captain on the bridge. I'm certain he heard some of the catcalls, but he never said anything. It was common knowledge that the deckhands wished there never was a sea anchor, praying that this bad dream would just quietly disappear. As a group, they showed a different face, defiant to any harassment of their division. Boats Oldervick could be credited with this show of esprit de corps.

Eventually the captain gave up on this wet dream. The deck apes' prayers were answered. Why the sea-anchor project in the first place? Had the project been a success, the skipper would certainly have benefited. Moreover, the idea was consistent with the prevalent navy can-do philosophy. The material costs for the project were small, and the potential benefits great. The *Vance* was viewed as one of the least impressive ships in the squadron. Here was one way to look better. The failure of the sea-anchor project could hardly be a black mark, especially if the effort were kept a private endeavor until successful. If the captain talked up the project to the squadron commander, its failure would not help our image. I am fairly certain the squadron commander was aware of the sea anchor.

CIC Watch Standing

The calm weather required for the sea-anchor launch was brief. We soon were experiencing forty-five-foot seas and winds to fifty-five knots. Christmas Day arrived as I sat on watch in the Combat Information Center (CIC). Now that Harvey, Jim, Fred, and I were actually fairly senior, we stood CIC watches on ocean station and deck watches when enroute to and from station. In CIC, we no longer froze. Now we sat in a large, dark room, bored most of the time, and we still worked to stay awake on the midwatch.

I learned that staying awake in the darkened CIC, with several sailors present, was more troublesome than being alone on a cold, isolated bridge watch. I usually brought something to read in CIC to help pass the time. The real difference was that on the bridge, I was isolated from the watch section in the pilothouse. The bridge watch offered time for reflection and daydreaming as I pressed my butt against the small bulkhead-mounted heater. In difficult seas, I was kept busy, my eyes trained on the wave patterns and my hands firmly gripped to a handrail. Ocean station was much the same as in the Antarctic, a designated spot sixty miles in diameter in which we slowly fought our way across, heading into the seas, turned through the trough, and then were swept along by a following sea. Upon reaching the station limits, we would turn and do it all over again and again until the fuel tanks were low and we headed home.

The alertness and personal isolation of bridge watches contrasted with the quiet CIC community environment. The CIC was the electronics nerve center of the ship. Located forward in perhaps the largest space in the ship, CIC was lined with radar screens and plotting boards. Several radarmen and electronics technicians were on watch, manning the scopes in the dark, while I sat at an elevated desk in the center of the room. Here the ship's three radars were monitored: the huge air-search radar that scanned for aircraft, the smaller, less conspicuous surface-search radar, and the enormous ungainly SPS-8 height-finding radar antenna mounted on the after-deck house.

With CIC located forward, deep in the ship's bowels on the second deck, the rolls were less severe here than on the bridge. Yet the ride remained very uncomfortable, as did the ride in all forward spaces. The deck apes' berthing area below the fo'c'sle, just forward of CIC, was the most uncomfortable habitable compartment on board. There, forward in the bow, the heaving and pitching were most intense. As the ship cut through the seas, the bow slammed down into the trough and then rose to meet the next wave. At high speeds, this action was at its worst, with the bow constantly slamming down, like a marble bumping down a slanted washboard. On station in rough seas, even at slow speeds, we suffered the slamming of the bow.

On the bridge, the fresh air and openness made the bucks and rolls easier to endure. Below in the dark, enclosed CIC, with hissing air vents and the green glow of radarscopes, the movement played games with the stomach and mind. The bridge was a rodeo cowboy's bull ride. The CIC experience was that of the rider blindfolded. In difficult weather, I preferred the bridge. Occasionally, a radarman bent over his scope would lose his lunch. After the barf was scraped up, wintergreen, from a big gallon jug in the corner, was sprinkled throughout the space. We couldn't exist in this enclosed space without the wintergreen.

Surprisingly, rarely was I seasick in CIC. Queasy, yes, but rarely did I lose my lunch. I did my barfing in the first three days underway to ocean station. By the time we reached the station and I started CIC watches, I had my sea legs and a settled stomach. You could never be certain. I kept a pail at hand near the desk, but out of sight.

The CIC watch standers were an efficient collection of radarmen and electronics technicians, who were far better equipped to operate the equipment and do the plotting than I was. Better educated but less colorful than the deck apes on the bridge, the CIC crew tended to generate more interesting conversations and less grandstanding. Less supervision was required. Being immersed in the engineering department, I had had little contact with electronics, radar, electronic warfare, or communications. Smart and well-trained sailors carried the load during my CIC watches. A more ambitious officer would have tried to learn all he could about the equipment while on watch. I was not interested in ever setting foot on a ship again. Perhaps I missed the opportunity to be the Renaissance man, that ideal naval line officer who knew all facets of shipboard systems. Knowing I would never be in the operations department helped me justify to myself the path of least resistance. I realized my limitations and was unwilling to make a serious effort to broaden my knowledge of the operations department. I brought a novel to CIC.

Cookies and Wontons

What made Christmas in the North Pacific cheerful was Fred Levin, Jim Kunz, and me alone in the bunk room sharing a couple of mason jars of cookies that Fred's wife had prepared for the trip. Why cookies in mason jars? The cookies were rum balls floating in rum-filled jars, technically baked goods, thereby skirting the forbidden-booze taboo on navy ships. I had mentioned that Fred was clever. The cookies and their juices were heartily appreciated. Nothing more exciting happened that holiday at sea. No attempts were made to tell the world we were here defending the nation from nuclear attack. I had heard that one previous Christmas, Captain Penny approved a flash message to NORAD, stating we had a contact in the northern sector and then identifying it as Santa Claus. Ho, ho, ho, this was not appreciated. No fighter intercept aircraft were launched, so why get excited? I could imagine Christmas at NORAD command, the air force personnel tucked away underground in their cozy Colorado Springs mountain retreat. With the change of the watch, they went home to a nice Christmas with their families. We crawled into our bunks to ride out the miserable weather.

On the twenty-ninth, the *Vance* was poised on the southeast edge of ocean station, maybe even a little beyond the station boundaries, awaiting the arrival of the USS *Savage* (DER 386), our relief ship, and then we could make a dash for home. Contact was made, and we headed for Pearl. At five in the evening New Year's Day, we arrived in Pearl Harbor. The year began well. Joan was there to meet me. Oahu was now a paradise. I had completed one and a half years as an officer. It was time for my automatic promotion to LTJG. You had to have done something really terrible not to be advanced to LTJG. A small increase in pay was forthcoming, as was the need to buy new collar devices and shoulder boards and throw a wetting-down party. Fred, Jim, and I decided to have a single party since we all advanced at roughly the same time. Harvey's friend Jane volunteered her house. We stocked it with cases of champagne and tons of fried wontons from Wu Fats in Honolulu, and then threw open the gate to the wardroom officers, wives, and friends. A memorable night it was. A few attendees didn't know how they managed to navigate down the mountain. Don Dunn's wife took a taxi home, letting Don, who insisted on driving, go it alone. Myself, I don't remember the details, although I was told it was a memorable party.

Ship Handling

Back aboard ship, we faced the usual in port routine: deck force making the ship's exteriors pretty while building another version of the sea anchor, snipes working on the machinery, operations sailors fixing electronics equipment, and supply department provisioning the ship. Occasionally there were exercises at sea for the day and return to port by five in the evening. These were opportunities to perform perhaps the most admired skill in the destroyer force, ship handling. Destroyer skippers were noted for their ability to maneuver their sleek greyhounds. Destroyer Flotilla Five consisted of three squadrons, two of which were comprised of real destroyers, and in the third, Destroyer Escort Squadron Five, were our seven DERs. The real destroyers gracefully slipped in and out of this busy harbor, while the DERs tried their best to look sharp. The DER was less maneuverable because of the large freeboard area that caught the wind, and the direct-drive diesel engines that responded ever so slowly.

The harbor was a stage on which destroyer skippers performed. Because ship handling was important, flotilla and squadron staffs often observed their ships entering and leaving port from the vantage of the harbor watchtower. Never underestimate the importance of well-executed destroyer maneuvers, particularly when entering and leaving port. Impressive ship handling could bring tears to the eyes of the old sea dogs in the watchtower.

Getting underway was a challenge, especially when several ships were jockeying for position to leave port at the same time. But real skills came into play when guiding the 1,680-ton *Vance* to the pier. This was white-knuckle time for the skipper. He was not a born ship handler. I've observed any number of great ship handlers, from bo'sun's mates to ensigns to ships' captains. The good ones were outwardly calm and confident. Our skipper was tense. Once I witnessed his pipe stem snap off in his hand on a cold, windy day while trying to reach the pier at Adak, Alaska.

Probably uncertain of his own abilities, the skipper was not about to let his junior officers maneuver the ship in the harbor. We all wanted the opportunity, and captains were encouraged to teach their junior officers. On the other hand, if I were to damage the ship bringing her into port, the captain would suffer the consequences. In this environment, Captain Beyer probably felt that if anyone were to make mistakes, it should be him. I never had the opportunity under this skipper to handle the ship except in the open ocean. The *Vance*'s next captain let me take the ship out several times and once allowed me to bring her in to the Bravo Piers. This was the extent of my ship-handling experience. I might have developed into a decent ship handler, but unfortunately I'll never know.

Most embarrassing was a bad approach to the pier in Pearl Harbor, especially at the conspicuous Bravo Piers, where the audience included the crews of neighboring ships, the squadron staff in the watchtower, and darn near anyone walking along the busy pier. One sunny day as we entered the harbor after a day of operating up the coast, I stood on the fantail watching the skipper maneuver toward our assigned berth. One DER was moored ahead of our assigned space, another behind. Both captains stood on their respective decks watching us, possibly out of concern for the safety of their ships. The momentum of 1,680-ton ships colliding even at a snail's pace could do considerable damage. The loud grinding screech of steel against steel as the ships come to rest against each other results in some buckling of the quarter-inch-steel sides, and if lucky, that is the worst of it. All ships have dented steel plating from gently bumping against piers and other ships.

This time the captain overshot the berth and glided gently into the fantail of the neighboring DER. Its skipper looked pissed, but controlled himself as he stared over at our bridge. Captain Beyer, with a guilty red face, called down from the bridge a weak, "Sorry." Several of our stanchions, the vertical posts on the edge of the deck that support the lifelines, were torn from the deck where the bow scraped along the neighboring ship. I noticed my easygoing shipfitter Williams standing there with a tired look on his face. Williams, a quiet, slim, black sailor from the rural South, rarely displayed his emotions. My life would have been so much less stressful had we ten more sailors as competent and dependable as Williams. With the sound of crunching of metal, Williams knew his evening and tomorrow would be spent welding stanchions to the deck. No need for me to tell him to do the job. And his welding was beautiful. I was thankful for Williams being aboard.

This time the stanchions were the worst of it, just a few more sizable indentations and scrapes in the steel hull well above the waterline. No real harm done that a little cosmetic paint wouldn't cure. The real damage involved pride and egos. Although we bitched among ourselves, both wardroom and crew were proud of the *Vance*. Embarrassing public exhibitions hurt. The audience of sailors on the neighboring ships grinned and fired a few salvos of comments and catcalls to our deck crew. There was a shortage of proud, cocky sailors on our fo'c'sle that day. Had the *Vance* glided gracefully up to the pier, the crew would have stood bold and quiet, proud of the ship's performance and proud to be a *Vance* sailor. Alas, it was not to be that day.

A Leaky Port Side

On January 25, 1963, we were once again underway for ocean station, my eleventh patrol. The weather quickly turned nasty and living conditions miserable. Heading north to ocean station placed us at the mercy of the prevailing western winds, which drove the waves against the port side. Waves breaking amidships on the port side leaked seawater into the crew's living space on the main deck.

When the *Vance* was modified to become a DER, the midsection of the ship was enclosed to provide additional living space, thereby disrupting the ship's sleek lines, leaving her looking bloated. Sensitive to adding more topside weight to the already top-heavy new radar antennas, the designers used aluminum rather than steel to create living and equipment spaces on the main deck. The modification brought two forces into play. First, the sheets of aluminum plate corroded due to electrolysis, the chemical reaction of the new aluminum bulkheads in the proximity of the original steel hull in a saltwater environment. The aluminum began to break down. Second, the extended aluminum sides were located over an expansion joint at frame 96. Expansion joints ran amidships in the main deck, effectively compensating for the lateral expansion and contraction of the ship's hull. This movement, together with electrolysis, eventually cracked the aluminum bulkhead at the expansion joint. We attempted every conceivable permanent solution, yet the cracks always reappeared in rough weather. I wish I had a dollar for every hour the shipfitters spent welding this area. The best solution, although temporary and ugly, was to tar burlap over the cracks.

In rough weather with waves slapping high against the port side, the burlap would give way. We then took in seawater on the main deck from each wave. Flooding was minimal, just seepage, except that it played hell with the living conditions for the operations-department sailors living in the space. Picture this narrow passageway of a space, sixty feet long stretching fore and aft. It reminded me of a bowling lane, with water substituting for the ball. Each time the bow pitched down into the sea, the seepage grew to a wall of seawater racing forward down the passageway, creating havoc. When the bow then rose again, the accumulated water reversed course and grew in size as it raced aft. The teeter-totter effect continued until we could find a better course and the water was swabbed up. Both sides of the passageway were lined with built-in drawers for personal gear. Above them were bunks stacked three high. The best a sailor could do was hope the passageway waves didn't run into the lockers or the lower bunks. Fortunately, we rarely had to contend with large amounts of seepage. Unfortunately, we never solved the problem of cracked aluminum at the expansion joint.

Airborne Early Warning Squadron Pacific

Nothing especially exciting happened on this patrol. We had another airdrop of electronics parts shortly after arriving on station and managed to pick the canister from the water without incident. The weather remained nasty for most of the time. After twenty-one days at sea with no opportunity to drift, we stopped at the Midway Islands to refuel before heading home. The Midway Islands visits were not especially exciting. For the crew, Midway was just another fuel stop, a long 1,150 nautical miles and three days steaming from Pearl Harbor and liberty. The islands provided a home for both hundreds of thousands of seabirds and the navy air squadron that flew the DEW Line.

Airborne Early Warning Barrier Squadron Pacific, twenty-five hundred men strong, was headquartered at Barbers Point NAF on Oahu, with a detachment at Midway and a re-

An Atlantic Barrier US Navy Lockheed WV-2 flying over USS Sellstrom *(DER 255) off the coast of Newfoundland, Canada, in March 1957. (US Navy photograph.)*

pair facility at Honolulu International Airport. Their mission was to keep four to five aircraft on barrier patrol at all times, just as we kept one or two ships afloat beneath them at all times. The aircraft took off every two and a half hours, flew the fifteen hundred miles from Midway north to the Aleutians, and returned, about a fourteen-and-a-half-hour flight, often in difficult weather. The planes and crews deployed for eighteen days from Oahu to Midway, and flew seven barrier missions, approximately 102 flight hours, per deployment.

To fly the barrier route, the navy employed an interesting, if ugly, airplane, the Lockheed WV-2, referred to as a *Willie Victor*. This workhorse of a plane, a modified Super Constellation, had four piston engines, which permitted a maximum speed of 285 knots and a range of 3,850 miles. Like the DER, the *Willie Victor* was also subjected to an ugly modification designed to do the job. The DER lost its sleek lines by enclosing the midsection of the ship. The designers were absolutely merciless with the *Willie Victor*. On the sleek Super Connie body were attached two large radomes, one below the fuselage containing air-search radar and one above the fuselage equipped with a height-finding radar. The net visual effect was that of a pregnant camel, its popular name for those of us who didn't have to fly in it.

The *Vance* and the *Willie Victor* were both radar platforms. Ours was afloat for twenty to thirty days, and theirs was in the air for fourteen hours. The difference had to do with the intensity of the experience. An aircrew of twenty-seven was crammed into the plane and stood a two-section watch, four hours on and four hours off, with blurry-eyed radar and sensor operators rotating frequently. This mass of humanity squeezed into the aircraft was to search for and, if possible, identify air and surface contacts. If warranted, NORAD fighter aircraft were launched to intercept any reported unknown or hostile radar contact.

Rarely was there a real alert on the barrier patrols. The aircrews found the job boring, repetitive, and tiring. My guess is that when they encountered rough weather, the boredom evaporated. The *Willie Victor* did not easily fly above the turbulence. I understood that when crossing 40° north latitude, the aircrews put on rubberized immersion suits. Without the suits, there was no chance of survival in the cold North Pacific. With the rubberized suits, their chances weren't much better because we were the folks assigned to retrieve them from the sea.

Sea-air rescue was something we practiced but not very confidently. The concept of having a rescue plan and drills was valid. You had to do something should a plane go down. The problem was that in rough weather, we were unlikely to save a single *Vance* sailor in the water, let alone rescue an entire downed aircrew. If the aircraft were able to control the landing, we were taught to empty large cans of firefighting foam over the fantail, making a long white trail in the water to guide the plane to our location. It was essential that the plane put down near us because time was everything. Privately among ourselves, we debated the chances for a successful rescue and concluded that the seas must behave, visibility must be good, and the plane must set down on our doorstep. Other factors were the sharks that fed on our garbage and our ability to locate and retrieve people from an angry ocean. If Mother Nature and luck were with us, then we might be successful. Fortunately, over the history of the squadron, an aircraft never went down at sea on the Pacific Barrier.

I often wondered if I would trade places with the navigator on these flights. In college, I turned down the opportunity to join the brown-shoe navy. My eyes were not good enough to be a pilot, and thus I likely would have ended up a navigator or CIC officer flying *Willie Victors* on barrier patrols. These squadrons absorbed a large percentage of reserve officers. The thought of long, tedious, and dangerous hours in the air, flying from unexciting desolate airbases like Midway, was not inviting. Still, they slept on terra firma every night.

At times, I was jealous over their short-term isolation. As they flew overhead, we occasionally chatted on the radio. The aircrews appreciated us being down here, yet who could resist a few digs given our miserable condition? "We'll be thinking of you tonight while having a drink at the O Club on Midway," or "We're heading back to Hawaii tomorrow and to the women of Waikiki." The bastards. We were jealous. Yet there was a stupid, stubborn pride exhibited by the DER sailor, like a boxer who gets the shit knocked out of him and goes on to brag about how he could take the punishment. Yes, we gave up precious years of our young lives stoically riding the rough seas. We received scant recognition or compensation. Still, there was a sense of pride in having taken whatever Mother Nature doled out, meeting the demands of the captain, squadron, navy, defense department, and everyone else tasking the *Vance*. We barked back at the aircrews overhead. Were we jealous of their short trips? Yes, but we were too proud to show it.

The macho sea-dog mentality melted upon hearing a sweet female voice in the middle of the barren Pacific Ocean. On occasion, when identifying civilian airline contacts, we spoke with Pan American stewardesses overhead. Now, 1960s-vintage stewardesses were a select group of beautiful creatures. A female voice over the radio connection was all that was necessary to set me off in a fit of depression. A beautiful woman was talking to me, in that, "Honey, I feel sorry for you" voice as she jetted by for an exciting weekend in Seattle, San Francisco, or the Far East. The patrol suddenly seemed longer, the situation more miserable, almost unbearable. I was spending my prime years in the middle of the fucking ocean with maybe 140 other unhappy men. The happy ones, and there were a few, were in need of professional help. I wished I had never heard her voice.

Lighthouse or Warship?

Refueled and all four engines cranking out sixteen knots, we departed Midway to arrive in Pearl Harbor at two in the afternoon on February 21 after a three-day dash home. The following days in port, the crew was busy preparing for an inspection by Rear Admiral F. Virden, Commander Cruisers and Destroyers Pacific. Shortly after surviving the admiral's inspection, the *Vance* was subjected to an intense week of daily exercises in the operational training area off the Oahu coast. At times like this, I was thankful for being a snipe. Operational training focused on the gunnery department firing their popguns and dropping depth charges, with the operations department assisting in CIC and communications. All the officers were actively involved, either on the bridge, CIC, or weapons-fire control—all, that is, except the supply officer and the engineers. We engineers down in our holes were responsible for keeping the ship moving and at times responding to a few engine or steering casualty drills. We were experts in engine-room casualties. As the damage-control officer, I had my teams respond to a few drills, nothing we couldn't handle well.

The emphasis was on testing the fighting capability of the ship. The first few days, the program called for antisubmarine-warfare (ASW) drills, during which the *Vance* dueled with a boat from the Pearl Harbor Submarine Base. The bridge, sonar, and CIC frantically worked together plotting submarine contacts. Originally built to fight submarines, the *Vance* was impressively armed with hedgehogs, homing torpedoes, depth charges, and a respectable sonar system. While our ASW weapons systems were adequate for the 1960s, the hull and power plant were World War II vintage, when slow, submerged German U-boats chugging along at a few knots could be run down by a twenty-one-knot destroyer escort. War games with nuclear-powered submarines capable of twice our speed tended to be discouraging. When the submariners felt sorry for us and sent out the slower, older, diesel boats, we had a chance to be taken seriously.

Never involved in the ASW exercises, I received the details of the day's events from exhausted fellow junior officers over beers at the officers' club, stories of considerable tension and frustration and captains having temper tantrums when the exercise was a bust, which it often was. I cannot recall these bull sessions ever being positive, never a claim that the day went well, only tired, worn-out shipmates and an occasional effort at humor. The exercises were coordinated team efforts involving a large number of men. A perfect exercise was a fantasy. Harvey Payne reported the bridge scene to me after one such failed exercise. A frustrated, raging, red-faced Captain Beyer threw his steel battle helmet across the bridge. It crashed into the bulkhead, rolling to a stop at Harvey's feet. The ever-cool

Harvey picked it up, walked over to the captain, and quietly with a sober expression said, "Your helmet, sir." This Rumpelstiltskin performance, straight from the *Brothers Grimm*, was no fairy tale to the crew, nor was this an isolated incident. Commanding officers were under considerable pressure to perform. These were the times I was happiest to be a snipe.

The fantail scuttle hatch continued to be my favorite spot for observing what was happening topside. Air attacks were real shows, and I loved to watch them. Of course, the hatch was supposed to be closed, but everyone was too busy on deck to notice a spectator. The aircraft for the exercises were from a fighter squadron at Barbers Point Naval Air Station, located in the cane fields on the south shore of Oahu. The pilots must have gotten a kick out of the exercise. They probably fought for the job. I concentrated, knowing how easy it was to miss the fun with the planes coming at us a hundred feet off the surface to avoid radar detection, the scream of the jet engines heard only after the attack. Our radar was late in picking up a pair of fast-moving A-4 Skyhawks hugging the surface, coming in low and fast off the starboard beam. In desperation, our battery of two three-inch guns spun around to face the incoming threat only to arrive after the planes had passed overhead. Hello! They attacked and were gone before our gunners could lock on them.

As we watched their vapor trail, two more Skyhawks almost scraped our radar antenna as they roared by from stern to bow. Again our guns proved too slow. I could not take this exercise seriously. We were no match for modern aircraft. There was nothing to get angry about. Trying our best was not enough. The *Vance* was an outdated weapon of war. We served a purpose as a long-range radar platform that floated in midocean, an extension of land-based early warning radar. I guess the drills were necessary in that the *Vance* was classified a navy warship and had armament. Being outperformed by modern submarines and jet aircraft didn't help our egos. In a different environment, against an opponent lacking modern weapon systems and with our control of the air, we might have performed well. The job we did day in and day out could be carried out by a civilian ship or noncombatant vessel with the appropriate radar and communications equipment.

On the fourth exercise day, our boss, the Commander Escort Squadron Five, went to sea with us to observe a refueling-at-sea exercise. Refueling was always an interesting demonstration of seamanship. Boats Oldervick's deck apes hauled in and attached the fuel line from the oiler on a rolling deck, while maintaining the proper tension on the fuel hose as both ships steamed close together on a parallel course. We looked good. No helmet throwing or cursing today. We did well, and the boss was aboard. The next and last day of exercises called for shore bombardment; the three-inch guns were noisemakers, as was the skipper over some poor shooting that day.

My Twelfth Patrol

Monday, March 25, two days after our last exercise, the *Vance* was underway for barrier duty, my twelfth patrol. The high point was the final sea-anchor dunking. Captain Beyer accepted defeat. The last and strongest of the anchors snapped and shredded within minutes after hitting the water. Privately the deck apes were relieved. The captain finally gave up on the project. Deck apes, normally great showmen, were tired of the abuse from the crew that went with the sea-anchor pageant. Sailors would ask with tongue in cheek, "How's the sea anchor coming?" "You guys still sewing canvas?" "That's one beautiful wooden cross." "Maybe two crosses would work, or three?" I never heard another word from Boats or his men about sea anchors, nor did the skipper bring up the subject again.

Everyday life at sea was the same from patrol to patrol: the routine of watch standing, a normal workday, dinner and a movie, then the bunk. Bull sessions rarely happened at sea. Privacy was lacking. The wardroom was too public for airing one's feelings. The bunk room was private, but there was no space for lounging, only three desk chairs along a narrow aisle. The bunks would be ideal, except someone was always asleep early in anticipation of the midwatch. All bull sessions took place ashore over a drink at the bar.

At sea, the wardroom was the fiefdom of the captain, whether he was present or not. When the captain entered, we all stood out of respect. After dinner, pipe in hand, he would settle in his reserved seat for the evening movie. The junior officer would operate the 16mm projector, while the rest of us would settle in a chair or on the deck for a movie, which for a brief time had us forgetting we were in the middle of the Pacific Ocean. Movies were the most popular pastime at sea. I can only recall one movie session in three years that I despised. On a Sunday afternoon, the skipper decided he wanted to see, for the second time that week, *The Ten Commandments*, with Charlton Heston as Moses. Charlton's facial expressions, those of a man under stress, had me wondering how he managed this look of constant agony in all his movies. My guess was that the prop people fastened a paper clip onto his penis. Regardless of how the look was achieved, I was stuck operating the projector, five full reels, just me, the skipper, and his pipe on a Sunday afternoon. I saw this as inhumane, possibly a violation of the Geneva Conventions.

This is not to say there were not moments of humor at sea—perverse perhaps, but humor nonetheless. We lived in close quarters, seven of us in the junior officers' bunk room. At all times of the night, sailors came in to either wake someone for the next watch or receive authorization for an outgoing message. Now Harvey liked to sleep on his back in the nude, usually without covers. When at sea, Harvey's aerographer mates launched weather balloons every four hours, the resulting data to be sent by message to the weather center in Hawaii. After a night launch, one of his sailors, usually the junior man, a young impressionable kid, entered the bunk room, message clipboard and flashlight in hand, to obtain Harvey's signature to release the message. The young sailor was confronted with a peaceful, sleeping Harvey uncovered and in the nude. The poor kid approached Harvey's chest-high bunk, his flashlight beam revealing a huge penis, perhaps the largest penis on board, sticking straight up above the sleeping Harvey. The sailor tried to wake the soundly sleeping Harvey without touching him and without staring at the pink monster. "Mr. Payne, Mr. Payne." Once awake, Harvey would ask a few questions, routinely sign the message, and go back to sleep, having taken no notice of his huge appendage or the discomfort it was causing the kid. Occasionally in frustration, one of us awakened by the noise would sign the message release and let the poor sailor be on his way while the laid-back Harvey slept on.

Harvey, a math major in college, was a focused person, who would concentrate on a specific event, often ignoring or being unaware of the peripherals. His perception was a rifle shot, rather than a shotgun blast. Harvey dealt in logic, never to be swayed by convention or peer pressure. He could not be rushed. This was a very logical, thinking man with the unfailing ability to tell a five-minute story in twenty minutes. The man was generous with his time, fair, and always courteous. He was a wonderful friend, and he was liked and respected by his men.

After sixteen days in an unruly ocean with no opportunity to drift, we set a course for Adak to refuel. The next day I was on the bridge as we entered Adak. Twenty-six knots of wind and five-foot seas were giving us trouble as we tried to enter the port. The pilot was on board, and two harbor tugs were assisting us. Captain Beyer had his hands full. We encountered strong gusts of wind, keeping the ship away from the pier. The *Vance*'s excessive freeboard area played hell with our ability to maneuver. The harbor pilot was there to advise, but the skipper was responsible for the ship. Watching the skipper nervously directing the tug at our bow while overseeing the *Vance*'s efforts to combat the strong offshore wind, I was happy this was his responsibility, not mine. I respected the man for the responsibility he shouldered. Knuckles white, his turkey nobble prominent and rigid, and pipe stem about to snap, Captain Beyer was trying his best to ease the *Vance* to the pier.

Eventually we arrived. Lines were doubled up, and we began taking on fuel.

After five hours in port, topped off with diesel fuel and king crab legs, we were underway once again for ocean station, but not before I scrambled ashore to the officers' club for the first time. After a brief stay on ocean station, we headed for Pearl Harbor, arriving on April 18, at which time we learned the *Vance* was scheduled for an R&R trip to Japan following the next patrol.

CHAPTER 14

Japan

April 18–July 13, 1963

When I lost my rifle, the Army charged me 85 dollars.
That is why in the Navy the Captain goes down with the ship.
—Dick Gregory

Escape Impossible

Three and a half weeks in Pearl Harbor, then two-plus months deployed, first underway for ocean station on the DEW Line, then to Japan, back to ocean station, and finally back to Oahu in mid-July. No question about it, I was excited by the prospect of visiting Japan. Still, I was tired of the long periods at sea and depressed by the thought of another year and a half on the *Vance*. I had completed twelve long patrols and had at least ten more to look forward to. Did I have an alternative? Was there a way off the ship? Several officers transferred off the *Vance* in less than three years, but most were career navy. Fred Levin and Jim Kunz, both like me, were in the naval reserve. They were applying for orders and hoped to eventually make the navy a career. Fred was looking for a shore billet, and Jim wanted a command-at-sea billet.

Perhaps I too could work something out with the navy, a trade of sorts. I would consider extending my obligation for one year if they assigned me a favorable shore billet. I would then have served two years on the *Vance* and two ashore before becoming a civilian once again. The navy showed an interest in me that suggested I might have some bargaining power. Out of the blue, BUPERS offered to change my status from reserve to regular navy, which meant a commitment to a twenty-year career. The navy sought to retain good officers, which meant that every junior reserve officer who wasn't an obvious loser

247

received the same letter. I had no intention of accepting the offer. If they thought so highly of me, I would offer my services for an extra year on the condition BUPERS got me off the ship and onto dry land in Europe or Japan.

I submitted the request, only to be turned down by BU-PERS. Others had gotten off their ships in two years, so why not me? I was uncertain what role the skipper played in the negative response. Did he provide a positive endorsement? I believe he meant well, but I have since learned that skilled and effective writers are rare. If the endorsement was of the same quality as my fitness reports, I doubted the document would be persuasive. I was confident he would not have intentionally sabotaged my attempt to escape the *Vance*. There was no logical reason to keep me aboard. I was just a quiet junior officer with no particular flare or impressive achievements. On my semi-annual fitness reports, the skipper rated me in the middle of the pack of junior officers. Perhaps I needed the friend I didn't have in BUPERS. I would never know the reason my request was denied.

There were other ways off the ship, none of which my pride would allow. Although I was always seasick for several days when underway, I came to accept this curse and never attempted to be excused from sea duty because of chronic seasickness. It never entered my mind that seasickness was a way off the ship. When writing this memoir, I learned that allowances were made for a seasick senior radioman on the *Vance*. He received a transfer to a shore billet.

There were other ways to get ashore. An officer from one of our sister ships, whom I noticed periodically at the O Club, sat at the bar for over four months waiting for the navy to do something with him. Rumors were that he was a kleptomaniac and that a number of penknives and other small missing items were found in his desk. He was immediately removed from his ship and given a room at the BOQ, the very establishment that Jim Kunz and I unsuccessfully tried to talk our way into just to have a place to live off the ship. In other situations, captains went to great lengths to transfer incompetent officers, usually to shore billets. I was just not clever enough to find a way off the *Vance*. Apparently I was being groomed to become the next engineering officer, and there was nothing I could do about it.

As much as I dreaded ceremony and spit and polish, I was desperate enough to wish for a berth on the USS *John S. McCain* (DL-3), a huge frigate always moored in the prime berth at the Bravo Piers. Three times our tonnage, almost five hundred feet long with a crew of four hundred, she was the flotilla flagship. Sailors referred to the *McCain* as Permanent Building #3. I was impressed with the fact that the *McCain* never seemed to go to sea. I liked that. I heard that she was a newer ship and that her 1,200-pound steam propulsion plant, newer technology, was plagued with problems. The other greyhounds in the flotilla were World War II–vintage ships, older but with proven steam plants. Fortunately, I never tried to have my wish come true. I am certain the *McCain* eventually got underway and was a credit to the navy.

Charity Begins at Home

I put my dreaming and scheming aside when the skipper invited the wardroom officers and their ladies to a day on a private island on the windward side of Oahu. What a lovely time sipping a glass of wine on the veranda under the palms. The house overlooked a tidal swimming pool that abutted the ocean. The island, lunch, and drinks were ours for the day. I never learned who owned the island or who paid for the refreshments. Someone said there was some affiliation with an insurance company.

I began to better understand the opportunities and temptations that availed themselves to a ship's captain. All commanding officers controlled a market. Our skipper was the gateway to a captive audience of 160 men. He controlled access. In port, I never gave a second thought to the civilian insurance salesman huddled with a sailor at the last table in the mess decks. The man, a frequent visitor when in port, was selling life insurance, and there was no way he could be there without the captain's blessing. There were no competitors. One time an encyclopedia salesman made a presentation to the assembled crew in the mess decks. The silver-tongued salesman, with the captain's strong endorsement, even nailed me for a subscription. Stupid me. It is difficult to believe that the captain or the ship's recreation fund did not receive something in return for his cooperation—insurance, a set of encyclopedias, a party, whatever the vendor was hawking.

The most common civilian service was the laundry truck. Logically, one laundry truck could efficiently service the ship. I never paid much attention to the laundry truck servicing us in Hawaii, although we always had the same one. Someone probably approved the arrangement. In Japan I noted to a fellow officer how punctual the designated laundry service was. He laughed, telling me how his destroyer deployed under classified orders to the Inland Sea. Their laundry truck was waiting for them at the pier when they arrived. Years later, a high school friend told me how he negotiated laundry services for aircraft carriers in San Diego. Another friend, who commanded a major warship in the Mediterranean, described to me the vendor offerings for access to the crew. The gatekeeper to the crew has probably always been presented with enticements—free laundry services, encyclopedias, meals ashore, and whatever. Some skippers accepted this as their due; others, including the next captain of the *Vance*, avoided the practice. I recall he only encouraged the crew to join the Navy Mutual Aid Society, an excellent organization, an action with no accompanying personal benefits.

Captains, like office managers, face real or at least perceived pressure to have their crews contribute to a local charity drive. Everyone in the American workforce has experienced this call to contribute for the unit to achieve 100 percent participation. We have all been there. The inference is that strong participation by the crew or office staff implies that morale is good and the captain or boss is doing a good job. A memorable moment in our annual squeeze for charity was when the XO applied pressure for 100 percent participation. Neither my snipes nor I were excited about participating. Most of them probably qualified for charity, considering the size of their paychecks. I would announce the drive and the benefits of the charities. I applied no pressure.

The pressure was applied from above. The snipes were behind the other divisions in contributions. Told to try harder, I was gently addressing the topic with a group of snipes huddled in the rear of the mess decks, when the XO joined us. He came on with the hard sell, stressing the importance of giving to the needy. The men were uncomfortable at being directly shaken down by the XO. They dared not appear negative. Executive officer was a powerful position, though not quite the magnitude of captains, who were godlike. Still, they were to be respected and obeyed. Obviously, the snipes weren't buying his charity pitch, but could not bring themselves to openly disagree or challenge the XO's assertions. A meek, faceless voice from the back of the group asked, "What do we get out of it?" Taking advantage of this opportune question, the XO cited the benefits they received through the Honolulu YMCA, a recipient of the charity funds.

Herbert Key, our rural Mississippian and troublemaker, blurted out, "They're all fuckin' queers at the YMCA." Engles and I looked at each other and rolled our eyes. The XO froze. His expression was blank, a deer in the headlights. He was caught off guard, stunned at being challenged. I guess he realized there was no effective comeback. He stiffened, gained control of himself, and just walked off. I never heard another word about the incident or the snipes' poor showing in the charity drive. I hoped the captain and XO now better understood the enormity of my job, rather than attributing the incident to my poor leadership.

Which Half Would Float the Longest?

We waved good-bye as the *Vance* backed from the pier. My thirteenth patrol was underway. The date was May 13, and the weather was fair. My focus was on Japan rather than Joan. Soon she would leave for a work-related position on the mainland for the summer months. I wouldn't see her again for four months. I realized our relationship was showing signs of wear. I certainly enjoyed our time together and wanted to continue being with her, and yet I avoided the idea of a commitment. Joan most likely read me correctly. She probably understood that my hesitation meant our relationship had no real future. Or perhaps she was growing tired of me. All I understood was that Joan made life wonderful in my present predicament. The problem was I was living in a temporary environment. Over the horizon, there were no more ships in my life, just a lot of the world yet undiscovered.

After three days in transit and an uneventful eleven days on ocean station, we steered a course for Adak to refuel. Entering the Adak harbor, the ship had a steering casualty, a serious condition that necessitated turning the rudder by hand from the after steering room. The problem, a loss of oil in the hydraulic system, was quickly corrected. We entered port and took on sixty-eight thousand gallons of diesel oil and two ensigns who were hitching a ride to Japan. In five hours, we were underway for ocean station once again, and the two young officers were experiencing their first taste of the DER navy. They did not opt to return from Japan aboard the *Vance*.

On the thirty-first after being relieved on station, we set a course for Yokosuka, Japan. I spent my free time reading books on Japanese history and culture. Old hands who had been to Asia were reaching into their repertoire for juicy sea tales about liberty in Japan. Others were researching the great bargains on stereo and photographic equipment available on the Japanese market. The weather was fair and the crew excited over the prospect of R&R in Japan.

Posturing was not limited to the crew. In the wardroom, the

captain, XO, and Don Dunn had all been to Japan before. Of the three, only Mel Huffman, the XO, had the need to inform us of his vast experience with non-Western cultures. As the ship's navigator, Mel was sometimes on the bridge when I had the watch. Occasionally I had to put up with his antics. On one occasion, friendly Mel pulled out his Zippo lighter with what appeared as black lines of Japanese script covering the case. He encouraged me to look more closely. The supposed script was actually stick figures demonstrating thirty or forty positions for intercourse. He then threw out a few Japanese words, demonstrating his firm grounding in the culture with a vocabulary of perhaps twenty words. Pronunciation was another matter.

Three days from Japan, we had an event that diverted my interest from the adventure ahead. A favorite spot for the chiefs and senior petty officers to complete their paperwork, play cards, or bullshit was the last table in the crew's mess, just forward of the expansion joint in the deck on the starboard side. A chief who happened to be sitting there one afternoon mentioned to Don Dunn that there were low squeaking sounds in the deck beneath him. Don and I went to investigate. We had the green asphalt floor tiles removed beneath the table. Finding the steel deck plates cracked, we followed the crack line across the main deck from starboard to port, paralleling the after expansion joint at frame 96. We removed the asbestos insulation below in the engine room, revealing the underside of the crack. To our amazement and chagrin, the steel-plated main deck was severed, extending the full thirty-six feet across the ship from starboard to port.

This was serious! The ship's two major strength members, keel and main deck, flexed to absorb the forces along its 306-foot length. The potential to break in half was very real. Each time the bow rose to meet a wave and then crashed down into the trough, tremendous stress was placed on the flexing keel and main deck. In rough weather, I had witnessed the movements of other ships in the squadron and the *Rotoiti* in the Antarctic, their hulls protruding half out of the water as they reached out over the crest of a wave. I could readily visualize the danger of the forward half of the ship's weight suspended and twisting, placing considerable stress on the main deck with each wave we plowed through. Was the cracked deck the result of extreme stress from having carried ten thousand gallons of diesel in the forward void for two years or more? Or was the crack just the result of age and rough seas?

Too late to be concerned with possible causes, I found myself walking softly, as if another 150 pounds would make a difference. Word spread quickly, and the crew immediately understood that the situation was serious. For me, the danger was especially vivid. I was fresh from Damage Control School and probably one of the few people aboard with formal instruction, scant as it was, that addressed a ship's structural integrity. There was little we could do in the middle of the Pacific Ocean but tell our bosses and seek terra firma.

Our flash message to the squadron commander resulted in an order to proceed directly and carefully to Japan for repairs and have an officer witness the micrometer readings of the keel along all 175 frames. Engles grabbed his micrometer, and the two of us spent a day and a half crawling through voids and bilges, measuring and recording. There were no problems with the keel. For the next three days steaming to Japan, I was sensitive to every squeak and groan from the old hull. I continued to walk lightly, as did the crew for the most part. Few spoke openly about their concerns. Still, one could detect that the crew was a bit more subdued, except for the usual few blowhards seeking an audience with their devil-may-care posturing.

The skipper thought this an opportune time for an abandon-ship drill. The previous times we drilled, the crew waltzed lightheartedly through the exercise with laughter and open life jackets. This time the drill was a sober, quiet affair. Men quickly lined up on the open deck beside their assigned life rafts. Life vests were strapped around bodies as tight as sausage casing. The deck apes took the time to carefully check the emergency rations in the life rafts as we steamed carefully those last few long days across the Pacific.

A Tourist in Japan

The weather was kind to us. We steamed happily into Tokyo Bay on June 7. The *Vance* followed in the path of US Naval Commodore Matthew Perry, who in 1853, with his Black Fleet, sailed into this same bay. While Perry went on to open trade and diplomatic relations between Japan and the United States, we ignored diplomacy and focused on trade, cash for: cameras, turntables, speakers, tape decks, pearls, and china. And yes, we were interested in R&R and ship repair. The *Vance* headed for the naval shipyard at Yokosuka.

Now that we were safely in port, I saw the positive side of the cracked-deck problem. The *Vance* would be in the Yokosuka shipyard for at

> **Yokosuka Naval Base**
> Yokosuka was a small quiet fishing village when Commodore Perry sailed into Tokyo Bay in 1853. With the opening of Japan to the modern world, there was an obvious need for the ability to build and maintain oceangoing vessels. First Yokosuka became the site of an ironworks, and by 1886 had evolved to become a naval shipyard. In the twentieth century, Yokosuka was a main arsenal of the Imperial Japanese Navy, reaching its peak during World War II with 40,000 workers in 1944.
>
> Following the war, in 1947 the US Navy reactivated the facility for the maintenance of its naval ships. The navy base became increasingly important with the outbreak of the Korean War in 1950, and since has been the major maintenance and repair facility for the US Seventh Fleet in the Far East. Located at the entrance to Tokyo Bay, Yokosuka is conveniently located twenty miles from Yokohama and forty miles from Tokyo.

least two weeks. I was hoping for three weeks. Unlike the Pearl Harbor yardbirds, the Japanese workers quickly swarmed over the ship and were doing a good job. This time efficiency was working against my tourist ambitions. My worry was, could I get leave in Japan or was I stuck with the responsibility of staying aboard to oversee the repair job? Bless you, Captain Beyer and Don Dunn. I was granted seven days' leave. Don would oversee the repair job. He had been to Japan a few times and had no great desire to be a tourist.

Jim Kunz and I took off for a quick cultural tour after a few days in the Shinbashi and Ginza districts, Tokyo's main shopping, dining, and entertainment areas. In the early 1960s, the hotels and food were still affordable—but just barely—on a junior officer's pay. Following the famous Tokaido Route, we took the fast train to the old imperial capital of Kyoto. With a student guide, who was practicing his English, we spent a few days walking the city. Kyoto was one of the best-preserved cities in Japan, with its two thousand Buddhist temples and Shinto shrines, as well as palaces, gardens, and architecture, all still intact after World War II.

Although the great economic miracle was well underway, goods and services were affordable and cities still lingered in tradition. I usually made an effort to be inconspicuous in foreign countries. This was not a possibility in Japan. There was no hiding our foreignness and our size. Most everyday items, including train seats, beds, bathtubs, shower stalls, and cars, were miniaturized. I didn't envy Larry Hanson at six four or Bob Baker at six six as they strolled together in Ginza, like a walking freak show. Normally Japanese are scrupulously polite; that day in Ginza, they stopped and stared.

Our guide found Jim and me a little inexpensive, traditional Japanese inn on a back street in Kyoto. We were the only foreigners in residence. Sleeping on the floor, meals in the room, and a community washroom were interesting features. In the communal washroom, while sitting on the Western toilet, I discovered that my knees stuck out, preventing the stall door from closing. I could see a lady approaching. Embarrassed, I frantically attempted to turn sideways on the toilet, tuck in the knees, and pull the door closed as she passed by on her way to the communal hot tub. Shelving my modesty, I soaped down, rinsed, and then joined the other guests, mostly families, in the large hot tub. They came in all shapes and sizes, offering polite hello nods while focused on their bathing. No one spoke English. My Japanese vocabulary included yes, no, hello, please, good-bye, and thank you. Thankfully, there were no young beautiful girls bathing.

Returning to Tokyo, we traveled north to Nikko and the Toshogu, the lavishly decorated shrine and mausoleum of Tokugawa Ieyasu, the founder of the Tokugawa Shogunate. The shrine was especially noted for its woodcarvings, including the famous three monkeys depicting hear, see, and speak no evil. They brought back memories of how my snipes depicted me in the Deep Freeze cruise book as the division officer who knew nothing. The hurt was still there.

On return from leave, I was able to explore the local scene. Yokosuka, at the entrance to Tokyo Bay, once the center for Japan's World War II naval forces, was now the home of the US Seventh Fleet. In short, Yokosuka was a sailor's town—narrow streets riddled with bars, whorehouses, massage parlors, noodle cafes, pochinko parlors, and more. The US Navy was here in force. Several destroyers, a cruiser or two, and a massive attack aircraft carrier were in port, along with thousands of sailors on liberty and shore patrols to keep order. The bars and brothels were filled with drunken sailors, loud sailors, and sailors and women peeing in the open benjo ditches, and probably some positive events and establishments that I missed.

Here, led on by tales of the Orient, I experienced my first and last foot massage. I anticipated an exotic setting with beautiful little women washing me down, taking me into a hot tub and steam room, caring for my every need, and finally, the famous foot massage and a quiet moment of reflection. What I endured was a quick scrub down by two girls, followed by my head sticking out of a commercial steam box. In the next box, a reeking drunk sailor, unable to hold his head up, was half asleep. With a towel around my waist, I was led to a row of mats. The few strings of beads dangling between each mat were intended to suggest privacy. Stretched out on my mat, I could take in the entire noisy operation of perhaps forty men being washed, cooked, and stomped on. A cute little lightly clothed Japanese girl, between age twelve and twenty-six, walked on my back for a while, then popped each finger and toe joint. I paid up and left, realizing the place was ideal for sailors to sober up before returning to their ships and nothing like the romantic postwar Japan of the silver screen.

Not knowing my way around Yokosuka was the problem. I would never have enough time ashore to learn much about the area, let alone Japan. We were tourists, as was the fleet. Traveling with the fleet on a real destroyer, I would have had similar experiences in Hong Kong, Subic Bay, and wherever thousands of sailors were let loose on liberty. Being slow and ugly, the *Vance* didn't travel with the big boys, the fast-moving task force. Nor did we have to endure sharing liberty ports with thousands of fleet sailors. I couldn't be happier. Steaming independently usually allowed us to be a big fish in a small pond. Attached to a task force, we would never have experienced the personal attention and care shown us in New Zealand, Australia, and Tahiti. With the fleet in Yokosuka, I was just another of the hundreds of junior officers streaming ashore at liberty call. The experience reminded me somewhat of a large cruise ship disgorging thousands of anxious tourists in a Caribbean port for the day. They work their way through a gauntlet of merchants, as do the fleet sailors, only different merchants, merchandise, and ports.

CVA-387

We were definitely in Yokosuka with the Seventh Fleet. Destroyers were moored alongside us. A huge aircraft carrier loomed across the harbor, and a cruiser was in the area. Captain Beyer was very aware that we were among the big boys, the real US Navy, which he emulated. Rubbing shoulders with the Seventh Fleet called for the *Vance* to make a positive impression, so he fervently believed. Although yardbirds were still crawling over the ship repairing the main deck, the skipper nevertheless insisted on a high level of formality and militarism. This came as a surprise. After all, we were in the shipyard for repairs. If this were the Pearl Harbor shipyard or if the Seventh Fleet were not in port, it would have been business as usual.

The skipper couldn't resist trying to make an impression. Out came the *Vance*'s honor guard, with their rifles, white helmets, scarves, spats, and gloves. Each day a four-man honor guard in full dress uniform with shiny rifles marched to the fantail, raised the flag in the morning, and lowered it each evening, to martial music piped topside over the 1MC loudspeaker. The sailors on the neighboring destroyers were astounded. I could hear their catcalls, and one yelled out, "It's CVA-387." The letters CVA designated an attack aircraft carrier, the 387 our hull number. They mocked us for mimicking the daily ceremony aboard a four-thousand-man attack carrier that had a band-and-bugle ceremony. The word was out. Each day we drew a crowd of hecklers on the neighboring destroyers, sailors who enjoyed starting the day with a mug of hot coffee and a little humor. We never disappointed them.

Our sailors of the once-proud honor guard begged to stop the flag detail and just raise and lower the flag like every other ship in port. The twice-daily humiliation was too much to take. Men tried in vain to avoid color guard duty. I noticed the captain observing the spectacle one evening from the 01 deck; he then turned and left without a word. He was well aware of the problem but chose to ignore it. The music continued to blare forth, and the color guard did as ordered. The only way I could understand the skipper's refusal to relent was that he must have considered rescinding the foolish order as a loss of face.

A Romantic Night in Atsugi

With a duty-free weekend coming up, I planned an overnight trip to the US Naval Air Facility at Atsugi, a reasonable taxi ride away. My old college roommate Bob Yohe, who hung out with me on Oahu, was full of stories about the great liberty there. Bob, a navigator in a Hawaii-based naval air squadron, often flew the Hawaii-to-Atsugi route. He told wondrous tales of visiting the local Atsugi girlie clubs. I was enticed by his description of how the clubs operated. Buy a few drinks, find an interesting girl among those working there, and if she approved, arrange to go home with her after closing. At her apartment, she would prepare tea or your favorite drink, perhaps a small late dinner or snack, watch some TV, make you comfortable in this domestic setting, and settle in for the night. Japanese girls pampered you with a night of bliss at a reasonable price. Now this appealed to me because it appeared civilized, private, and domestic. Bordellos didn't interest me. The pound of flesh on exhibition, selected and paid for, the room upstairs, and the clock running were repugnant. I was just horny enough to believe that Bob's Atsugi love nests were different.

To share the taxi cost, I linked up with Salts McKillop, a new ensign on board. Salts was a likable, easygoing guy, a good-hearted person who was not meant for a military organization. When Salts reported aboard for the first time, he forgot to wear the collar devices that indicated his rank. Jim Kunz immediately bestowed the name "Salts," suggesting a crusty seafaring man. The name stuck.

Salts and I arrived by taxi at one of the two clubs Bob had suggested. After a few drinks and talking with the girls, we agreed to find our own way back to the ship the next day. I chose to go home with a pleasant little Japanese girl. In the dark of night, I had no idea where the taxi dropped us off. Her apartment was a bedroom in a house with the usual paper-thin walls, no kitchen, no food, just an old double bed with an open spring mattress, nested in a huge 1890s Victorian-style wood frame. A small TV was across the room. I had envisioned something more snug and domestic, but I remained optimistic.

Down the hall, I found the bathroom. I tried the latch. Locked. Then it opened, and a little old lady padded out, bowed, and smiled. A couple of little children and a man peered around the corner in the hall, bowed, and waited their turn for the bathroom. Back in the room, I asked the young lady who these people were. Apparently she was relatively new to the business and was renting this room from the family until she could afford her own apartment. Like most Japanese houses, the paper-thin walls allowed sound to travel freely. I was in a fishbowl with a family: a mamasan, papasan, and who knew how many little children in residence. So much for a quiet, comfortable evening of refreshments, sex, TV, and being waited on. I was very uncomfortable, self-conscious, and ashamed with the family sharing the house. I was mortified when the lot of them knocked, then entered our room, to stand at the foot of the bed, bow, and I think wish me good night, as I sat there nude under the sheets.

They probably rented out a room from necessity, while the big-spender, conquering Yankee ravished a Japanese girl on the premises. I could not be comfortable in that house. Very early in the morning, I asked the bewildered young lady to call me a taxi, placed her money on the nightstand, and fled back to the *Vance*. So ended my ill-conceived attempt to buy a night of domestic bliss. I guess I always knew deep down inside I couldn't buy what I really wanted.

Back aboard the *Vance*, there were more important matters to be addressed: the purchase of Japanese stereo equipment, cameras, flatware, dishes, and pearls, all at bargain prices. I focused on stereo equipment. Amplifier, tuner, turntable, tape deck, and speakers for me; twelve-piece settings of flatware, glassware, and china for the family. The ship's hold was filled as we departed Japan. The yard workers did an excellent job of gluing the *Vance* back together, just too quickly for my tastes. On June 21, we were underway for Adak.

Back on Ocean Station

Five days later, we steamed into Kuluk Bay and moored at the Adak fueling pier. Besides the need to take on fuel and king crab, there was Don Dunn's promotion to lieutenant to celebrate. The message of his promotion arrived while we were in transit to Adak. The captain loved a party. At the skipper's suggestion, Don threw the traditional wetting-down party at the Adak Officers' Club. Most of the wardroom was in attendance.

With Lee Cole in the States attending DCA School, Don and I were the only engineering officers aboard, a guarantee that I would have the duty. We couldn't have both engineers off the ship. While the ship took on fuel, the party attendees took on alcohol. The celebration quickly consumed Don, as did the bottle of champagne the skipper produced and directed Don to empty immediately. He was dumped onto his bunk, and to this day doesn't remember much of the event or how he got back to the ship. At six in the evening, we were underway for the one day of steaming to ocean station.

After fourteen days on ocean station, the *Vance* started for Hawaii. On a hot sunny July 13, we doubled up the lines at the Bravo Piers, the completion of my fourteenth patrol. With almost two years on board, any hope of getting off the ship in less than my full three years was fading fast. A more realistic scenario was that Don's promotion meant he would soon have orders off the *Vance*. Guess who would be the new engineering officer.

CHAPTER 15

My Department

July 13–September 7, 1963

Hold faithfulness and sincerity as first principles.
—Confucius

The New Executive Officer

As we doubled up the lines at the Bravo Piers, a short, muscular officer reported aboard. He was a bit old for a lieutenant, probably in his late thirties, meaning he came up through the enlisted ranks before securing a commission. His name, Hainyard L. Horne, had a nautical ring to it. Understandably he preferred the middle name, "Les," or to us underlings, XO. Yes, a new executive officer was reporting aboard. My guess was that the man lifted weights. A barrel chest, hard biceps, and a flat stomach filled the short-sleeved white uniform shirt. The tight upper lip, serious eyes, and bald head suggested a quiet, sober approach when introduced. BUPERS continued to keep us off-balance, sending a replacement who appeared to be the exact opposite of Green Jeans, a bulldog to replace a poodle.

We wardroom officers were reserved and careful from the start. The captain's new enforcer for the next year and a half didn't look friendly, especially after we had become accustomed to the convivial Green Jeans. Les Horne's arrival was to be the major turning point of my life on the *Vance*. Only years later, when reflecting on the events of 1963–64, did I come to understand the importance of Les to my last year aboard. As with most notable events, time must pass before we understand the factors influencing the changes that took place.

The return to Pearl Harbor was significant. The *Vance* was to undergo a much-needed shipyard period, free from the DEW Line patrols for the next six months. First, there would be

263

an administrative inspection, followed by a period at the destroyer tender at Ford Island, then into the shipyard. After the yard period, we would undergo testing of the ship and retraining the crew in preparation to once again resume our job on the DEW Line. A busy schedule, all on terra firma.

My recall of the administrative inspection is dim except for Mel Huffman's swan song, an indelible event on my brain. I am uncertain of the timing of the inspection except that it occurred before Les Horne took over as XO. Counter to the natural response of trying to look one's best, we engineers again showed all our warts and willingly took our lumps, reasoning that by presenting our true condition, we would receive the time and funding needed to correct the discrepancies. The squadron commander, his staff, and the ship's officers sat under the canvas awning on the *Vance*'s fantail as the chief inspecting officer summarized the inspection results.

The strengths and discrepancies were noted, and each department head was permitted a rebuttal. We engineers accepted the criticism. In the navigation area, it was noted that the navigational charts had not been updated. Green Jeans, our ship's navigator, leaped to his feet in defense of his area of responsibility. He had failed to ensure that the quartermaster keep the charts updated. With both hands on the podium, he leaned toward the audience with his best "I've got you this time" grin and proudly stated, "The charts for Hawaii and Japan are up-to-date." Poor fool. The inspecting officer happened to be Sam Gravely, the Jackie Robinson of the US Navy. He was the first black man ever to command a US Navy ship, the USS *Falgout* (DER 324). It didn't take much upstairs to realize that this commander was an outstanding officer, chosen to be in the forefront of the long-overdue effort to integrate the conservative naval officer class. This man, preordained to be the first black admiral, returned to the podium, smiled, and stated, "It is heartening to learn that the condition of the *Vance*'s navigational charts permits the ship to operate in two places on earth, Hawaii and Japan."

We junior officers slouched down in our chairs, embarrassed once again by association with our leadership. Several months before, in Dunedin at the Miss *Vance* Coronation Ball, I experienced this same deep sense of embarrassment. *Am I on a ship of fools? We worked our asses off and had pride in the ship, only to be identified with this public embarrassment.* Had I not been young and idealistic, perhaps I could have just laughed off the event. Or was I proud of my ship? Did the captain feel the embarrassment I felt? He must have. Yet Green Jeans was leaving us as a lieutenant commander, having been promoted several months earlier. Obviously the wardroom officers did not hold the man in high esteem. We were just happy to see him depart.

Finally Chief Engineer

Lee Cole was back from DCA School ready to take over R division. Don Dunn was awaiting orders, and I anticipated leading the department through the overhaul. The yard period promised about four months of uninterrupted *cold iron*, which meant all services were to be provided from the pier. The engines would be silent. The crew would eventually move into barracks, except for the few daily watch standers when the ship went into drydock. The Pearl Harbor Shipyard was to address ship modifications and hull repairs. They would not overhaul engines. Yet our main propulsion engines were key to the rebirth of the engineering plant.

Together, Lee Cole, Chief Mooney, and Engles approached me with the idea of overhauling all four main engines, a monumental task. They had talked it over with the men, and together we committed to overhauling all four main engines before departing the shipyard. To accomplish this major undertaking, the men volunteered to work in two twelve-hour shifts six days a week. This said a lot for the chief's and Engles's leadership and the men's pride in the department and the ship. Sensitive to double standards, we snipe officers and chiefs worked when the men worked. The worst possible message was to flaunt the benefits of rank by going on liberty when your men have to work. I was amazed, impressed, and humbled that the plan to work twelve-hour shifts was not dictated from above, that it came from the crew.

I was never self-deceived enough to think that the snipes were doing this for Lee or me or even for Engles. They committed to the task because they knew the work needed to be done and they had pride in their work and the ship. I liked to think that the snipes believed that Don, Lee, and I cared about them and the engineering plant. I liked to believe I was respected for my attempt to treat them fairly, punishing the lazy and incompetent and rewarding those who tried their best. I liked to believe that despite my obvious technical ignorance, I gained some respect by trusting and supporting the leading petty officers. I was certain that Lee's and my relationship with Chief Mooney and Engles was positive, or the snipes' voluntary offer would not have been forthcoming.

If one were to select an animal to characterize my first two years in the *Vance* wardroom, it would be a tortoise. I played at being Ensign Pulver. I avoided calling attention to myself and stayed clear of the captain and the wardroom. The less perceptive officers with whom I had little personal contact may have seen me as quiet and perhaps by extension weak. On a one-to-ten flamboyancy scale, I probably registered a three. Perhaps by now the reader better understands my preference to play the tortoise. I lacked confidence my first year as main propulsion assistant, and I operated in the shadow of Don Dunn, a strong-willed and likable guy who had his own agenda and little support from the captain. In short, I had no power to change anything. With seniority and a changing cast of characters, the tortoise revealed his true nature, that of a snarling Chihuahua.

After two years aboard, I became the engineering officer, responsible for the efforts of sixty men and two officers in the two divisions. My ascent and coronation were to some extent in accordance with the simple tradition that seniority rules. Any officer with seniority and having done a passable job would be advanced to the next more-senior position. We waited in line. Now after two years in engineering, it was my turn to become department head, and after me it would be Lee Cole's turn. In my case, there were a few twists and turns before receiving the crown.

The skipper, now twice passed over for the next rank, that of commander, was destined to leave the navy after he completed twenty years of service. His naval career was to end. He was a lame duck to both the *Vance* and the navy. His future had been determined: one more assignment and then forced retirement on half-pay and a search for a second career. It was a difficult time for this man who loved the sea and cared about his crew and his officers. In his last months aboard, I believe the captain was trying to help his officers' careers, especially that of Don Dunn, by rotating department heads, a maneuver traceable to the concept that the naval line officer was a Renaissance man, capable of managing any and every department on board. The maneuver was intended to embellish the service records of his more-senior officers, to show they performed in a variety of positions, even if only for a few months.

This game, playing musical chairs at the department-head level, was poorly timed. We were nearing the crucial three-year shipyard overhaul cycle, when the ship was to be repaired and upgraded before enduring another difficult three years at sea. When the music stopped, Don Dunn went from engineering to operations, Bob Baker from gunnery to engineering, and Larry Hanson from operations to gunnery. In focusing on his officers' future, I believe the skipper ignored what was best for the ship.

Captain Beyer was trying to enhance Don Dunn's service record by assigning him to a different department after Don had served as the chief snipe for the past two years. Don was scheduled to receive orders off the *Vance*. What was the value of a month or two as operations officer? Larry Hanson, who spent almost three years in operations, was near the end of his three-year obligation and couldn't care less about taking on a new job. He would be a civilian in a few months. Bob Baker, a late arrival on the *Vance*, was also due for orders. As a result of these moves, each man's service record would reflect experience in having managed two different departments aboard the *Vance*.

I didn't like the unintended implication of this game of musical chairs, that it made no difference which officer headed the department on a destroyer escort. Were department heads only figureheads? Bob Baker, my new boss, knew nothing about engineering, and worse still, he had no appreciation of our two-year struggle for resources and respect and our objective of having a first-class engineering plant when the *Vance* emerged from the shipyard. He and I were on a collision course. The collision occurred in the first week of his reign. I cannot recall Bob's precise order, except that his order required that we temporarily pull the snipes off the critical engine overhaul schedule. This was major. The work schedule was already stretched too tight. Our objective was to overhaul all four main propulsion engines before leaving the shipyard.

The damage from Bob's order would occur months later, when both the skipper and Bob were long gone. Bob was reacting to something the captain wanted. Lacking a background in or loyalty to the department, Bob was not equipped to advise the captain otherwise. It was easier to say, "Aye, aye, sir," and do the captain's bidding. I explained why the order was detrimental to the ship. Perhaps I was too rigid by implying that my snipes were untouchable. I certainly wanted to ensure that they were not available for the usual "all hands" tasks. Bob brushed my objections aside rather than attempt to convince the captain. It was easier to do what the skipper wanted.

Two dynamics were at work here. First, Bob wanted to clearly communicate to me that he was the boss. He had been at the job a week, and this was our first disagreement. Here was a six-foot-six tower of a man unaccustomed to doing the bidding of a Chihuahua, a junior Chihuahua at that. What better time to establish his position? In the military, we were taught to carry out orders, a necessary rule to ensure we were all rowing together. However, there was an obligation to speak up when the question was, "Are we are rowing on the correct course or heading for the rocks?" Perhaps I might have handled the situation better. Unfortunately, my personality did not permit a more effective response, if there was one.

A second factor was that Bob didn't want to argue a point with the captain. With no experience in the engineering department, he may have lacked the confidence to go this route. If he had brought me into the discussion with the captain, this could be interpreted as an open admission that he could not handle the job. I had been in this same position several times because I could not sufficiently explain a technical problem or engine casualty. You swallowed your pride and brought the CPO or senior petty officer with you to help explain the issue. It undermined your position, vividly portraying to the captain your technical shortcomings. For myself, there was never an alterative because I was not a good bullshitter and I wanted to do the right thing, even at the risk of showing myself to be inadequate. In this instance, Bob was just carrying out the captain's wishes, the easy choice. Why listen to me and put himself at risk with the skipper? A good officer salutes and carries out the order. After all, this was the captain's ship. Bob's decision was logical, safe, and self-serving. Had the issue been with gunnery, an area more familiar to him, I am certain Bob would have argued the point.

I was left with the option of carrying out Bob's order or I could fight. In this situation, my first loyalty was to my snipes and our goal. The stubborn tenacious Chihuahua within me refused to carry out the order, thinking Bob would come to his senses and listen to reason. I was wrong. Bob put me in *hack*, restricted to the ship. Department heads had this power to discipline the junior officers in their charge. I had never before witnessed it on the *Vance*. Being in hack didn't bother me, but stopping work on the engines did.

Les Horne, who had recently relieved Mel Huffman as XO,

defused the confrontation by suggesting that cooler heads prevail. I was no longer in hack. Knowing I was heading for Waikiki after work and his car was still on the mainland, Les Horne asked me for a ride to Waikiki, where he was to meet his wife. We squeezed into my MG roadster for the thirty-minute drive. Les had only been aboard for a few weeks, and we were already impressed. The clean-shaven bald head, thick muscular body, immaculate appearance, and quiet reserve suggested this man had a large dose of self-control in a body that screamed out, *don't trifle with me.* Our wardroom of college-boy officers had little in common with Les Horne, who probably had never set foot on a college campus and was at least ten to fifteen years our senior. This man was no kid and no greenhorn. What Les Horne did have was experience, brains, integrity, and intense loyalty to his shipmates and the US Navy.

I was wired and ready to explode after the confrontation with Bob. In the passenger seat was this man whom I scarcely knew. Les was a man of few words, and he selected these words carefully. He rarely raised his voice and was courteous to a fault, and yet I knew the man could be explosive. Our conversation led to engineering, and I became emotional, dumping on the man the problems and frustration of two years of trying to square away the engineering plant. Intuitively I knew I could be honest and direct with Les. I explained that the yard overhaul was our one chance and that I had no intention of compromising or backing down from this objective. My snipes had been shortchanged on equipment and felt ignored by the command. In a burst of energy, I let it all hang out, a release of emotions too long constrained.

Les Horne was what he appeared to be, a sincere man interested in the good of the ship and the navy. What I did not know was that he was a friend and past shipmate of the new captain of the *Vance,* due to report in a few months. Whatever I said to Les apparently was the right tonic because my life and that of the snipes changed in September with the arrival of the new captain.

The next day, the captain's request that started the uproar was forgotten, and the snipes continued with the engine overhaul. With the XO's guidance, Bob backed off, probably realizing that the exhibition of power was hasty and constituted overkill. Shortly after, Bob moved back to gunnery. Within a month, Larry Hanson and Don Dunn departed the *Vance*. Bob Baker left shortly after. Either Captain Beyer realized that logically I was the next in line for engineering officer, or perhaps the new XO recommended I be moved into the position as quickly as possible for the sake of continuity. We were scheduled to begin the shipyard overhaul in a few weeks, during which time the engineering officer ran the show. Changing engineering officers in the midst of an overhaul was best avoided.

Why did the XO champion me for the position? Aside from being the logical choice by having the seniority and experience, I believe the day we had the heart-to-heart conversation on the road to Waikiki cemented our relationship, an unspoken bond. I can't recall ever having a drink with Les. Well, maybe once or twice as part of a group at the Pearl Harbor Officers' Club. His life was private, or maybe he was just a bit old for us boys. Yet we got on well. I must have impressed him with my sincerity and passion over fixing the engineering plant. I was willing to gamble all just to keep the department on the right track.

My relationship with Les Horne continued to be positive during this, my last year aboard. Only once did I test his self-control. We were alongside the tender prior to going into dry dock. I was on the fantail talking with my officers when the 1MC loudspeakers barked out, "Engineering officer, report to the XO's stateroom on the double." I hurried forward and looked for him in his stateroom. From the forward officers' head, Les Horne's unmistakable voice erupted with an icy, "Get in here." There stood the XO, his immaculate white uniform covered from head to toe with his own shit. His face was red, and he was trembling. "Get this fixed and report back to me" was all he could manage to say as he fought to control himself. "Aye, aye, sir," was all I dared to say as I beat a hasty retreat.

Apparently one of our shipfitters had removed a valve from the fire main for repair and then replaced it, but forgot to bleed the air from the system in the forward officers' head. The fire main ran fore and aft through the ship, distributing saltwater for firefighting, toilets, and urinals. With the system back in operation under pressure, an air hammer built up in the forward officers' head. The XO came in to work that morning decked out in an immaculate white uniform, took a dump in the small enclosed-toilet compartment with the door closed. Les must have stood up before flushing, judging from the shit pattern on the bulkheads, door, overhead, and of course on Les. The moment he flushed, the man didn't have a chance. He must have liked me because I survived this incident. A year and a half later, when Les Horne, now a lieutenant commander, was captain of his own ship, a minesweeper, he offered me the XO billet, to be his second-in-command. Needless to say, I had no intention of leaving dry land ever again, but I appreciated the generous offer and Les's confidence in me.

A Changing Wardroom

The composition of the wardroom was changing. Les Horne took charge of the *Vance* in his own quiet way. There were two months at most before Captain Beyer was to be relieved. His heart was no longer in the job. He was doomed to become a civilian landlubber in a few years. The man always preached that a sailor belonged at sea and that he loved being underway. I felt sorry for him. He was a good person. Yet I was happy to see him go. I never understood how he could place his emphasis on ceremony over substance. Nor did I understand his love of the sea given that he had a lovely wife and family ashore. To me, the sea was like the desert, empty of people and the dynamics of human society. Perhaps the sea is an excellent refuge for quiet reflection, away from the ding of human activity. I prefer the mountains for isolation.

Wardroom of the USS Vance. *(Left to right, seated) Fred Levin, Bob Baker, Hank Beyer, Les Horne, Harvey Payne, the author. (Left to right, standing) Salts McKillop, Con Murray, Bruce Young, Jim Kunz, Ken Wood, Lee Cole, Richard Rightmyer. Pearl Harbor Shipyard, Summer 1963. (US Navy photo.)*

Captain Beyer had a final wardroom group photo taken in the shipyard. There he sat, Les Horne to his left and Bob Baker on his right. The three new department heads were Harvey Payne, Jim Kunz, and me. Fred Levin remained CIC, Bruce Young stayed in communications, and a new ensign, Richard Rightmyer, was the electronics officer. Ken Wood was now the ASW officer and Salts McKillop the first lieutenant. Lee Cole had returned from DCA School to take over the repair division, and a new ensign, Ed Furher, was due to report as the main propulsion assistant. The supply officer remained Con Murray.

Con Murray had joined the *Vance* some months earlier as we said aloha to Robbie. Con, a quiet, efficient supply officer, sported a thinning hairline, glasses, and a chunky but solid five-foot-eight frame. He seemed capable of absorbing considerable information rapidly. I don't think Con was overly challenged by the job. Perhaps this was why he volunteered to stand bridge watches. Supply officers were not expected to stand watches, nor were they expected to learn seamanship skills, such as ship maneuvers or navigation. Con Murray wanted to do it all, and he did it better than many. He became a dependable OOD underway.

After three years on the *Vance*, the big Dane, Larry Hanson, returned to civilian life. Larry was a friend who helped me out of a few scrapes. I would miss him. With his departure, I was now the longest-serving officer on the *Vance*. Then Don Dunn left for a new duty station. I had worked under Don for two years. We had fought the good fight together. Don's departure was necessary for the engineering department to be truly mine. I was too long his apprentice. Next, Bob Baker received his orders and departed.

I was happy, finally the chief snipe and six months on terra firma. What more could one ask for? Yet I did have more. I didn't have to live on board for the next three months. The ship was not habitable during much of the yard period. Single sailors were assigned a barracks, and the single officers were provided a stipend for civilian housing. All three department heads happened to be single and close friends. Harvey Payne had the operations department, and Jim Kunz took over the gunnery department. Together the three of us rented a neat little hideaway in Waikiki: two bedrooms, a living room, and kitchen opening onto a tropic courtyard with fishpond, banana trees, and flowers, a small but beautifully furnished tropical paradise. Our three stipends were required to afford this paradise. Rarely were we all at the house at the same time because we continued to stand a four-section watch on board even while in dry dock. After a sweaty day in the shipyard, an evening at our little Waikiki paradise was as good as it got for this single seagoing officer.

A Lean Year for Engineering

Why was the department in such poor condition? The nine months on Deep Freeze took its toll, as did our lack of senior petty officers while deployed. Most important, since our return from Deep Freeze, the department had been inadequately funded and the plant overly taxed. Neither helped morale. Why didn't we have funds for simple basic needs? I have no solid answers for this situation. The departments did not operate on budgets. Certain items, such as fuel and oil products, had a separate funding classification, as did ammunition. They were mission-related and handled outside the command. The *Vance*'s supply officer managed a budget for normal supplies and materials. Recently, Robbie explained to me that Captain Beyer personally approved these requests from the various departments. The skipper determined the funding priorities, and we never knew the size of the pot, although I am certain it was small. Most items were in the ship's spare-parts allowance. Deployed on Deep Freeze, we were fully supported. I was told we received whatever we asked for. Back with the squadron, I believe all DERs operated on very tight budgets. As with most organizations, there are benefits associated with not going to the pump too often for special consideration. We all made do with what we were allotted: squadron, ships, and departments.

Shortage of funds led to a number of growing problems and makeshift solutions. We strived to overcome and be rid of the pervasive jury-rigging mentality that was ingrained after months of doing without and poor morale. For example, a couple of our enginemen were barbarians among machinery, masters at jury-rigging equipment. Why go through the trouble of ordering a repair part when a quick temporary fix worked? Why not jury-rig the unit while awaiting the part on order, and then never follow up by eventually installing the part? "Hey, the unit's running, why bother?" Or we didn't have the funds to order a part. Jury-rigging became a way of life, which could only lead to a ship being precariously held together by rubber bands and paper clips. We had been on this road. Aware of the problem, together with strong leadership in the trenches, we were headed in the right direction.

Periodically we would spend a week alongside the tender. Their limited services often were disappointing because our needs were great. We had been there before, took what they had to offer, and searched elsewhere for most basic needs. We begged, borrowed, and bartered for tools, materials, and machine parts. But now I sensed in the snipes a new missionary zeal in the search for solutions. For well over a year, the engine-room snipes had lacked basic hand tools and rags for cleaning equipment and themselves because we had no funds.

In these bleak days, the enterprising snipes discovered the air force discarded-equipment yard, a junkyard for usable items that the service no longer needed. We were not allowed to reclaim discarded navy equipment, while army and air force castoffs were fair game. The air force in particular was viewed as a land of plenty. EM2 Avery, a short skinny electrician's mate, and several other snipes, drove up to the ship in a borrowed flatbed truck with a huge air force missile launch unit. Frustrated, I blurted out, "What the hell are we going to do with a missile launcher, Avery?" Apparently in the drawers of the large discarded unit were usable hand tools, and the only way to get them was to take the entire launcher. The snipes unloaded the hand tools and dumped the launcher at the navy's discarded equipment yard. All this effort for a few basic hand tools.

The resourcefulness continued in the good navy tradition of cumshaw, the ability to barter goods within the naval community. I also remember EM2 Avery as our lead cumshaw artist. The wiry little guy was like a ferret, full of energy, searching, sniffing out opportunities. Our best source was the submarine base on Ford Island. Submariners were an elite group, and as such, they had excellent personnel, adequate budgets, and first-class engineering support for their boats. Their diesel boats were driven by the same Fairbanks-Morris diesel engines as the *Vance*. Since our return from Deep Freeze until the shipyard period, we would beg the submariners for their used cylinder liners. Other DERs did the same. We had no recourse; funding was scarce. Anything to keep the engines operating.

The only item of value that we had to barter was coffee, and the submariners couldn't get enough of it. Tools, sheets of stainless steel, and other items traded hands. A five-pound can of coffee was the coin of the realm. Fortunately our cooks could always be relied upon to supply the coffee. Resourceful as the snipes were, it was just not possible to trade for most of our needs. Still, every little bit helped, and the men's enthusiasm in their searches was heartening.

In the Shipyard

As the engineering officer, much of my time was spent overseeing the *Vance*'s shipyard work orders, most of which were modifications to communications

Vance in dry dock, Pearl Harbor Shipyard, August 1963. (Photo from author's collection.)

and radar equipment and hull repair. Life was smoother. I was reporting to Les Horne; the captain was rarely involved. I was enjoying my new importance. All liaisons with the shipyard were through me. My office, a mobile trailer, was nothing fancy: a World War II relic about twenty feet long, large paneless windows with trapdoor-like hinged wood shutters, and a couple of beat-up old desks inside with a telephone line. During the hot summer, tropical breezes blew through this open wooden shell, offering some protection from the heat. I couldn't be prouder of my office trailer. It was the only *Vance* office space during the yard period, and it was all mine.

For this, my third and final year on the *Vance*, I was the chief snipe, and I liked it. The responsibility was enormous for a twenty-five-year-old. One would be hard-pressed to find a civilian position with this magnitude of responsibility at my tender age. On the bridge or managing a department, we young officers were often responsible for the lives of the crew and, by one estimate, a ship valued at twenty-five million dollars (in 1957 dollars). Managing the engineering department and the *Vance*'s multimillion-dollar overhaul was my responsibility. Certainly there were limits placed on my role. I was there to achieve the most benefit from the funds available, prioritize the work orders, and press the shipyard for all we could get. The shipyard liaison officer, Lieutenant Larry Los, was a pleasant, energetic optimist. We worked well together, haggling over work orders, modifications, and anything that would secure more yard services for the *Vance*. On occasion tempers flared, but overall, we both did a creditable job and went on to be lifelong friends.

Vance in dry dock, Pearl Harbor Shipyard, August 1963. (Photo from author's collection.)

What impressed me most during the yard period was the ability to walk beneath the ship's hull while she was in dry dock. The month spent in dry dock provided an opportunity to clean and repair the hull and the sonar dome and to inspect the screws. I walked beneath this 306-foot-long mass of battered steel plating, thinking about how it had endured the last three years. Over the past year, organisms had attached themselves to the hull in the warm tropical ocean waters, eradicating traces of the cleansing benefits from the frigid Antarctic waters. This battered mosaic of welded steel plates had withstood constant pounding in some of the world's most violent seas. With difficulty, I tried to imagine how the forward half of this 1,680-ton mass was able to rise up from the sea, like a hooked fighting fish suspended at the crest of a fifty-foot wave, and then plunge down into the trough, accompanied by an audible bang and creaking of steel joints as the hull once again met the sea. I was impressed and amazed that the quarter-inch steel plating, supported by steel ribs and held together by the strength of the main deck and keel, could withstand this brutal, repetitive punishment day in and day out.

With these thoughts running through my mind, I walked beneath the hull with my new damage-control petty officer. We were forward on the port side when he poked his penknife at the quarter-inch steel hull. It went through like a hot knife through butter. Astonished, I urged him to keep jabbing. The hull in spots was paper-thin from corrosion. Apparently the sacrificial zincs attached to the hull for corrosion control were long gone. To the shipyard engineers, this was nothing new. The corroded sections of steel plate were replaced. I couldn't shake the feeling of vulnerability. For over two years, I had slept in a bunk within a few inches of this outer metal shell, listening to floating ice bang against the bulkhead in the Antarctic and an occasional whale rub against the drifting hull on a quiet summer night in the North Pacific. So little, a quarter inch of steel or less, separated us from an unforgiving sea. I kept pushing the knifepoint against the hull, looking for more weak spots, a foolish impulse, fearing that the shipyard might miss a weak spot. Obviously, they didn't. We had an excellent yard period, perhaps not achieving our full wish list, but what was accomplished was done well.

For a man who had spent the previous two years dreaming of nothing but women and liberty ashore in exotic ports, I was spending an extraordinary amount of time working on board or in my trailer office. Many a late evening, I drove home to Waikiki for a sandwich, a beer, and a bed. I was enjoying the job. I felt we were achieving something. The engine-room snipes continued to work their grueling schedule without complaint. Were we finally all rowing together? I was afraid to reach for this conclusion. With few exceptions, this was the same troublesome crew of snipes that was always well-represented at captain's mast. These were the ship's problem sailors. I kept waiting for the personnel problems to begin again.

I didn't work or worry all the time. Living in Waikiki was wonderful—weekends on the beach, concerts, and the nightspots. My social life improved with Joan's return in late summer. Hawaii, once again, was everything the travel agencies promised: the soft chanting of a native tune on a quiet beach after dark, surf and turf with a mai tai, cruising the Waikiki nightspots, cheap drinks and meals at Fort DeRussy, really cheap Thursday night one-dollar steak dinners at the Makalapa BOQ, and picking bananas in my garden yard.

The Captain's Farewell

I like to link the departure of Captain Beyer with another personality, a chief bo'sun's mate who reported aboard six months earlier. We now had one too many chief bo'sun's mates. The old salt of a chief with the cobra tattoo coming out of his ass was already comfortably situated in first division, with Boats Oldervick actually running the show. With one too many chiefs, the new arrival, a fleshy guy with a big mouth, was assigned as chief master-at-arms. This was a perfect spot because the man was not qualified to run the deck force. Since he passed considerable verbal gas, I'll call him Chief Gas. He was from the naval reserve, having spent most of his career as a weekend warrior, where advancement was a much easier road to travel. Having recently returned to active duty, he was terribly short on practical experience. Perhaps the casting was too good. The man was a born politician and industrious in feathering his own nest by focusing his energy on ingratiating himself with the captain.

Chief Gas's most memorable act was presenting a huge three-foot-square varnished wood plaque to Captain Beyer as a farewell gift from the crew. Of course, the crew had not been consulted. Mounted on the plaque was the usual presentation information, listing the dates Captain Beyer served aboard and a picture of the *Vance*. Especially interesting were the three-inch-high shiny brass letters "DER 387." The chief's presentation, made supposedly on behalf of the crew, took place on the 01 deck near the davits holding the ship's whaleboat. As I stood there in the crowd wondering how the man managed to get such nice, smooth, well-worn brass lettering for the plaque, especially when the paperwork would have had to cross my desk, my eyes locked onto the ship's whaleboat hanging from the davits. On the starboard side of the bow, the letters "DER 387" were faintly visible in faded gray paint, where once brass letters existed.

I looked into the crowd trying to make eye contact with Boats Oldervick. He wouldn't look my way. I just shook my head quietly in disgust, although I well knew that all kings were plagued with self-serving courtiers. Later, having given the event more thought, this wasn't a bad trade: the whaleboat's brass lettering for a new skipper.

CHAPTER 16

The New *Vance*

September 7, 1963–January 9, 1964

It was with a happy heart that the good Odysseus spread his sail to catch the wind and used his seamanship to keep his boat straight with the steering-oar.
—Homer

The Snipes Appreciated

On September 7, the crew in dress whites lined up in formation along the busy shipyard pier beside the dry dock in which sat the *Vance*, high and dry, the way I liked to see the ship, out of the water. The change of command was about to take place. Captain Beyer was turning over the *Vance* to Lieutenant Commander Ross Wright, a short wiry man, about five seven, with thinning hair. His thin face appeared even smaller under the broad visor and ballooning span of his hat, as if the hat would swallow his head. The position of the headgear contrasted sharply with Captain Beyer's, who always wore his lid cocked to the right and pushed back on his head, showing his entire forehead plus a bit of hair. Wright didn't show much forehead, but a pair of astute dark eyes was visible. Yes, we carefully studied our soon-to-

Ross W. Wright. (Photo courtesy of Anne Wright.)

be new master. We didn't know much about the man. He had been aboard for a week. I had escorted the man through my

283

engineering spaces and briefed him on the condition of the department. He was all business, no small talk, not unfriendly, just sober and noncommittal. At the podium, Ross Wright read his orders, and we had a new captain.

During the last ten days in the dry dock, the new skipper surprised me by going down into the engine rooms and talking with the men. Captain Beyer had limited his engine-room visits to weekly inspections when underway. I was uncertain of what to expect from the new man. The squadron staff was not blind, especially the older, experienced squadron engineer. It was well-known that the *Vance* had engineering problems. I wished I were a fly on the wall when Ross Wright received his welcome-aboard briefing from the squadron commander. I was certain he would get an earful about the poor performance and condition of the ship. Did we, the engineering officers, share responsibility for the ship's poor condition? Were we viewed as incompetent? I was uncertain of what Les Horne had said to the new skipper or what influence he had. The XO kept his thoughts to himself, although he knew my feelings and what efforts were underway in the department.

On his third day as captain, Ross Wright called me into the wardroom for a private talk and asked what he could do for the snipes. "How can I help, Tom? What do you need?" he asked. Before I could put together a reply, he offered, "Do the men have enough tools, rags? Do you think the snipes overhauling the engines might like work coveralls?"

I almost fell off the wardroom chair. In my two years aboard, the snipes were taken for granted, out of sight out of mind. You step on the gas pedal and the ship moves. Never bother to look under the hood. Here was a man who understood that yes, the electronics modifications were important and the guns had to work, but the mission of the ship, to travel to and sit in midocean for extended periods, deemed the condition of the engineering plant crucial. Therefore, the most important result from the shipyard period was that the hull and engineering plant be in good condition. The four big Fairbanks-Morse diesels, the centerpieces of the plant, were our responsibility, not the shipyard's, and the skipper understood this. I was a new man from that day forth, and engineering was a new department. Captain Wright began to regularly visit the engine rooms and talk with the men. The snipes received their rags and their tools. Most of all, they received recognition.

This may appear trite, but something as simple as clean rags was an important message to snipes who for months put up with scraps of disintegrating rags that had made too many trips to the ship's laundry. Did anyone care how the snipes were to clean the tools, machinery, and themselves? How about a trip down into the engine room with a few words of encouragement? An ideal time would have been when a gang of snipes was pulling a cracked cylinder liner. Well, the new skipper did all this and more.

On September 17, the dry dock was flooded, and the *Vance* was afloat once more. A tug maneuvered her to a shipyard pier. We doubled up the lines, took on shore services, and continued with the engine overhaul for the next month. In mid-October, Engles and Chief Mooney carefully tested each newly over-hauled main propulsion engine alongside the pier. By the big smile on the chief's face, I knew the tests were a success—four beautifully running engines. You had to know the snipes to re-alize how proud they were. No great fanfare, the usual "fucks" and "shit" were heard, but there was no edge on the banter. Best never to let on that you might be a damn proud and happy sailor. No way a snipe was going to show his true feelings, es-pecially to an officer.

Morale in engineering was excellent. Even the bad boys were behaving. In the previous two years, M division, and to a lesser extent R division, sailors were constantly in trouble. Don, Lee, and I were continuously in attendance at captain's mast. Men lost their stripes, forfeited pay, were restricted to the ship, and on occasion served brig time. Surprisingly, there had been no disciplinary problems since entering the shipyard overhaul. This suggested the beginning of a new era. I rarely had a disciplinary problem over the next year. Our snipes were basically the same bunch of sailors who had been so difficult to manage over the past few years, peppered with some new men and a few more strong leaders. I was amazed that even the bad boys joined the effort willingly. The atmosphere in the engine rooms changed to a new healthy defiance. "You're fuckin' right, we'll get these fuckin' engines overhauled." The men were tired of the criticism and equipment failures and being the brunt of jokes. They wanted to walk down the Bravo Piers proud of the USS *Vance* patches on their uniforms, telling the world they were serving on the best fuckin' ship in the squadron. Don't let all the bitching fool you. They always wanted to be proud of their ship, a ship with a failing engineering plant. Here was the opportunity to change it all.

Why the change? A simplistic explanation was that the new captain brought on the change. The officers and senior petty officers had started the ball rolling months before Ross Wright became CO. If the wrong man had been selected, all our efforts could well have been unsuccessful. Under LCDR Wright, the engineering plant, morale, and the ship in general blossomed. Initially I credited the senior enlisted leadership, especially the three first-class petty officers and Chief Mooney. Engles, in his quiet way, was the longtime key man in the division. Mac, the competent, newly arrived single man was popular with the younger sailors, and Alex was the brains and energy behind the record keeping. Add to this Chief Mooney, a knowledgeable and conscientious technician. These men supervised the months of work in the engine rooms. They led the team effort to overhaul the engines. If there were problems, and I'm sure there were, they were solved internally.

We might emerge from the shipyard with newly overhauled engines, but the engineering plant and morale would degrade rapidly without a captain who understood their importance. So where did we engineering officers fit in this dynamic? I had learned over the previous year and a half that without the support of the commanding officer, we junior officers could accomplish little. The captain was the ship. I liked to think that the senior enlisted men understood that Don, Lee, and I supported and protected the department as best we could. We carried out the captain's wishes as if the orders were our own. That's the way any good management system must work. Still, you can't fool the crew. Everyone understood who was in charge.

We engineers always showed our warts in hopes of attracting more funding. It didn't work. The funds weren't there for us or our sister ships in Escort Squadron Five. I was never privy to the navy's support policies for our squadron. I can only guess that we received funding commensurate with our importance to the navy's mission. Engineering's full-disclosure approach won no points with the CO and probably enhanced the squadron commander's belief that the *Vance,* beset with engineering problems, was the worst ship in the squadron. I am certain Captain Wright received an earful on the subject at his first squadron meeting. He also received an earful from his XO, Les Horne, about my feelings, the loyalty and pride of my men, and what we were doing to raise this phoenix from the ashes. Somehow the new captain, the shipyard period, the chief's and Engles's leadership, the snipes' pride, and Lee's and my determination all came together. There were no heroes here, just a bunch of men thrown together who cared about their ship.

While gaining a new captain, I said farewell to my close friend Harvey Payne, who headed home to California and law school. The electronics technicians presented Harvey with a farewell gift, a thank-you for being a good division officer and a nice guy. The gift, a book titled *All I Know About Electronics* by Harvey Payne had all blank pages. Harvey, a college math major, knew little about electronics. He learned to work with and trust his men. We all faced this challenge, managing areas in which we lacked technical expertise. I would miss this good friend.

Harvey's departure and the completion of the shipyard overhaul signaled the end of our housing allowance. Jim and

I returned to our bunks aboard ship. In our final days at the Waikiki house, we held a wardroom party, welcoming the new captain and celebrating the completion of the yard period. I got seriously drunk.

The next week was my last date with Joan. The coming breakup had been obvious since her return in late August. I wasn't especially bothered by it at the time. After a few more patrols, I missed her very much.

A Master Ship Handler

Nor was life perfect aboard ship. There were times I wished I wasn't in engineering. One such time was Captain Wright's first day on the bridge. He had taken command ten days prior to the ship leaving the dry dock. Several weeks later, after the newly overhauled engines were tested and back online, we prepared to get underway for the first time, to move the *Vance* to a new berth. The newly overhauled engines were cranked up, everything checked out, and the special sea and anchor detail was set as we prepared to get underway. The new skipper was on the bridge, maneuvering to back out of the slip, a narrow channel with piers and moored ships on both sides. I was in main control, listening to the engine-order telegraph bells briskly ringing. Our LP air tank was depleting rapidly. We warned the bridge that the reserve HP air was all that was left; we could respond to a few additional bells and nothing more.

There was panic on the bridge. The new captain was never briefed on the limitations of direct-drive diesels. He was never told that the engines must be completely stopped before reversing direction and that air pressure was essential to starting and stopping the engines. The bridge, initially, had about eleven bells available, and then a fifteen- to twenty-minute wait for the air compressor to replenish the air storage tank. The skipper had assumed that the *Vance,* like most any other navy combat ship, could instantaneously reverse and change speed without such stringent limitations and lag time. This was true for steam or diesel electric systems, but not for the direct-drive diesel ships of the Pacific Barrier DER squadron. No one on the bridge had thought to mention this little fact to the new skipper. Les Horne, the XO, who would normally have warned him, was also new to the ship. As engineering officer, I should have briefed the new skipper on the limitations of the engines. We were too caught up in preparing our respective departments to realize this major oversight. This was serious. The ship was moving. The skipper was conning the *Vance* for the first time, maneuvering in a tight spot a ship whose maneuvering characteristics were new to him. Then he learned that the ship's engines were about to be no longer available.

What comes to mind is Thucydides's famous quote, "A collision at sea will ruin your entire day," or in this case, an entire career. Instead, the crew was treated to the most masterful ship-handling display they had ever witnessed. The skipper used the rudder and the few remaining bells to avoid a collision with ships moored on both sides of the slip. Using primarily the rudder, he maneuvered the *Vance* safely back to the pier. Captain Wright was too exhausted from having escaped this potential career-ending situation to tear into us. I felt like shit, having let the new skipper down so soon. He received his briefing on the engines, and we officers, for the first time since I'd been aboard, began to receive ship-handling lessons. Ross Wright taught me how to spring off the two forward mooring lines to push the fantail away from the pier and neatly back out into the channel. God, we looked good. Eventually, we more-senior officers tried our hand at bringing the ship alongside the pier, a much more difficult feat. Unfortunately, the docking lessons were not frequent enough for me to develop self-confidence in conducting the maneuver. I would never know if I could have been a good ship handler.

My teacher, Ross Wright, was the best of ship handlers. The man knew ships well before coming to the *Vance*. Beginning with Liberty ships during World War II, he had ten years' experience in the US Merchant Marine. Leaving as chief mate, he switched to the navy and served on various ships, including command of an LST. Now the *Vance* smartly entered and left port. A proud crew continued to be in awe of his ship handling.

Underway with New Diesels

Beginning in mid-October and throughout the remainder of the year, the *Vance* underwent a series of tests, ranging from radar pattern tests to engine test runs. The center of attention for engineering was the full power trial, to determine if the twin propellers could achieve their maximum of 400 RPM for an hour. The propellers were linked to the big Fairbanks-Morse diesels through reduction gears. To achieve full power, the big diesels had to turn over at 720 RPM. It was a sunny, calm day to the north off Oahu. We gradually built up speed, Engles at the throttles, snipes gathered around the main control panel in B-2, others tweaking the big diesels, keeping an eye on exhaust temperatures. The bridge was letting us control the final lunge forward. The *Vance* was already at her maximum of twenty-one knots in a calm sea. Our efforts were paying off. The newly overhauled diesels inched up to 720 RPM. They then soared beyond their maximum and held steady. The normally reserved Chief Mooney had a big grin on his face. Mac, Alex, and the other enginemen cheered, and Engles lit a cigarette with a sense of relief.

For the snipes, after success with the diesels, the remaining tests and drills were of minor concern. Local operations for the most part were to reacquaint the crew with the usual series of drills and to get better acquainted with our new skipper. New to us but not to ships, Ross Wright knew what he wanted and how to achieve it. First and foremost, he was a seagoing man demanding the most from his crew. His sinewy frame and thinking eyes were warning flags that strong emotions were penned up in this small but tense body. What a temper! The new skipper would scream at his officers, and he too would throw his battle helmet onto the bridge deck if an operational exercise went afoul. He demanded perfection. Again, being a snipe kept me off the bridge, out of sight and out of harm's way when conducting training exercises.

Only once did he verbally clobber me on the bridge. I had brought the ship close to the fleet oiler we were traveling with. We stood there together on the starboard wing of the bridge, the oiler a few hundred yards off our beam on a parallel course. The captain apparently didn't like my having us close to the oiler. He screamed in my face, "What will you do if you have a steering casualty?" I took the best option. I ordered a course change, kept my mouth shut, and endured the verbal dressing-down, rather than try to defend my actions and debate the allegation. The man could be frightening and unnerving at times, but he was competent and fair.

Generally I found Captain Wright to be pleasant and engaging aboard ship and on the beach in a social setting. He appreciated the engineers. I guess we were the favorites in the wardroom. Yet I was never truly relaxed in his company, knowing he had a hair trigger that could deliver a stinging verbal assault. Hank Beyer had been more congenial, more comfortable to be with. Being smart, demanding, and observant, the new skipper was a scary man. I am certain Captain Wright was compassionate on occasion. A few times when I couldn't readily explain a technical problem to his satisfaction, he held back the verbal broadside and appeared to make allowances for my shortcomings. I walked cautiously.

In January 1964, we started Pacific Barrier patrols with a smooth-running engineering plant and a highly experienced skipper.

CHAPTER 17

New Ship, Old Station

January 9–May 26, 1964

The sea is everything. It covers seven tenths of the terrestrial globe.
Its breath is pure and healthy. It is an immense desert, where man is
never lonely, for he feels life stirring on all sides.
—Jules Verne, *20,000 Leagues Under the Sea**

*In his lifetime, Jules Verne spent almost no time at sea. He was enamored by the
sea and the concept of submarines, yes. But he had no experience with them.

My memory of the last six months aboard the *Vance* is uneven.
The events that occupied my attention in these final months
are more coherently revealed in four subject groups rather than
chronologically. The first three—my time at sea, the changing
wardroom, and my social life—are addressed here. The fourth,
my exit from the *Vance*, is addressed in the next chapter.

Three Patrols on Ocean Station

The *Vance* was about to cast off all lines and be underway for
my fifteenth patrol, the first of the four patrols I would make
under Captain Wright and as the ship's engineering officer.
As we once again cleared the leeward side of Oahu, the January winds whipped through us. I grabbed for my old friend,
the barf bucket. On station, the seas were high, the winds
strong. The skipper was experiencing his first DER North Pacific sleigh ride. For the next ten days, the seas continued to
batter us mercilessly, up to forty-foot-high seas, and winds to
forty-five knots.

Captain Wright quickly realized that he was the skipper
of the worst-riding ship type in the fleet and that his living
quarters were in the most uncomfortable location on the ship.
High up in his stateroom behind the bridge on the 02 level,
over forty feet above sea level, the captain was learning how

293

to deal with our version of a rodeo-bull ride. During a modest roll, my old fart sack in the bunk room pivoted in an arc of four feet. This same roll swung the captain's bunk twenty feet from side to side. In desperation, the skipper had Lee Cole's shipfitters mount his bunk on a set of gimbals to minimize the roll action. There was no way to avoid the pitching motion. The gimbals were a great idea. I wondered why previous skippers hadn't thought of it.

My new quarters, forward on the main deck adjacent to the wardroom, offered a smoother ride than the captain's, but worse than my old bunk aft. I now had my own stateroom, with a sink, desk, wardrobe, a bunk with bedsprings beneath the mattress, and a porthole that I ignored. There was nothing to see through it but the sea. A sound-powered phone near my bunk linked me directly with the engine rooms. A second one linked to the bridge, the captain, and elsewhere. A curtain over the entrance provided privacy from the narrow passageway that separated the three other staterooms and the communal head. I preferred my old quarters aft.

I had gained more spacious living quarters and lost the privacy I had enjoyed in the bunk room for the past two years. Now my seniority placed me near the head of the dining table. I could no longer be Ensign Pulver and remain in the background. With my new status came increased responsibility and tension. Don Dunn was no longer there as a buffer between the captain and me. Ross Wright was demanding, and I felt the strain of long work hours in the shipyard, operational training, and now once again, Pacific DEW Line patrols. Two-plus years on this tub was wearing on me.

Life wasn't perfect. I couldn't understand why intelligent people, like Hank Beyer, Ross Wright, Jim Kunz, Les Horne, and many of my shipmates over the years, enjoyed a career at sea. There was nothing out here but endless water, which we avoided touching, and then feared when the seas were angry. We might gaze romantically on this enormous expanse of water, but that grew old rapidly. Once, the seas were the avenues to adventure that linked faraway places. Air travel put a stop to that. If the oceans alone were not the attraction for a life at sea, the answer must be in the ship and not the oceans. The cruise lines knew this. They indulged the passengers with food, drink, entertainment, ports of call, anything and everything to avoid the boredom of continuous water. A cruise can provide a short escape, a break from the pressures of daily life. A career at sea is another matter.

After eighteen days of punishment from the waves and winds, the *Vance* set a course for Pearl Harbor. The new skipper, as we expected, knew his stuff. He knew ships and how to run them effectively. Often, Captain Wright would be in his bridge chair looking out to sea. I could feel his presence, his silent evaluation of the bo'sun's mate on watch, the helmsman's steadiness, and my attention to the course being steered. I was more familiar with and less apprehensive dealing with Captain Beyer on the bridge. Beyer was more approachable and for some unexplainable reason, less threatening. The new skipper also was approachable and friendly, but formidable. I always expected he was going to ask for more than I could deliver. The man knew what he wanted, and he expected precise, factual information. Captain Wright might joke and engage in a light-hearted conversation, but one always knew that just beneath the surface, there was tension. The man was all business. What stress I had built up in my new position dissolved the moment we reached Pearl Harbor after twenty-one days at sea.

Following twenty-one days in port, we headed back to sea on February 20, the start of my sixteenth patrol. Midwinter in the North Pacific was full of surprises. On station steaming at six knots, the wind suddenly shifted 90° and radically increased to gusts of forty, then fifty-five knots, and the seas rose to thirty feet. Suddenly, a thirty-five-foot wave struck the port bow, carrying away the huge aluminum weather shield on the forward gun mount. Bruce Young remembered standing the bridge watch as fifteen feet of sheet aluminum torn from the forward gun mount passed overhead to clear the bridge and the main mast. The force of the wave bent the quarter-inch steel gun mount bulkhead, damaged the forward gun, and tore a hole in the main deck. With each wave, seawater poured into the hole, flooding the forward amplidyne room below on the second deck. Unable to approach the hole from the wave-swept open deck, we plugged the hole as best we could from inside.

Why the damage? We had sailed in rougher seas without incident. A rogue wave? Difficult wave patterns to read? Who knows? At sea, these things happen in tricky weather conditions. Time to head for home. Only five days into the patrol, we headed back to Pearl Harbor. We were back in Hawaii on March 2, looking forward to more than a month in port for repairs.

The in-port days passed quickly. The sea and anchor detail was set as we prepared to get underway once more for ocean station, my seventeenth patrol. After clearing the harbor and the channel entrance, I assumed the bridge watch. The rest of the officers were at dinner in the wardroom. Surface traffic was heavy. There was a submarine leaving port behind us, a couple of destroyers and an oiler heading for the Pearl Harbor channel entrance, and about twenty radar contacts of various ships in the vicinity. The *Vance* began to roll and toss about as the seas picked up. My stomach was churning. My mind told me that I was about to start my usual first day out barfing. There was no way I could afford to get sick. The ship was my responsibility. There was too much surface activity for me to be sick. I couldn't imagine barfing over the radarscope or the Polaris compass while conning the ship in this traffic.

I stood my watch and managed to hold down my lunch. For the first and only time in three years, I didn't barf the first day at sea, nor did I barf any other day that patrol. Nauseous, yes. Barf, no. This event made me a firm believer that there was a psychological factor to seasickness. Perhaps one must be familiar with the phenomenon, an experienced veteran of seasickness, in order for the mind to rule the stomach. I'll never know for certain, because I was seasick on my next and last patrol. There has been no further testing of the theory.

There was a positive side to my last four patrols on Captain Wright's ship. Engineering was proving to be an efficient and favored department. The skipper understood that if the ship could not get to where she was ordered to go, the other departments, no matter how proficient they were, could not function. He realized that the Pacific Barrier duty was all about endurance. The main propulsion plant was to be respected. No longer were the engines abused during operational drills and war games. The snipes had adequate tools and spare parts. Their labor was appreciated. The captain made a point of visiting the engine rooms. The snipes were appreciated, and they knew it. My days of dealing with disciplinary problems were at an end—well, almost.

As chief engineer, my daily chore at sea was to report to the squadron the amount of fuel on board. This could be a difficult number to gin up. The oil king, a sailor whose job it was to shift fuel as necessary and take on ballast, took daily soundings in the multiple fuel tanks, an inexact procedure when the ship was rolling in heavy seas, yet an important task. The daily tally was important to determine how long we could remain at sea and to coordinate the arrival of the relief ship. The oil king had to be a dependable sailor.

You would never have guessed that my oil king was Herbert Key, the Mississippi redneck who had been the department's #1 problem child for the past two years. His appearance hadn't changed. Key remained a sloppy sailor. His vocabulary and worldview were unchanged. His observations continued to be prefaced with "fuckin'," and he firmly believed the US Navy was not where he belonged. What had changed was his attitude. He was proud to be a *Vance* snipe, in the best "fuckin'" engineering department on the best "fuckin'" ship in the squadron. Of course, he would never admit this to me. Amazing that after two years of trying to be rid of him, the man proved salvageable and a credit to the ship. Strong senior petty officers and a captain who showed that he cared about the snipes were most responsible for this change and excellent morale among the snipes. The captain's role was crucial.

After twenty-three uneventful days at sea, we steamed into Pearl Harbor. I might note that our stack smoke was silky light gray, a sign of beautifully functioning big diesels. What a far cry from the previous year, when we limped into port in a smoky haze to the amusement of our sister ships. They would soon discover the *Vance* had the best engineering department in the squadron.

A Changing Wardroom

In the first six months of 1964, a number of new faces appeared in the wardroom and a couple of old friends said aloha. First to say farewell was Fred Levin, who had orders to a shore billet in Japan. He planned to make the navy a career as an intelligence officer, not as a ship driver. Fred might go to sea again, but he would never command a ship. I am certain this made him extremely happy. Fred was intelligent, hardworking, and extremely likable. He was resilient. He could get along with anyone. Well, almost anyone. Captain Beyer liked him, possibly because Fred could be entertaining and was always upbeat. I think it helped the captain to believe that he had a happy wardroom. I probably had the opposite effect on the skipper.

While he had the right personality for Captain Beyer, he was the wrong man to be aboard Captain Wright's ship, especially now that he moved up to operations department head. There was no longer a buffer between Fred and the new skipper. I can recall the captain screaming at him over misinterpreting our operational orders. Fred, a man of finesse and expansive rhetoric, had a difficult time working for this meat-and-potatoes skipper. Fred hastily departed after several difficult months under Captain Wright.

I missed Fred. We had been together for over two years, from lowly ensigns surviving together in the bunk room to being department heads together. I had seen Fred angry, disappointed, under pressure, and worried. I never witnessed him belittling or hurting another human being. I admired the man and respected his intelligence. Believing his sea stories was another matter.

Following Fred over the gangway was Jim Kunz, my other close friend, who with Fred and me survived for two years in the bunk room. Jim opted for a naval career and received orders as the XO of a small LST, an amphibious ship that took troops and equipment onto the beach. Jim and I were close friends despite our being very different. He was a correct naval officer, while I avoided military formality. Jim was a strict Catholic, and I fled from organized religion and resented my dictatorial Catholic childhood. Jim liked sea duty. Need I say more? Being single and sharing the shipboard experience, we tended to hang out together ashore. There was a kindness in Jim that his sometimes prickly personality and dry wit masked. People either understood and perhaps appreciated his sense of humor with its militant overtones, or they misunderstood it. Jim was efficient, correct, and orderly in all things. Yes, we were good friends. You had to look beyond the smoke screen of this very private man. With both my contemporaries gone, I felt abandoned, a dinosaur, the last of the Deep Freeze wardroom.

The wardroom was full of new faces. Tom Williams, a young career navy OCS graduate, replaced Jim Kunz as the gunnery officer. Tom was a pleasant, easygoing guy, whom I never had the opportunity to know well, probably because he was married. Phil Loggins, the sharp Californian who replaced Fred, was an NROTC graduate who would finish his last year on the *Vance* after having served on a real destroyer. Our electronics officer, a new ensign, Richard Rightmyer, had joined the wardroom in Japan. Ken Hamaker, a thin, quiet, easygoing ensign, came aboard as our new communications officer. John Wells, known as Cash because of a consuming interest in finance and the business world, transferred in from another ship to spend his final two years on the *Vance* as the CIC officer. Jim

Morrow, another recent OCS graduate, arrived to manage the deck apes.

Two more officers joined Lee and me in engineering. Hoppy Mason, who actually had an engineering degree, transferred to us from another ship in the squadron. In another year, Hoppy would take the reins of the department when Lee Cole departed. Ed Fuehrer, an architect and the new MPA, would spend his three years as a snipe. In his final year, Ed led the department following Hoppy's departure. I felt like an old man as I rapidly approached the end of my third year aboard.

A Loss of Balance

Since first stepping aboard the *Vance*, I dreamed of being somewhere else, anywhere but on her rolling decks. Enduring week after week at sea with hour after hour of lonely watches, I needed something to look forward to. I stood my dull bridge watches dreaming of the Irish girl I had met in New Zealand. When I was dating someone I cared for, the new girl occupied my daydreams at sea. Call my dreaming fickle and unreal, but I needed it. The loneliness of this profession was crippling.

Near the end of each patrol, I could see on the horizon that narrow strip of land called Oahu. As we drew closer, the land took on a greenish hue. Closer still, the green took the form of lush trees backed by green and bluish-gray highlands. Before life on the *Vance,* I took vegetation for granted. Now I worshiped anything and everything that grew on the earth. I was twenty-six years old, lonely, sick of the sea, and craving for a partner to give my life meaning. At sea, my life was on hold, at a standstill, while on terra firma, there was variety, options, choices to be made, and people busy making lives for themselves. At sea, we were isolated, locked in a rigid routine, each person assigned a position and status within a hierarchy. People had it wrong. We didn't go to sea. We went to shore. The sea was home; ashore was our deployment. We were conditioned for short stays of irrational living ashore.

I was back to trying to maximize my time ashore with my

shipmates, looking for women, lying on the beach, playing tourist, frequenting the bars, going anywhere but back to the ship. Bob Yohe, my old college roommate turned navy flyboy, and I hung out on the beach together when our schedules permitted. Through Bob, I met Sally, a sweet little freckle-faced strawberry blond who loved to party. Twenty years old, the daughter of an army colonel stationed on Oahu, Sally was pure fun and very popular. I was fascinated and sought every opportunity to date her. After my year with Joan, I realized how important a female companion on the beach was to my sanity. Unfortunately, between our difficult schedule and Sally's popularity, we didn't have the time together I would have liked.

In *Lucky Jim* by Kingsley Amis, a humorous novel dealing with illusion and reality, the observation is made that there are two requirements of love: wanting to go to bed with a woman and not knowing her very well, and that the years of disillusionment aren't those of adolescence, they are the ones immediately after, in the midtwenties, the false maturity when you first get thoroughly embroiled in things and lose your head. This passage summed up my plight with Sally.

On the beach with Sally, Hawaii once again became the tropical paradise depicted by the travel industry. She was used to attention, having a pert little figure together with a passionate and bubbly personality that readily attracted men. Competitive me, I tried to be first in line. She loved the attention. Sally was easy to be with, and I, for countless foolish reasons, preferred to overlook how incompatible we were and my place in her priorities. I didn't know her very well, or she me. We had such little time together. She seemed a perfect creature, except for one personality quirk. When we competed in the popular limbo dance contest at Fort DeRussy, she would ignore the rules to have her way. I was amazed that winning a stupid little limbo contest could mean so much to her. I was appalled by her willingness to ignore the rules. I knew she liked to be in the spotlight more than I could be comfortable with. So what? I was in love and had my blinders on. Sally could do no wrong.

Subconsciously, I knew it was a stretch to get serious over this girl. I was scheduled to leave Hawaii in four months, with no real objectives in my aimless life. I didn't want to let go of her. I never had her to let go of, a mere detail I ignored.

Sally and I arrived at Captain Wright's house party for the wardroom officers. This first social event at the skipper's house was enjoyable. As with most military families, moving every few years was a logistics challenge. The navy supplied the housing on expensive Oahu. His was a small but adequate duplex with a mix of navy and personal furnishings. There sat the family's baby grand piano. Anne, the skipper's wife, was tapping out a tune. Ross was especially attentive and sweet to her. Anne had recently given birth to their first child, a daughter. The proud father briefly rewarded us with a glimpse of his sleeping infant. Here was a warm, happy family. Again I realized that I did not want a career that would take me away from my loved ones for extended periods of time.

Foremost on my mind that evening was to have a serious conversation with Sally about a future together. I unsuccessfully tried to be alone with her at the captain's party and tell her how much I loved her. Failing that, on the way to her house, we stopped at an all-night outdoor snack shop, and I popped the big question. Sally gently turned down my proposal of marriage. Despondent at the rejection, some time was necessary for me to recover from a bruised ego and to realize how close to disaster I had placed myself. Starved for female comfort and companionship, I had conjured up a scenario. There I was traveling off into the sunset with Sally, bringing stability and meaning to my stress-ridden lonely life. Only much later did I learn my role in this sad saga. Sally was as ready for marriage as I was to stay on terra firma. Fortunately, I was not on her list of candidates. I hear she eventually chose an old boyfriend. Lucky me. I was shaken by my actions and the realization that I was seriously out of balance, my judgment impaired. Three insane years at sea in the prime of my life had me conditioned to dive into a very long-term commitment, not more seasickness or years at sea, just an unhappy marriage.

After the foolish encounter with Sally, I slipped into a quiet, reflective mood ashore. No more chasing women. More time was spent with my fellow single officers: snorkeling, talking shop, and hanging out at various bars. I recall a favorite hangout, sitting around the piano at a little club, sipping scotch and dreamily listening to a lovely girl singing, "Yellow bird, way up in banana tree. Yellow bird, you sit all alone like me," a then-popular Jamaican song of thwarted love. We snorkeled on the windward side of the island and at Hanauma Bay. There was the usual beach time at Fort DeRussy, although I no longer took an interest in cruising the beaches and bars of Waikiki. Chasing after women was of no interest. I looked ahead to when I would be saying aloha to Hawaii.

In May, we were underway for a three-day R&R trip to Kauai. The previous year, with Jim and Harvey aboard, I enjoyed the island visit. Now with my old shipmates gone, I truly was the last of the dinosaurs. In this mood, my second visit to Kauai was less spectacular. I had been there. I looked forward to leaving the islands, and I was tired. Only the snorkeling in an isolated cove held my interest. I was content counting the days I had left on board. A few days following our return from Kauai, we again set the special sea and anchor detail and were underway for ocean station, my eighteenth and final patrol.

CHAPTER 18

Request Permission to Go Ashore

May 26–July 9, 1964

Anyone who would go to sea for enjoyment,
Would go to Hell for a vacation!
—Old Saying

The Last Patrol

The last patrol may have been my best, certainly my most relaxed once I was over the usual couple of seasick days. The engineering department had an extra officer. Technically, I continued as department head despite the fact that Lee Cole would assume the job within a month. Hoppy Mason was now the DCA and Ed Fuehrer the MPA. They didn't need me. I had asked the skipper for leave, hoping to miss the patrol. I was told it was not possible: officers don't miss patrols, especially engineering officers. So I went along for the ride. The department's future was in Lee's hands. I stood my watches and made polite conversation at the dinner table. My mind was a million miles away.

My attention was riveted on the future in Europe. Most of our officers either planned for a navy career or had specific plans for when their three-year obligation was completed. I envied them. Jim Kunz and Fred Levin followed navy careers. Harvey Payne and Lee Cole would go to law school. Larry Hanson always knew he was headed for an MBA program. I knew that Bob Yohe's heart was in horses and the Wild West. They all knew what they wanted. I saw no civilian career that excited me, and there was a whole world yet to be explored. I would continue to lend my valuable services to the US Navy if they would assign me to terra firma in England or Germany. The navy offered Spain.

I accepted a two-year placement in Spain rather than returning to civilian life in the States. Not a practical decision given that I had no intention of staying in the navy. Yet the thought of a boring civilian job in America implied an end to traveling. Welled up in my head were memories of my father's work experience. Once committed to a civilian career with the practical concerns of career and responsibility, would I ever again have the opportunity to travel and experience more of the world?

I was still aboard the *Vance*, but for the first time in three long years, my attention was focused elsewhere, on a new adventure to Europe and sunny southern Spain. My wounds from the marriage proposal rejection healed more quickly than one would expect. I kept questioning myself. How could I have been so stupid? What had the *Vance* years done to my judgment? Once done with the *Vance*, I foresaw a normal life ahead and hopefully the ability to make sounder judgments. The marriage proposal had both scared and embarrassed me. How could I have proposed marriage when all the signs pointed to this being a big mistake? I didn't know the girl that well, we were not really compatible, and she never implied that I was the chosen one. Three years at sea had me going over the edge.

My eighteenth and final patrol was coming to an end. The date was June 18, Oahu was in sight, and I was in a state of extreme calm, a religious state of ecstasy. I couldn't care less about the engineering plant. Three years at sea had been a prison sentence. Finally the prison gates were opening. Nothing bothered me. I was impervious to problems. All engineering problems were now Lee Cole's problems. The patrol was ending. My seagoing years were over. I was floating on air as we approached the Pearl Harbor channel. The engines were running smoothly, generators screaming as usual, and a touch of fine gray smoke trailed from the stack as the *Vance* cut gracefully through the water. She was a good ship, and I was getting off her.

With Lee in charge in main control, I was free to wander

back to the fantail. As we began to enter the Pearl Harbor channel, I took off my scruffy Wellington seaboots and threw them overboard, watching them begin to sink in our churning wake. It was a symbolic gesture: my seaboots were no more, and I would never buy or wear another pair of Wellington boots. Three years before, during my first week on the *Vance,* as we prepared to leave for the Antarctic, Larry Hanson advised me to buy a pair of brown Wellingtons. The rationale was that you needed shoes without laces to slip into quickly during emergencies. This proved to be good advice. For three years, I kept the boots next to my bunk within reach each night, leaping into them at the sounding of general quarters or for an engine-room emergency. They served me well.

Moored at the Bravo Piers once again, I had twenty-one days left before being transferred. I packed a bag for ten days' leave, my first leave since Japan. The best I could negotiate with Captain Wright was ten days, while the ship was undergoing daily operations off the coast. Normally I saw no advantage to taking leave while the *Vance* was in Pearl Harbor. I would be avoiding the daily bouts of seasickness that went with the daily excursions underway. Besides, I would lose the leave if not taken. Rather than visit my old haunts on Oahu, I spent an interesting and uneventful week on the big island of Hawaii, tramping around the active lava flows of Kilauea Crater and feeling as if I were on a religious retreat.

A Surprise Farewell

A personnel inspection was scheduled for my last day aboard. The crew, all 160 sailors and officers in dress whites, lined the pier. I stood at attention in a grumpy mood in front of my two snipe divisions. *Why in hell do I have to put up with one more personnel inspection on my last day? The skipper could have excused me. I'm history to the* Vance. At the podium, Captain Wright called out the command, "Lieutenant Jaras, front and center." *He must be mistaken.* It finally dawned on me that the event was for me. I tried to look military, attempting to make smart 90°

turns as I marched to the podium and saluted. I never did cut much of a military figure. I was shortchanged in my gene pool. All five foot six and three quarters inches of me stood before the crew as the skipper read a letter of merit for my services to the ship. I had never witnessed an officer receiving this recognition on the *Vance*. Perhaps they were normally given in private. I had no idea. I just knew I was surprised, pleased, grateful, and humbled. I expected nothing and certainly never thought the crew would be turned out to witness the presentation. I was indeed humbled and realized I would deeply miss this old tub of a ship and the men who kept her alive.

The next morning before the *Vance* was underway for a day of local operations, I said my good-byes to the wardroom, especially to my lead snipes Chief Mooney, Alex, Mac, and Engles. To Boats Oldervick, I gave a nod and received one in return with a small grin. Boats didn't miss much. He knew how much I wanted to be ashore for the rest of my life. Without a word, I had wished him smooth sailing, and he smiled an acknowledgment that told me I was a good shipmate.

I stood on the Bravo Piers as the *Vance* smartly swung her fantail away from the pier, pivoting on #1 and #2 lines. Lines in, the skipper turned her elegantly toward the channel. The *Vance* headed to sea once again. I boarded the bus for Hickam Field and my plane to the mainland. My beloved 1961 MGA was sold to Jim Morrow, the new first lieutenant. Three years earlier, I had arrived in Hawaii at Hickam Field alone without fanfare and planned to depart the same way. My shipmates were at sea.

To my surprise, Harvey Payne's girlfriend, Jane, was waiting at Hickam to see me off. I was both delighted and embarrassed. Harvey had left six months previous, and I had neither seen Jane since nor made an effort to at least call her. Somehow she knew I was leaving and took time off from her job to say aloha. Thank you, Jane. A second surprise: joining us were Sally's parents, whom I had not seen since Sally had turned me down four months earlier. How did they know I was leaving, and why bother to see me off? Regardless, I was touched by the reception, the ceremonial flower leis around my neck, the farewell hugs, and the realization that these people went out of their way to say farewell and good luck. I held back the tears until seated on the plane, looking out the window waving aloha.

With no interest in returning to the continental United States and no career aspirations, I had elected to trade two more years of my life for a navy shore billet in Europe. First, I was heading home to see my family in Cleveland, and then I would go to Europe for thirty days' vacation in Scandinavia and Northern Ireland, where I would visit with the young Irish lady. Then to London, where I planned to catch a military flight to the naval base at Rota, Spain, my home for the next two years. My thoughts were on the future as the plane was preparing to depart the terminal. The lights flickered off, then on again as the plane changed power sources. I tensed up, ready to spring from my seat, and then realized that I was no longer aboard the *Vance*. For three years, I had lived and worked to keep the ship's generators operating. That was my job. Any flicker of the lighting meant there was a generator problem and we were in danger of losing all power. The *Vance* was still with me.

What I Took with Me

Six more months would pass before I no longer reacted to the flicker of lights. The *Vance* was then truly just a memory—or was it? Just as exposure to a different biological environment can influence our immune systems, so too can three years in a steel cocoon influence how we see ourselves. From my window seat, I gazed out at the ocean below, seemingly for hours, tranquil and mentally grappling with the change. I was aware that the experience had changed me. I was older, more confident, and hopefully wiser. Most of what the *Vance* bestowed on me would become apparent over time.

As we flew east to the mainland, my thoughts returned to Oahu. I was still grieving, saddened by the idea that *Vance* was underway without me and I was leaving friends and shipmates behind. I was having trouble distancing myself from the *Vance*, the ugly, unstable, little ship that I had long dreamed of being free of. Initially, I had viewed this ship as a large metal box, an inanimate object and nothing more. Somehow over the years, the crew, the agony of the job, the joys and blunders in port, the dull shipboard routine, the friendships made, and the wonder of living with the ocean metamorphosed this chunk of metal into a living, breathing entity, which was now a permanent part of my life. *Vance* was no longer a thing. Separation was necessary to permit me to view her as a living, human event. Perhaps this helps explain sailors' lingering fondness for ships on which they have served. The bucket of bolts I served on and would have traded "my firstborn" for a transfer off of was to be with me the rest of my life as a memorable experience.

The *Vance* experience left its mark in various ways. My sister's tears were necessary for me to realize how tough and demanding I had become. I was brutal when retrieving my phonograph record collection that I had left in her care during my years at sea. My response to her wanting to keep the collection was excessively demanding, as if I were dealing with a shipboard infraction. I realized this was another gift from the *Vance* that I had best rid myself of. Cursing was another shipboard habit, one I was unable to discard. Communicating with my snipes to stress the importance of an issue, I learned to employ: God damn it! Shit! Damn it! Son of a bitch! And a few other, more imaginative phrases. I discarded much of this vocabulary over time. Today when I swear, the words flow smoothly, in a normal, comfortable manner, as if a long-practiced part of my natural self. Prior to my navy experience, swearing required a conscious effort. It was an alien, uncomfortable act. This is no longer true, God damn it!

I arrived aboard the *Vance* a college boy and left a self-confident manager and an adult male. I had my first intimate relationship with a lady and benefited greatly from it. Thank you, Joan. I also came to understand how vulnerable I was as a lonely and love-starved sailor. I was determined to never again make serious decisions about marriage without much forethought, and I haven't. I left the ship a lonely person. I understood the importance of having someone to share my life with. I was beginning to learn how to manage my life.

The day I said good-bye to the *Vance*, I knew I could manage people. Although I had successfully managed people both in college and working summers, the *Vance* experience gave me tremendous confidence. I had a knack for inspiring people to work for me. Officers and crew worked well for me largely because I was fair and sincere. I supported them and could not be accused of self-promotion. I like to think I was respected, not always liked, but at least respected.

The irony in being a good manager was that the *Vance* experience told me that I didn't like managing people. Several more years were needed before I got the message. The captain or manager subordinates the welfare of the individual to the needs of the ship or firm. I didn't like being the middleman. The faster the crew rows, the more the institution benefits. Managing projects proved more fulfilling. I preferred the narrow focus, precise product, and limited responsibility for my fellow workers.

I cared about people, and this could be a problem, especially in the navy, where I was responsible for my sailors ashore and afloat, their marital problems, financial problems, legal problems, health problems, and any other problems that prevented them from being aboard when expected and doing an acceptable job. I preferred a work environment without involvement in the employees' personal lives.

The privileged life of the naval officer always bothered me. Despite a college education and being commissioned as a naval officer, I was tied to my working-class roots. A bit of guilt was always there just under the surface as I accepted the deference and perks of my rank. I was keenly aware of the enlisted man. Was our privileged existence essential to managing the ship? How much of this eighteenth- and nineteenth-century class-based tradition of privilege was necessary? My problem was with the class distinction, so important to a tradition-bound navy. I wasn't comfortable with the mandatory saluting, the collar devices announcing the rank or pecking order to be respected, or the special quarters, meals, and servants. I was uncomfortable with the stewards waiting tables, handling my laundry, and making up my bunk. I accepted these practices and benefits, but I always carried some guilt. I was no different from the sailors I managed or the stewards waiting on me.

I wasn't knocking the system, nor could I offer constructive criticism on how to improve the system. Rather, I was seeking to understand my own discomfort. I loved being in charge. I just preferred to avoid public recognition and aggrandizement. Some officers readily accepted every privilege as their just due. They were rarely in conflict with their elevated status. I downplayed aggrandizement of the individual. Success was the result of a team effort. The *Vance* experience helped me realize that, at heart, I am a bit of a leveler. I like the utopian idea of the class strata being leveled out.

Reflecting on this US Navy adventure, I realized that the reward for doing a good job was personal satisfaction. I was fortunate to finish my tour under Captain Wright, to know that my contribution was appreciated and that the engineering department would only get better. I'm not sure how I would have felt about the *Vance* experience today had my tour ended differently. Like most people, I could and did get upset when undeserving people were rewarded. From my brief experience, I found that the US Navy usually rewarded the correct person, especially the command-afloat billets. The navy reinforced my belief in Niccolo Machiavelli's observation that success was 50 percent effort and 50 percent luck and that the effort was necessary in order to take advantage of the opportunity when luck presented itself. The competent Captain Wright was lucky taking command of the *Vance* when she was at an all-time low. How could he not succeed considering his experience and ability? Captain Beyer faced a real challenge having to follow a popular captain and assume command in the middle of a stressful deployment.

I liked all three of my skippers—Penny, Beyer, and Wright—and would thoroughly enjoy their company had they not been my captains. A navy ship is a world unto itself, an insular environment ruled by the captain. With the advent of modern communications technologies, a captain's control has lessened somewhat from the life-and-death powers once exercised at sea. Today the captain by necessity still retains considerable power. He makes the ship what it is. I was always sensitive to this power and did my best to minimize my contact with the person possessing it. I saw the captain at lunch and dinner, the evening movie, special wardroom meetings, and occasionally on the bridge. I avoided the wardroom whenever possible and made it known that I was ignorant of their favorite pastimes, playing bridge or backgammon. No matter how nice a person, all recreational activity with the skipper was still a business meeting with a dictator. In the private sector, I could give my boss a hard time and get away with it or just quit.

As I gazed out the plane's window at the ocean below, I promised myself to never serve aboard ship again. But a part of me pulled in the opposite direction. I missed my fellow officers, my snipe chiefs, the men, the teamwork, the routine, and the pride in a mission well-done.

EPILOGUE

He who graduates the harshest school, succeeds.
—Thucydides

Down from the Ramparts

I was about to come down from the wall and turn in my spear, short sword, and shield. I knew how a Roman soldier must have felt, a sentinel in 130 AD on the ramparts of Hadrian's Wall, that seventy-three-mile-long wall across Britain, built to keep Roman Britain safe from the barbarians to the north. The Romans built with stone and peat. Radar, ships, and aircraft formed our wall, the Pacific Barrier. The Romans garrisoned theirs with auxiliary units, not the war-toughened legions. Ours were old ships with reserve sailors and airmen. The auxiliary soldier stood a boring, dreary watch on the cold damp moors. Ditto.

For the past three years, I was missing much that was happening in the world due to the tempo and isolation of this life. I was either at sea, aboard ship alongside the pier, or briefly ashore searching for a social life. I was about to rejoin society, to have the opportunity to smell the roses and be part of what was happening in society.

I was a product of the times, a 1950s college boy who went to sea as a naval officer. I was swept along on a big wave called the Cold War, which carried me through a three-year stint at sea. Unbeknown to me, when I left the *Vance*, I was to be caught up by a second great wave. The world was changing. America was expanding its role in Vietnam. The first bombings of North Vietnam were about to take place. Social rebellion was in the air. The first student protests and draft-card burnings over our role in Vietnam had already begun. Growing concerns for racial equality had led to the new Civil Rights Act, and President Johnson had declared war on poverty. Society's social mores

315

were being challenged. Even tastes in music were changing. The Beatles took the country by storm earlier in the year, quickly followed by the Rolling Stones. America was undergoing a tremendous social and political transformation. I would step cautiously into this changing world and become aware of how insular my shipboard years had been. In time, I would willingly ride this new wave.

Life on Terra Firma

If I learned anything from the *Vance* it was to never, no never, no never go to sea again. The next year, as a military courier in Spain, I was forced to spend a night aboard a US Navy supply ship moored at Valencia. Lying on my assigned bunk, I was having a conscious nightmare from the all-too-familiar hum of the ventilation system, the same putrid-green bulkheads, the dull gray decks, the cheap gray-green floor tile, and the smell of crusted salt and oil. I thought I was back on the *Vance*. I slept poorly and hurriedly left the ship at first light. Two years later as a naval reservist, I became nauseous sitting on the deck of a naval reserve destroyer transiting the Ballard Canal in Seattle, a difficult feat considering the ship only traveled a mile and with minimal motion. Several years ago, with a seasickness patch on my neck, I endured a bumpy uncomfortable afternoon off the Baja coast on an old thirty-foot Mexican fishing boat, diesel fumes spewing from its stack. I kept my lunch. Unfortunately, there were no patches in the 1960s. Although the patch solved my inner ear balance problem, there was still the mind to contend with. So many things associated with ships bring me back to the *Vance* and by association seasickness. The intensity of my first seasick weeks, from Hawaii to New Zealand, will always be nearby, awaiting resurrection. I have no desire to go there again.

My life eventually normalized. I enjoyed three weeks in Scandinavia and went on to North Ireland to visit with Rosemarie, the girl I met in Dunedin. We quickly found that we were not made for each other. I moved to Belfast to stay with her brother, a newspaper reporter, for the remainder of the visit. Farewell, fair Rosemarie, and thank you for being in my dreams, dreams that kept me company through lonely night watches in the North Pacific.

I enjoyed two years in Spain, roaming the European continent and the countries bordering the Mediterranean. Eventually I met, courted, and married a wonderful woman, an American schoolteacher on the Rota naval base. With my navy obligation drawing to an end, we returned to the United States. So ended my lonely existence and so began a life of responsibility and goals.

Old Shipmates

What of my old shipmates? I continued to correspond with several, but occupied with a family and earning a living, I lost touch with all but a few of them. Five years ago, we attempted a small wardroom reunion in San Diego. Small because some had passed away, others we had lost contact with, a few wanted nothing to do with a reunion, and several were incapacitated or had conflicting obligations. After all, almost fifty years had passed. Planning the reunion did bring me up-to-date as to what became of most of the officers I served with.

My first skipper, Commander Penny, retired a captain after a successful naval career. My guess is that it was a colorful career. He passed away in the early 2000s. Tom Jewell, his executive officer, also went on to an impressive career in destroyers, retired a captain, and died of cancer in 1980. My second skipper, Hank Beyer, retired from the navy in the late 1960s and reportedly returned to his home state, Oregon. We lost contact with both him and his executive officer, Mel Huffman, who went on to command an LST. Ross Wright, my third commanding officer, went on to command a real destroyer and eventually retired from the US Navy with the rank of commander. In retirement, unable to resist the sea, Ross was master of two cruise ships, taught at the Massachusetts Maritime Academy, and was master of their training ship. While dean of students at the Academy, he also wrote a seafaring novel. Ross passed away in 2009 at age eighty-three after a long battle with cancer. His executive officer, Les Horne, had his own ship, the USS *Esteem* (MSO-430) and in time retired in Northern Virginia. Les passed away in 2010 at age eighty-two.

So what happened to the wardroom of young men who shared in this unique experience? Jim Kunz, Fred Levin, and Bruce Young made the navy a career. Within two years of leaving the *Vance*, Jim was the commanding officer of an LST in Vietnam. He eventually retired, and unfortunately, I have since lost track of him. Both Fred and Bruce earned their four stripes, retiring as captains. Bruce, with an impressive career in destroyers, was considered admiral material, but was forced into retirement for health reasons. Fred and Janet retired to the Pensacola area after his successful career in navy intelligence.

Lee Cole and Harvey Payne established successful law practices, Lee in Akron, Ohio, and Harvey in Los Angeles, California. I frequently visit with Lee. We laugh and joke over our days as snipes on the *Vance.* You had to have been on those rolling decks to appreciate the humor. Following our first and only wardroom reunion in San Diego in April 2009, Harvey Payne was diagnosed as having advanced prostate cancer. He passed away a few months later, at age seventy-two. I mourn him still. Ken Wood, a rugby enthusiast and a manager at the US Environmental Protection Agency, passed away in his early fifties from a heart attack. Chuck Laipply, who retired from the navy, passed away in the early 2000s.

Our supply officer, Robbie Robinson, completed his twenty years in the navy and went on to a second career as a clinical psychologist. Con Murray, our second supply officer, went on to be an attorney and retired after a career with a major corporation in New York. Doc Gersenfish retired a few years ago after a long career in pathology in La Jolla, California. Tom Milligan retired after a successful career with Boeing in Seattle. Larry Hanson completed graduate school as planned, and eventually retired as comptroller for a major company in California. Don Dunn, our Annapolis graduate, left the navy a few years after leaving the *Vance*. He recently retired from the presidency of a leading ballistics company.

Much of my information is sketchy. I know that Frank Collins taught at a Texas university and Ray DeMott retired to Florida. I have no idea what happened to Tom Williams, Bob Baker, or Hank Fox, although I believe all three followed naval careers. Hoppy Mason returned to Savannah and worked for a major manufacturer. Ed Fuehrer was involved in real estate in Washington, DC. Kent Hamaker still has a real estate business in Northern Virginia. John (alias Cash) Wells is a partner in an investment firm in Seattle. I lost track of Dick Rightmyer, Phil Loggins, Salts McKillop, and Jim Morrow and my 1961 MGA.

I have few details on most of the wardroom officers. Some just disappeared from the radar, a few I never really knew because we served together only a few brief months, and a few prefer to forget that period of their lives. We certainly were a diverse group. That was one of the beauties of universal military service.

Of the *Vance*'s snipe population, I know almost nothing. I learned that Senior Chief Mooney passed away in 2004. Engles, Mac, and Alex I was unable to trace. Nor have I been in contact with other shipmates who shared these years afloat. Fifty miles north of Yellowstone National Park each summer, you will find my college roommate, Bob Yohe, working from horseback, herding greenhorns and livestock at the 63 Ranch near Livingston, Montana.

The Vance *Sailed On*

As young men, it was not possible to comprehend that we were just passing through. After a few generations, we are likely to not even be a memory. There may be a tombstone or perhaps a publication or photo album left behind, but little else will survive, certainly not the truth. This will be the fate of our accomplishments as well. I left the *Vance* proud of helping turn around an engineering department. Over the next three years, Lee Cole, Hoppy Mason, and Ed Fuehrer, each in his own turn as the engineering department head, ensured that the *Vance* excelled in engineering. The ship won the coveted red "E" for best engineering plant in the Pacific. In 1965, the Pacific Barrier lost its importance, and the squadron was deployed to patrol the coastal waters of Vietnam. In the *Vance*'s several deployments to Vietnam and to the Taiwan Strait, the engineering department continued to excel.

Ross Wright completed his tour as skipper, to be relieved by Marcus Aurelius Arnheiter. Then begun a short but infamous ninety-nine-day period for the *Vance*. Fortunately I was not aboard for one of the US Navy's major public relations mistakes of the Vietnam Era, the assignment of Arnheiter as commanding officer of the *Vance*. This was a man who, reportedly inflated with his own importance, would go to any length to impress his superiors and endangered his crew for a chance at superficial glory. My fellow officers suffered through his reign until they did the unforgivable. They worked to have the captain relieved, risking a court-martial for their efforts. A fair and revealing account of this sad event is Neil Scheen's excellent book *The Arnheiter Affair*.

The US Navy, not the *Vance*'s officers, was the culprit here for placing an unfit man in command of a ship. Even today, forty-five years later, some naval officers still shake their heads in disgust that *Vance* officers conducted the equivalent of a mutiny on a navy ship. The position of commanding officer of a navy ship is sacrosanct. The Arnheiters are to be obeyed. I understand the need for this position, but I just do not want ever again to be subjected to such total control of my life by any one person. Who can guarantee a competent and rational dictator? BUPERS couldn't.

The *Vance* continued to deploy to the Far East for the next few years. With improved radar and satellite early-warning capabilities on the DEW Line, the DER ships became obsolete. In 1969, five years after my leaving the *Vance*, the ship was decommissioned and mothballed on the West Coast. In 1975, she was struck from the US Navy's list of ships and scheduled to be a target ship. The life and death of a small warship is strangely similar to that of a new business enterprise. The start-up is a flurry of media releases and celebration. When the venture folds, there is only silence. The life of a ship follows the same pattern. A good bottle of champagne broke on the *Vance*'s bow and the band played as she slipped into the warm waters of Galveston Bay on July 16, 1943. The celebration continued at her commissioning four months later. Freshly painted, brass polished, and signal flags streaming from the bow over the main mast to the stern, the *Vance* hosted another celebration, a warship joining the fleet. Recommissioned a DER in 1956, she was splashed again with another bottle of bubbly, the band played, and speeches were made.

After forty-plus years, stripped of memorabilia and a few valued parts, the *Vance* was on its last mission, that of a target ship. I can envision a submarine on a training run off the California coast. The captain leaned on the periscope, and with the prey in sight, launched a torpedo at the defenseless *Vance*. The torpedo tore a massive hole in the hull at the after engine room, collapsing the watertight bulkhead to the adjoining space, main control. The ocean waters, having waited patiently all these years, came rushing into the hull. The keel and main deck snapped, breaking her back, sending the *Vance* to the bottom. She lies in a quiet grave a mile or two down in the Pacific Ocean, a scattered batch of steel on the ocean floor. Gone are those beautiful Fairbanks-Morse engines that turned over hour after hour, year after year, carrying the *Vance* over three oceans in her lifetime.

Gone to the bottom are the ship service generators, those finicky GE units that made life on board possible and the lives of the snipes impossible. Gone are the spotless engine rooms, the pride of the snipes, who spent years living and working in them. All their labor and sacrifice are forgotten, gone, rusting away on the ocean floor. The cursing, bitching, bad grammar, and laughter of these oil-stained snipes is imbedded in those bulkheads, as are the impressions of the middle-aged New Zealand housewife who put on trousers so she could go down the ladder to see an engine room. Returning, she poked her head out above the hatch and exclaimed, "This space be cleaner than my house. You could eat off them deck plates."

Newly commissioned ships are celebrated with a champagne christening, speeches, a navy band, streamers floating down, and considerable media coverage. The execution of the *Vance* was a routine affair, quietly recorded in sanitized terms, not abandoned or sunk or destroyed, rather "struck from the Navy list." The fatal stroke was with pen and paper.

About the time the *Vance* went down, I was building sand castles on the Rhode Island beaches with my children. When completed, we would turn over our creations to an admiring audience of children. With a sand castle, I knew the joy was solely in the construction, because the ocean would wash it away with the incoming tide. Sand castles and ships have much in common. I never realized how frail and temporary were our labors and accomplishments on the *Vance*. We were young, strong, idealistic, and naïve. We were invincible.

The Demise of Destroyer Escort Squadron Five

USS *Falgout* (DER 324):	January 12, 1972, sunk as a target off California.
USS *Finch* (DER 328):	September 27, 1974, sold for scrap to Levin Metals Corp., San Jose, California.
USS *Forster* (DER 334):	September 25, 1971, transferred to South Vietnam. Written off by the navy as transferred to Vietnam April 30, 1975. Renamed *DAIKY (HQ-03)*. Stripped and in harbor as a training hulk as of 1999.
USS *Haverfield* (DER 393):	December 15, 1971, sold for scrap to Chi Shun Steel Co., Ltd., of Kaoshiung, Taiwan, for $35,000.
USS *Koiner* (DER 331):	September 3, 1969, sold for scrap.
USS *Lowe* (DER 325):	September 3, 1969, sold for scrap.
USS *Savage* (DER 386):	October 25, 1982, target ship.
USS *Vance* (DER 387):	1980s target ship.
USS *Wilhoite* (DER 397):	July 19, 1972, sold for scrap to General Metals, Inc., Tacoma, Washington.